On Canadian Literature
1806-1960

On Canadian Literature
1806-1960

A CHECK LIST OF ARTICLES, BOOKS,
AND THESES ON ENGLISH-CANADIAN
LITERATURE, ITS AUTHORS,
AND LANGUAGE

Compiled by
REGINALD EYRE WATTERS
INGLIS FREEMAN BELL

UNIVERSITY OF TORONTO PRESS

© UNIVERSITY OF TORONTO PRESS 1966

Reprinted 1967

Reprinted with corrections and additions 1973

Printed in the United States of America for
University of Toronto Press
Toronto and Buffalo

ISBN 0-8020-5166-9
LC 66-1582

Preface

On Canadian Literature is a listing of the biographical, critical, and scholarly writings about English-Canadian literature, its authors, and its language.
Not listed, however, are items in standard reference works such as encyclo-
paedias, biographical dictionaries, and *Who's Who*s. Book reviews also are
normally excluded; the relatively few exceptions are some "book-review
articles" and some unusually significant or lengthy reviews by outstanding
reviewers. The aim of the compilers of this list was to facilitate the study of
our national literature and thereby promote its understanding and enjoyment.
Because the focus is therefore on *belles lettres* and closely related categories,
Canadian authors whose publications fall into quite different categories are
not covered. No attempt was made to screen the material to eliminate the
trivial or ephemeral, since the very publication of even slight comment has its
own significance. On the other hand, also listed here are those critical and
scholarly treatments of our literary culture which are of the highest
importance.

The overwhelming bulk of the material listed was published in recent
decades, but some items are included which appeared more than a century
ago. The effective terminal date of this compilation is 1960. However, reference
material published subsequently may be located through the bibliographies
published annually in *Canadian Literature* (covering the years 1959–1970).
A similar annual compilation was begun in 1965 by *The Journal of Common-
wealth Literature* and is still being continued. The list of materials on language
and linguistics can similarly be kept up to date by consulting the bibliography
published annually in the *Canadian Journal of Linguistics*.

The compilers are under no delusion that they have discovered and
exhausted all possible sources or references, but they hope they have at least
made a substantial beginning that will prove useful to readers and scholars of
today and tomorrow. They would be deeply grateful to anyone who will
draw their attention to significant material not included here.

Preparation of this list has spanned more years than the compilers like to
contemplate; but the task could never have been accomplished at all without
the help of many persons whom they delight in remembering. In the early
years, a grant from the Board of Governors of the University of British
Columbia made possible the organizing and recording of material gathered

up to that time, and in the final stage the Royal Military College of Canada provided indispensable help in the typing of the complete manuscript. This work has been published with the help of a grant from the Humanities Research Council of Canada using funds provided by the Canada Council, and with the aid of the Publications Fund of the University of Toronto Press.

Librarians in some dozen libraries have generously contributed of their time and experience. The labours of other bibliographers have been equally indispensable. Dr. Walter S. Avis made available the results of his own bibliographical endeavours in the section on Canadian English, and Dr. Carl F. Klinck provided many items of value by his annual lists of graduate theses written on Canadian literature. Two other examples are the Malcolm Lowry check list prepared by Earle Birney and Margerie Lowry and the bibliography included in V. L. O. Chittick's biography of Thomas Chandler Haliburton. Needless to say, our chief debt is to the compilers of such standard indexes as the *Canadian Periodical Index*, *Poole's Index*, *Readers' Guide to Periodicals*, *Essay and General Literature Index*, etc. Most of the references obtained from such sources have been individually verified, but it was not possible to examine all such items.

To our wives we are indebted not only for patience and understanding but also for more tangible, and only slightly less onerous, assistance in such matters as checking, typing, and proofreading.

Kingston, Ontario
Vancouver, British Columbia
June, 1965
October, 1972

R. E. WATTERS
I. F. BELL

Partial List of Abbreviations

The following list includes the titles of fewer than half the periodicals referred to in the pages of this *Check List*. Omitted are the many periodicals whose titles are either cited in full (e.g. TIME, CURTAIN CALL) or shortened only in a minor and unmistakable fashion (e.g., BLACKWOOD'S MAG, JEWISH WESTERN BUL). Indeed, we hope that most persons using this book will find all our abbreviated forms instantly intelligible. However, the list is provided to assist readers, especially those outside Canada, who may be relatively unfamiliar with some of the abbreviations (including those for the names of some Canadian provinces).

ACTA VIC, *Acta Victoriana*
L'ACTION UNIV, *L'Action universitaire*
ALTA HIST R, *Alberta Historical Review*
AMER HIST R, *American Historical Review*
AMER J PHILOLOGY, *American Journal of Philology*
AMER LIB ASSOC BUL, *American Library Association Bulletin*
AMER LIT, *American Literature*
ANGLO-AMER R, *Anglo-American Review*
ANN AMER ACAD POL SOC SCI, *Annals of the American Academy of Political and Social Science*
ASSOC CAN BKMN LIT BUL, *Association of Canadian Bookmen's Literary Bulletin*
ATLAN ADV, *Atlantic Advocate*
ATLAN MO, *Atlantic Monthly*
BC HIST Q, *British Columbia Historical Quarterly*
BC LIB Q, *British Columbia Library Quarterly*
BC MO, *British Columbia Monthly* (also *Westminster Hall and B.C. Monthly*)
BKS ABROAD, *Books Abroad*
BK NEWS, *Book News*
BKMN (London), *Bookman* (London)
BKMN (New York), *Bookman* (New York)
BRIT ANN LIT, *British Annual of Literature*
BUL HUMAN ASSOC CAN, *Bulletin of the Humanities Association of Canada*
CAN ANNUAL R, *Canadian Annual Review*
CAN ART, *Canadian Art*
CAN AUTH, *Canadian Author*
CAN AUTH & BKMN, *Canadian Author and Bookman*
CAN AV, *Canadian Aviation*
CAN BKMN, *Canadian Bookman*
CAN BUS, *Canadian Business*

CAN COMMENT, *Canadian Commentator*
CAN COUNCIL BUL, *Canada Council Bulletin*
CAN GEOG J, *Canadian Geographical Journal*
CAN HIST ASSOC REP, *Canadian Historical Association, Report*
CAN HIST R, *Canadian Historical Review*
CAN J ECON, *Canadian Journal of Economics and Political Science*
CAN J INDUSTRY, *Canadian Journal of Industry, Science and Art* (1856–1866)
    [successor to *Canadian Journal* (1852–1855)]
CAN LIB ASSOC BUL, *Canadian Library Association Bulletin*
CAN LIT, *Canadian Literature*
CAN MAG, *Canadian Magazine*
CAN MAG & LIT REPOSITORY, *Canadian Magazine and Literary Repository*
CAN RECORD SCI, *Canadian Record of Science*
CAN MED J, *Canadian Medical Journal*
CAN MO, *Canada Month*
CAN MO & NATL R, *Canadian Monthly and National Review*
CAN MUS, *Canadian Musical Journal*
CAN POETRY, *Canadian Poetry Magazine*
CAN THINKER, *Canadian Thinker*
CHRISTIAN CENT, *Christian Century*
CHRISTIAN SCI MON, *Christian Science Monitor*
CONTEMP VERSE, *Contemporary Verse*
CURRENT BIOG, *Current Biography*
DAL R, *Dalhousie Review*
DIALECT N, *Dialect Notes*
DOM ILLUS, *Dominion Illustrated*
EDUC RECORD (Quebec), *Educational Record* (Quebec)
EMP CLUB CAN, *Empire Club Speeches* (or Addresses)
ESSAYS AND STUDIES BY MEM ENG ASSOC (LONDON), *Essays and Studies by Members of the English Association* (London)
FOR & OUTDOORS, *Forest and Outdoors*
FOREIGN TR, *Foreign Trade*
HARVARD THEOL R, *Harvard Theological Review*
HUMANITIES ASSOC CAN BUL, *Humanities Association of Canada Bulletin*
INTL FORUM, *International Forum*
J CAN LING ASSOC, *Journal of the Canadian Linguistic Association* (becomes *Canadian Journal of Linguistics*)
J E & G PHILOLOGY, *Journal of English and Germanic Philology*
J EDUC NOVA SCOTIA, *Journal of Education for Nova Scotia*
J NFLD TCHRS ASSOC, *Journal of the Newfoundland Teachers Association*
LIB WORLD, *Library World*
LIT DIGEST, *Literary Digest*
LIT R, *Literary Review*
MACL MAG, *Maclean's Magazine*
MAN ARTS R, *Manitoba Arts Review*
McGILL U MAG, *McGill University Magazine*
McMASTER U MO, *McMaster University Monthly*
MINNESOTA HIST, *Minnesota History*
MOD LANG R, *Modern Language Review*
NATL MO, *National Monthly*

NATL R, *National Review*
NEW ENGLAND MAG, *New England Magazine*
NEW ENGLAND Q, *New England Quarterly*
NFLD Q, *Newfoundland Quarterly*
NORTH AMER R, *North American Review*
NS HIST SOC COLL, *Nova Scotia Historical Society Collections*
ONT HIST, *Ontario History*
ONT HIST SOC PAPERS, *Ontario Historical Society Papers*
ONT LIB R, *Ontario Library Review*
ORBIS, *Orbis: Bulletin international de documentation linguistic* (Louvain)
P M, *P M Magazine* (Vancouver, 1951–1952)
PUB AFFAIRS, *Public Affairs*
PUB AMER DIALECT SOC, *Publications of the American Dialect Society*
PUB WKLY, *Publishers' Weekly*
Q J SPEECH, *Quarterly Journal of Speech*
QUE LIT HIST SOC TRANS, *Quebec Literary and Historical Society Transactions*
QUEBEC, *Quebec: A Monthly Journal devoted to the Interests of the Province* . . .
QUEEN'S Q, *Queen's Quarterly*
QUEEN'S R, *Queen's Review*
R DE L'UNIV LAVAL, *Revue de l'Université Laval*
R DE L'UNIV D'OTTAWA, *Revue de l'Université d'Ottawa*
REV OF REV, *Review of Reviews*
ROSE-BEL CAN MO, *Rose-Belford's Canadian Monthly*
ROY BANK MAG, *Royal Bank Magazine*
ROY SOC CAN PROC & TRANS, *Royal Society of Canada Proceedings and Transactions*
SASK HIST, *Saskatchewan History*
SAT EVE POST, *Saturday Evening Post*
SAT N, *Saturday Night*
SAT R, *Saturday Review*
SAT R LIT, *Saturday Review of Literature*
TAM R, *Tamarack Review*
THEATRE ARTS MO, *Theatre Arts Monthly*
TIMES LIT SUPP (London), *Times Literary Supplement*
TRANS ILLINOIS ACAD SCIENCE, *Transactions of the Illinois Academy of Science*
UBC ALUMNI CHRONICLE, *University of British Columbia Alumni Chronicle*
UNIV MAG (Montreal), *University Magazine*
UNIV TOR MO, *University of Toronto Monthly*
UNIV TOR Q, *University of Toronto Quarterly*
VAN DAILY PROV MAG, *Vancouver Daily Province Magazine*
WESTMINSTER (Vancouver), *The Westminster* (Vancouver)
WESTMINSTER HALL, *Westminster Hall* and *Westminster Hall and Farthest West Review*
WESTMINSTER R (Vancouver), *Westminster Review* (Vancouver)
WILSON LIB BUL, *Wilson Library Bulletin*
WOMEN'S CAN HIST SOC OTTAWA TRANS, *Women's Canadian Historical Society of Ottawa, Transactions*

Contents

PART ONE

General Bibliographies

ANON. "Alphabetical List of Books in the Dominion Archives, 1902," CAN ARCHIVES REP (1902) pp 1–123.

────── "Alphabetical List of Pamphlets in the Dominion Archives, 1902," CAN ARCHIVES REP (1903) pp 3–272.

────── "Canada: A Reading Guide for Children and Young People, 1951–1958 Supplement," ONT LIB R 43: 40–46 (Feb. 1959).

────── "Canadian Books of the Year." An annual listing in CAN ANNUAL R (1900–1938), ed. J. Castell Hopkins.

────── "Canadian Heritage Books," CAN LIB ASSOC BUL 16: 267–275 (May 1960).

────── "Linguistica Canadiana: A Linguistic Bibliography and Supplement for Previous Years," J CAN LING ASSOC 6: 85–89 (Spring 1960).

────── "The Literature of Education in Canada," ROSE-BEL CAN MO 4: 593–600 (June 1880).

────── "Northwest Bookshelf: Checklist of Crown Colony Imprints," BC HIST Q 1: 263–271 (Oct. 1937).

BEALS, HELEN D. *A Catalogue of the Eric R. Dennis Collection of Canadiana in the Library of Acadia University* (Wolfville, N.S., the University, 1938).

BELL, INGLIS FREEMAN, ed. "Canadian Literature—1959: A Checklist," CAN LIT no 3: 91–108 (Winter 1960). [A continuing annual compilation.]

BERTON, PIERRE. "Gold Rush Writing: The Literature of the Klondike," CAN LIT no 4: 59–67 (Spring 1960).

BOURINOT, JOHN G. "Bibliography of the Members of the Royal Society of Canada," ROY SOC CAN PROC & TRANS 1st ser 12: 1–79 (1894).

BOYLE, GERTRUDE N. *A Bibliography of Canadiana—First Supplement* (Toronto, Public Library, 1959).

BROWN, EDWARD KILLORAN *et al.* "Canadian Classics Chosen for Unesco," CAN LIB ASSOC BUL 5: 68–71 (Sept. 1948).

BROWN, MARY MARKHAM. *An Index to* The Literary Garland (*Montreal 1838–1851*) (Toronto, Bibliographical Society of Canada, 1962).

BULL, WILLIAM PERKINS. *M'N N Canadiana* (Brampton, Charters, 1933).

BURPEE, LAWRENCE J. "Bibliography in Canada," PUBLIC LIBRARIES 12: 401–405 (1907).

────── "A Canadian Bibliography for the Year 1901," ROY SOC CAN PROC & TRANS 2nd ser 8: 233–344 (1902).

BUSTERD, I. A. "What Do They Read? Books for Canadian Children," CAN LIB ASSOC BUL 15: 40–44 (July 1958).

CAMPBELL, CATHERINE, comp. *Canada's Two Heritages . . . as Revealed in Their Writings of the Present Century: A Bibliography to the End of 1952* (London, Ont., University of Western Ontario Library, 1954).

CANADA FOUNDATION. *Canadian Cultural Publications: English Language List*. Rev. April 1952; August 1956 (issued jointly by the Canada Foundation and the Canadian Citizenship Council, Ottawa, 1952; 1956).

CANADIAN ADVERTISING AGENCY. *Canadian Magazines and Society Papers* (Toronto, the Agency, 1896).

CANADIAN ASSOCIATION FOR ADULT EDUCATION. *A Selective Bibliography of Canadian Plays* (Toronto, the Association, 1957).

Canadian Index to Periodicals and Documentary Films: 1948–1959 [cumulated in one volume]; 1960— [monthly, Sept.–June, with annual cumulations] (Ottawa, Canadian Library Association and National Library of Canada, 1960—).

Canadian Periodical Index, 1st annual cumulation, 1931 (Windsor, Ont., Public Library, 1932). [Forms the first printed and cumulated number in the series of quarterly indexes issued in multigraphed form since Jan. 1928. Continued 1932 by quarterly multigraphed numbers which index 41 periodicals. Not published 1933–1937.]

Canadian Periodical Index, 1938–1947 (Toronto, Public Libraries Branch, Ontario Dept. of Education, 1939–1949), 10 vols. [A cumulation of the quarterly indexes published in the *Ontario Library Review*.]

Canadiana: A List of Publications of Canadian Interest (Ottawa, Bibliographic Centre, National Library, 1950—). [A continuing serial, issued monthly, with annual cumulations.]

CARNOCHAN, JANET. "Rare Canadian Books," CAN MAG 43: 236–238 (July 1914).

CROMBIE, JEAN BREAKELL. *Bibliography of Canadiana, 1944* (Montreal, Sir George Williams College, 1944).

DEACON, W. A. "Book-List." In his *Poteen, a Pot-Pourri of Canadian Essays* (Ottawa, Graphic, 1926) pp 221–229

——— "The First Histories of Canadian Literature," WILLISON'S MO 1: 263–264ff (Dec. 1925). Also in his *Poteen* (Ottawa, Graphic, 1926) pp. 207–217.

——— "A Guide to the Anthologies." In his *Poteen* (Ottawa, Graphic, 1926) pp 187–203.

——— "Know Canada in Ten Easy Books," PUB WKLY 141: 2196–2199 (June 13, 1942).

DEVERELL, A. FREDERICK. *Canadian Bibliography of Reading and Literature Instruction (English) 1760–1959* (Toronto, Copp Clark, 1963).

DIXON, R. F. "Some Old Books on Canada," CAN BKMN 2: 49–51 (July 1920).

DOUGLAS, ROBERT W. *Catalogue, Bibliotheca Canadensis* (Toronto, Douglas, 1887).

DROLET, A. "Early Canadiana in Laval University Library," CAN LIB ASSOC BUL 14: 107–108 (Dec. 1957).

DUFF, LOUIS BLAKE. "The Earliest Canadian Travel Books," PHILOBIBLON, ZEITSCHRIFT FÜR BÜCHERLIEBHABER, 8 Jahrgang, Heft Nr 7 (1935): pp 317–324 in German; pp 325–333 in English.

EVERITT, CORA. "List of Source Material Used for Canadian Biography by the Cataloguing Division of the Toronto Public Library," ONT LIB R 20: 131–134 (Aug. 1936).

GARRETT, ROBERT MAX. "Canadian Short Stories from Periodicals," CAN BKMN 4: 42, 44, 46 (Feb. 1922).

GOGGIO, EMILE, BEATRICE CORRIGAN, and JACK H. PARKER. *A Bibliography of Canadian Cultural Periodicals (English and French) from Colonial Times to 1950 in Canadian Libraries* (Toronto, the University, 1955).

GUSTAFSON, RALPH BAKER. *Poetry and Canada, a Guide to Reading* (Ottawa, Canadian Legion Educational Services, 1945).

HAIGHT, WILLET RICKETSON. *Canadian Catalogue of Books, 1791–1895* (Toronto, Haight, 1896).

HARLOWE, DOROTHY. *A Catalogue of Canadian Manuscripts* (Toronto, Ryerson, 1946).

HAYWOOD, CHARLES. *A Bibliography of North American Folklore and Folksong* (New York, Greenberg, 1951).

HERBERT, WALTER. "Periodical Literature in Canada: The Humanities," CAN LIB ASSOC BUL 16: 289–290 (May 1960).

HORNING, LEWIS EMERSON and LAWRENCE J. BURPEE. *A Bibliography of Canadian Fiction (English)* (Toronto, Briggs, 1904). [Victoria University Library Publication no 2.]

HUMANITIES RESEACH COUNCIL OF CANADA. *Canadian Graduate Theses in the Humanities and Social Sciences, 1921–1946* (Ottawa, King's Printer, 1951).

HURTIG, M. "Books in Canada," HUMANITIES ASSOC CAN BUL no 27: 8, 18 (April 1959).

JACK, D. R. "Acadian Magazines," ROY SOC CAN PROC & TRANS 2nd ser 9: 173–203 (1903).

JAMES, CHARLES CANNIFF. *A Bibliography of Canadian Poetry (English)* (Toronto, Briggs, 1899). [Victoria University Library Publication no 1.]

JEFFERYS, CHARLES WILLIAM. *A Catalogue of the Sigmund Samuel Collection, Canadiana and Americana* (Toronto, Ryerson, 1948).

KINGSFORD, WILLIAM. *The Early Bibliography of the Province of Ontario . . .* (Toronto, Rowsell & Hutchison, 1892).

KLINCK, CARL F., ed. "Canadian Literature—1959, a Checklist: Theses," CAN LIT no 3: 108 (Winter 1960). [A continuing annual compilation.]

―――― "Some Anonymous Literature of the War of 1812," ONT HIST 49: 49–60 (Spring 1957).

KNISTER, RAYMOND. "List of Canadian Short Stories in Books and Magazines." In *Canadian Short Stories*, ed. Raymond Knister (Toronto, Macmillan, 1928) pp 329–340.

LAMB, W. KAYE. "Seventy-Five Years of Canadian Bibliography," ROY SOC CAN PROC & TRANS 3rd ser 51: sect II, 1–11 (1957).

LANDE, LAWRENCE M. *Old Lamps Aglow* (Montreal, the Author, 1957). [Articles listed separately in this bibliography.]

LAURENCE, ROBERT G. "A Descriptive Bibliography of the Manuscript Material in the Rufus Hathaway Collection of Canadian Literature, University of New Brunswick" (Thesis, University of New Brunswick, 1947).

LONG, ROBERT JAMES. *Nova Scotia Authors and Their Work* (East Orange, N.J., the Author, 1918).

LOOSLEY, E. W. and E. WICKSON. "Canada, a Reading Guide," ONT LIB R 25: 119–125+ (May 1941).

LUNN, A. J. E. "Bibliography of the History of the Canadian Press," CAN HIST R 22: 416–433 (Dec. 1941).

―――― "Milestones in Canadian Bibliography," CAN LIB ASSOC BUL 16: 311–314 (May 1960).

McDowell, M. "A History of Canadian Children's Literature to 1900, Together with a Checklist" (Thesis, University of New Brunswick, 1957).

MacFarlane, William Godsoe. *New Brunswick Bibliography* (Saint John, N.B., Sun Print, 1895).

McGill University, Library School. *A Bibliography of Canadian Bibliographies* (Montreal, McGill University Library, 1930).

MacTaggart, Hazel I. *Publications of the Government of Ontario 1901–1955* (Toronto, printed and distributed by the University of Toronto Press for the Queen's Printer, 1964).

Matthews, William, comp. *Canadian Diaries and Autobiographies* (Berkeley, University of California Press, 1950).

Meikle, W. *The Canadian Newspaper Directory* (Toronto, 1858).

Moir, Elizabeth. "List of Books on Canadian Bibliography in the Reference Department of the Toronto Public Library," LIB WORLD 13: 111–113 (1910–1911).

Morgan, Henry James. *Bibliotheca Canadensis; or, a Manual of Canadian Literature* (Ottawa, Desbarats, 1867).

Morse, William Inglis. *The Canadian Collection at Harvard University* (Cambridge, Mass., Harvard University, 1944–1949) 6 vols.

New Brunswick, University of, Library. *Catalogue of the Rufus Hathaway Collection of Canadian Literature, University of New Brunswick* (Fredericton, the University, 1935).

Ontario, Department of Education. *Catalogue of the Books Relating to Canada, Historical and Biographical, in the Library of the Educational Department for Ontario* (Toronto, Warwick, 1890).

Pacey, Desmond. "Areas of Research in Canadian Literature," UNIV TOR Q 23: 58–63 (Oct. 1953).

Park, M. G. "Canadian Poetry," MEANJIN (Australia) no 78, vol 18: 350–352 (no 3, 1959).

Peel, Bruce Braden. *Bibliography of the Prairie Provinces to 1953* (Toronto, University of Toronto Press, 1956; Supplement, 1963).

Pierce, Lorne. *Unexplored Fields of Canadian Literature* (Toronto, Ryerson, 1932).

Playwrights' Studio Group. *Catalogue of Original Canadian Plays Suitable for the Little Theatre by the Playwrights' Studio Group Successfully Produced at Hart House Theatre, Toronto* (Toronto, 1936).

Porteous, Janet S. *Canadiana 1698–1900 in the Possession of the Douglas Library, Queen's University, Kingston, Ontario* (Kingston, the University, 1932).

Quebec Literary and Historical Society. "Index of the Lectures, Papers, and Historical Documents Published by the Literary and Historical Society of Quebec . . . comp. by F. C. Wurtele . . . ." QUE LIT HIST SOC TRANS no 18 (1883–1886).

Ray, M. "Project in Canadian Bibliography," ONT LIB R 30: 392–395 (Nov. 1946).

Samuel, Sigmund. *Catalogue of the Sigmund Samuel Collection, Canadiana and Americana* (Toronto, Ryerson, 1948).

Scadding, Henry. "Some Canadian Noms-de-plume Identified," CAN J 15: 259–276 (Oct. 1876); 15: 332–348 (Jan. 1877); 15: 436–458 (April 1877).

Simon, B. "Canadian Bibliographical Tools," ONT LIB R 23: 204–206 (May 1939).

STATON, FRANCES M. *The Canadian North West* (Toronto, Public Library, 1931).

STATON, FRANCES M. and MARIE TREMAINE, eds. *A Bibliography of Canadiana* (Toronto, Public Library, 1934). [*First Supplement*, ed. by Gertrude N. Boyle, 1959.]

TANGHE, RAYMOND. *Bibliography of Canadian Bibliographies* (Toronto, published in association with the Bibliographical Society of Canada by University of Toronto Press, 1960; Supps., 1962, 1965). [2nd ed. by D. Lochhead, 1972.]

THOMAS, CLARA EILEEN. *Canadian Novelists, 1920–1945* (Toronto, Longmans, 1946).

TOD, DOROTHEA D. and AUDREY CORDINGLEY. "A Bibliography of Canadian Literary Periodicals, 1789–1900: Part I—English-Canadian," ROY SOC CAN PROC & TRANS 3rd ser 26: sect II, 87–96 (1932).

—— *A Check-List of Canadian Imprints, 1900–1925* (Ottawa, King's Printer, 1950).

TORONTO PUBLIC LIBRARY. *Books and Pamphlets Published in Canada, up to the Year Eighteen Hundred and Thirty Seven, Copies of which are in the Public Reference Library, Toronto* (Toronto, the Library, 1916; Supplements Dec. 1919 and Jan. 1926).

—— *The Canadian Catalogue of Books Published in Canada, Books about Canada, as Well as Those Written by Canadians, with Imprints of 1921– 1949* (Toronto, the Library, 1922–1950). [Consolidated into two volumes, with cumulated author index (Toronto, Public Libraries, 1959).]

TREMAINE, MARIE. *A Bibliography of Canadian Imprints, 1751–1800* (Toronto, University of Toronto Press, 1952).

—— "Canadian Pseudonyms," WILSON'S BUL 6: 52–53 (Sept. 1931).

University of Toronto Quarterly. "Letters in Canada." Published annually since vol 5, 1936. [Various editors.]

WALLACE, W. S. "Bibliography of Canadiana," CAN HIST R 5: 4–8 (March 1924).

—— "The Bibliography of 'Canadiana,' " UNIV MAG (Montreal) 11: 284– 288 (April 1912).

—— comp. *A Dictionary of North American Authors Deceased before 1950* (Toronto, Ryerson, 1951).

—— "Literature Relating to the Selkirk Controversy," CAN HIST R 13: 45– 50 (March 1932).

—— "Periodical Literature of Upper Canada," CAN HIST R 12: 4–22 (March 1931); 12: 182–188 (June 1931).

—— "Periodicals." In *Encyclopaedia of Canada* (Toronto, University Associates of Canada Ltd., 1937) vol 5, pp 105–106.

—— *The Ryerson Imprint.* A Check List of the Books and Pamphlets Published by the Ryerson Press since . . . 1829 (Toronto, Ryerson, [1954]).

WATTERS, REGINALD EYRE. *A Check List of Canadian Literature and Background Materials 1628–1950* (Toronto, University of Toronto Press, 1959).

WEBLING, LUCY. *Catalogue of the John Clarence Webster Canadiana Collection (Pictorial Section) New Brunswick Museum* (Saint John, N.B., Museum, 1939).

WHITE, WILLIAM JOHN, ed. *Canadiana, a Collection of Canadian Notes* (Montreal, Gazette Print., 1889–1890).

WILSON, C. P. "Hobby for Booklovers," BEAVER 276: 7–9 (Dec. 1945).

WINNIPEG PUBLIC LIBRARY. *A Selective Bibliography of Canadiana of the Prairie Provinces* (Winnipeg, the Library, 1949).

Canadian Culture and Background

ANDREW, G. C. "The Canada Council: A National Necessity," QUEEN'S Q 61: 291–303 (Autumn 1954).

ANON. "The Arts from Coast to Coast," FOOD FOR THOUGHT 10: 53–58 (May 1950).

———— "The Canada Council," CAN FORUM 32: 27–28 (May 1952).

———— "Fine Arts in the West," CAN FORUM 31: 99 (Aug. 1951).

———— "Highlights of the Massey Report," CAN UNIONIST 25: 202–203, 215 (June 1951).

———— "The Massey Report," CAN FORUM 31: 73–74 (July 1951).

———— "Massey Report: Second Anniversary; Editorial," CAN FORUM 33: 51–52 (June 1953).

ARTS & LETTERS CLUB OF TORONTO, comp. *The Yearbook of Canadian Art 1913–* (Toronto, Dent, n.d.). [Articles are listed separately in this bibliography.]

AYRE, ROBERT. "Painting." In *The Arts in Canada*, ed. Malcolm Ross ([Toronto], Macmillan, 1958) pp 9–32.

BECKWITH, JOHN. "Music." In *The Arts in Canada,* ed. Malcolm Ross ([Toronto], Macmillan, 1958) pp 43–51.

———— "Music." In *The Culture of Contemporary Canada*, ed. Julian Park. (Ithaca, N.Y., Cornell University Press, 1957) pp 143–162.

BISSELL, CLAUDE, ed. *Our Living Tradition*, First Series (Toronto, published in association with Carleton University by University of Toronto Press, 1957). [A continuing serial, *see under* McDougall.]

BONENFANT, JEAN CHARLES. "Culture in Quebec Today," UNIV TOR Q 27: 386–397 (April 1958).

BOURINOT, ARTHUR S. (ed.), *At the Mermaid Inn.* Being Selections from Essays on Life and Literature which Appeared in the Toronto *Globe* 1829–1893 (Ottawa, Bourinot, 1958). [Selections from a column series conducted by A. Lampman, W. W. Campbell, and D. C. Scott.]

BOURINOT, JOHN GEORGE. *The Intellectual Development of the Canadian People* (Toronto, Hunter Rose, 1881).

———— "Literature and Art in Canada," ANGLO-AMER MAG (London) 3: 99–110 (Feb. 1900).

———— "Literary Culture in Canada," SCOTTISH R 30: 143–163 (July 1897).

———— "Our Intellectual Strength and Weakness," ROY SOC CAN PROC & TRANS 1st ser 11: 3–54 (1893).

BREBNER, J. B. "Canadianism," CAN HIST ASSOC REP (1944) pp 5–15.

BRIDLE, AUGUSTUS. *The Story of the Club* (Toronto, Arts & Letters Club, 1945).

BROOKER, BERTRAM, ed. *Yearbook of the Arts in Canada . . . 1928/29* (Toronto, Macmillan, 1929). [Articles are listed separately in this bibliography.]

———— ed. *Yearbook of the Arts in Canada 1936* (Toronto, Macmillan, 1936). [Articles are listed separately in this bibliography.]

BRUCHÉSI, J. "Culture in Canada," ROY SOC CAN PROC & TRANS 3rd ser 45: sect II, 141–157 (1951).

BUCHANAN, DONALD WILLIAM, ed. *Canadian Painters* (Oxford, Phaidon, 1945).
———— *The Growth of Canadian Painting* (London, Collins, 1950).
CALLAGHAN, M. E. "We're on the Wrong Track in Our Culture Quest," MACL MAG 70: 8, 86–87 (May 25, 1957).
CANADA FIRST [pseud.]. "A Question for All Canadian Readers and Homes," BC MO 26: 1 (April 1927).
CHAPIN, MIRIAM. "Salvaging our Indian Languages," QUEEN'S Q 60: 79–87 (1953–1954).
COLGATE, WILLIAM G. *Canadian Art: Its Origin and Development* (Toronto, Ryerson, 1943).
DALE, WILLIAM S. A. "Sculpture." In *The Arts in Canada*, ed. Malcolm Ross ([Toronto], Macmillan, 1958) pp 33–41.
DAVIES, BLODWEN. "Quickening of the Arts in Canada," CAN FORUM 26: 34, 36 (May 1946).
DAVIES, ROBERTSON. *A Voice from the Attic* (Toronto, McClelland & Stewart, 1960).
DENNISON, MERRILL. "Canada's Vital Story," CAN AUTH & BKMN 24: 30–40 (Sept. 1948).
DOUGLAS, R. W. "The Intellectual Progress of Canada during the Last Fifty Years, and the Present State of Its Literature," ROSE-BEL CAN MO 7: 465–476 (Jan. 1875).
DURNFORD, A. T. GALT. "Handicrafts." In *The Arts in Canada*, ed. Malcolm Ross ([Toronto], Macmillan, 1958) pp 155–159.
EGGLESTON, WILFRED. "Canadian Geography and National Culture," CAN GEOG J 43: 254–273 (Dec. 1951).
———— "Canadians and Canadian Books," QUEEN'S Q 52: 208–213 (Summer 1945).
———— *The Frontier and Canadian Letters* (Toronto, Ryerson, 1957).
FAIRLEY, BARKER. "Canadian Art: Man vs Landscape." In *Our Sense of Identity* ed. Malcolm Ross (Toronto, Ryerson, 1954) pp 230–234.
FAWCETT, W. McRAE. "Canada Climbs Parnassus," DAL R 11: 383–388 (Oct. 1931).
Food for Thought. "The Arts in Canada"; entire issue 10: 1–60 (May 1950).
FRASER, C. F. "The Crisis in the Arts, Letters and Sciences," DAL R 30: 35–45 (April 1950).
GLOVER, GUY. "Ballet as a Canadian Art," QUEENS Q 60: 501–513 (Winter 1953–1954).
———— "Film." In *The Arts in Canada*, ed. Malcolm Ross ([Toronto], Macmillan, 1958) pp 103–113.
GOMERY, PERCY. "Do Canadians Care for Canadian Literature in Any Form?" BC MO 26: 1–3 (Feb. 1927).
HAMBLETON, JOSEPHINE. "Sculpture," FOOD FOR THOUGHT 10: 36–38 (May 1950).
HAMMOND, MELVIN ORMOND. *Painting and Sculpture in Canada* (Toronto, Ryerson, 1930).
HARTE, W. B. "Intellectual Life and Literature in Canada," NEW ENG MAG n.s. 1: 377ff (Dec. 1889).
HERBERT, W. B. "Canada Foundation," CAN ART 16: 29, 65–66 (Winter 1959).
———— "Who Supports the Arts?" FOOD FOR THOUGHT 10: 49–52 (May 1950).

HOUSSER, FREDERICK BROUGHTON. "The Amateur Movement in Canadian Painting." In *Yearbook of the Arts in Canada 1928–1929*, ed. Bertam Brooker (Toronto, Macmillan, 1929) pp 83–90.

——— *A Canadian Art Movement* (Toronto, Macmillan, 1926).

HUBBARD, R. H. "Growth in Canadian Art." In *The Culture of Contemporary Canada*, ed. Julian Park (Ithaca, N.Y., Cornell University Press, 1957) pp 95–142.

——— "Painting," FOOD FOR THOUGHT 10: 31–34 (May 1950).

HUTCHISON, BRUCE. "The Canadian Personality." In *Our Sense of Identity*, ed. Malcolm Ross (Toronto, Ryerson, 1954) pp 39–45.

INGRAM, KENNETH. "Music," FOOD FOR THOUGHT 10: 44–48 (May 1950).

IRVING, JOHN A. "Philosophy." In *The Culture of Contemporary Canada*, ed. Julian Park (Ithaca, N.Y., Cornell University Press, 1957) pp 242–273.

JACKSON, A. Y. "The Birth of the Group of Seven." In *Our Sense of Identity*, ed. Malcolm Ross (Toronto, Ryerson, 1954) pp 220–230.

JACOB, FRED. "The Background of Canadian Literature," CAN BKMN 3: 43–45 (June 1921).

JOHNSTONE, KEN. "Ballet." In *The Arts in Canada*, ed. Malcolm Ross ([Toronto], Macmillan, 1958) pp 53–60.

KENNEDY, WARNETT. "Architecture and Town Planning." In *The Arts in Canada*, ed. Malcolm Ross ([Toronto], Macmillan, 1958) pp 133–148.

KIDD, J. R. "Films," FOOD FOR THOUGHT 10: 16–19 (May 1950).

KIRKCONNELL, WATSON and A. S. P. WOODHOUSE. *The Humanities in Canada* (Ottawa, Humanities Research Council, 1947).

LAMBERT, RICHARD STANTON. *The Adventure of Canadian Painting* (Toronto, McClelland & Stewart, 1947).

LANDON, F. "Canadian Scene, 1880–1890," CAN HIST ASSOC REP (1942) pp 5–18.

LASSERRE, FRED. "Architecture," FOOD FOR THOUGHT 10: 39–40 (May 1950).

LAVERE, G. F. "State of Canadian Culture: a General View," CULTURE 15: 83–90 (mars 1954).

LEBEL, MAURICE. "The Problems and Advantages of Bilingual Culture in Canada," CULTURE 12: 35–42 (mars 1951).

LEWIS, D. E. "Timid Renaissance," CULTURE 7: 48–53 (mars 1946).

LISMER, ARTHUR. "Art Appreciation." In *Yearbook of the Arts in Canada 1928–1929*, ed. Bertram Brooker (Toronto, Macmillan, 1929) pp 59–71.

LORTIE, L. "Canadian Universities and a Canadian Culture," L'ACTION UNIV 16: 46–56 (avril 1950).

LOWER, A. R. M. "Colonialism and Culture [reply to H. Lundie]," CAN FORUM 14: 264–265 (April 1934).

LUNDIE, H. "Colonial Literature; a False Analogy," CAN FORUM 14: 181–182 (Feb. 1934).

MAHEUX, J. T. A. "Dilemma for Our Culture," CAN HIST ASSOC REP (1949) pp 1–6.

MACDONALD, THOREAU. *The Group of Seven* (Toronto, Ryerson, 1944).

McDOUGALL, ROBERT L., ed. *Our Living Tradition*, Second and Third Series (Toronto, published in association with Carleton University by University of Toronto Press, 1959). [A continuing serial.]

McDOWELL, F. E. D. "Record of Achievement: A History of the Governor-

General's Awards . . . ," CAN AUTH & BKMN 28: 14–19 (Winter 1952–1953).

MacLennan, Hugh. "Canada between Covers," SAT R LIT 29: 5–6, 28–30 (Sept. 7, 1946).

―――― "Culture, Canadian Style," SAT R LIT 25: 3–4ff (March 28, 1942).

McRae, Douglas George Wallis. *The Arts and Crafts of Canada* (Toronto, Macmillan, 1944).

MacTavish, Newton McFaul. *The Fine Arts in Canada* (Toronto, Macmillan, 1925).

Markham, Mary. "An Index to the Literary Garland, 1838–1851, with Three Essays on Colonial Fiction" (Thesis, University of Western Ontario, 1949). [Published in part as *An Index to The Literary Garland (Montreal 1838–1851)* by Mary Markham Brown (Toronto, Bibliographical Society of Canada, 1962).]

Massey, Vincent. *On Being Canadian* (Toronto, Dent, 1948).

―――― *Speaking of Canada* (Toronto, Macmillan, 1959).

Mazzoleni, Ettore. "Music in Canada," QUEEN'S Q 60: 485–495 (Winter 1953-1954).

Moore, Mavor. "Radio," FOOD FOR THOUGHT 10: 20–24 (May 1950).

―――― "Radio and Television." In *The Arts in Canada*, ed. Malcolm Ross ([Toronto], Macmillan, 1958) pp 115–124.

Morris, Edmund Montague. *Art in Canada: The Early Painters* (Toronto, 1911?).

Neel, Boyd. "Opera." In *The Arts in Canada*, ed. Malcolm Ross ([Toronto], Macmillan, 1958) pp 61–66.

Nicol, E. P. "Aid for the Arts [radio talk]," FOOD FOR THOUGHT 15: 28–31 (Feb. 1955).

Park, Julian, ed. *The Culture of Contemporary Canada* (Ithaca, N.Y., Cornell University Press, 1957). [Articles listed separately in this bibliography.]

Penfield, Wilder. "The Liberal Arts in Canada," DAL R 38: 497–507 (Winter 1959).

Perry, M. Eugenie. "Give the Canadian Author a Chance," BC MO 26: 15–16 (Feb. 1927).

Phelps, Arthur L. "Canadian Literature and Canadian Society," NORTHERN R 3: 23–26, 31–35 (April–May 1950).

Phillips, Alan. "Are We Getting Our Money's Worth from the Canada Council?" MACL MAG 72: 26, 72–75 (Dec. 5, 1959).

Phillips, Charles E. "Education." In *The Culture of Contemporary Canada*, ed. Julian Park (Ithaca N.Y., Cornell University Press, 1957) pp 293–326.

Pierce, Lorne. *A Canadian Nation* (Toronto, Ryerson, 1960).

Priestley, F. E. L. "Creative Scholarship." In *The Arts in Canada*, ed. Malcolm Ross ([Toronto], Macmillan, 1958) pp 98–101.

Queen's Quarterly. "Our Lively Arts"; 60: 476–513 (Winter 1953–1954).

Rayski-Kietliez, K. "The Canadian Cultural Pattern," DAL R 30: 169–178 (July 1950).

Robbins, J. R. "Canada between Covers [*Encyclopedia Canadiana*]," FOOD FOR THOUGHT 18: 171–178 (Jan. 1958).

Robson, Albert Henry. *Canadian Landscape Painters* (Toronto, Ryerson, 1932).

Ross, Malcolm M., ed. *The Arts in Canada* ([Toronto], Macmillan, 1958). [Articles listed separately in this bibliography.]

———— *Our Sense of Identity: a Book of Canadian Essays*, ed. with an introduction by Malcolm Ross (Toronto, Ryerson, 1954). [Articles listed separately in this bibliography.]

ROYAL COMMISSION ON NATIONAL DEVELOPMENT IN THE ARTS, LETTERS, AND SCIENCES 1949–1951. *Report* (Ottawa, King's Printer, 1951).

———— *Studies. A Selection of Essays Prepared for the Royal Commission on National Development in the Arts, Letters and Sciences* (Ottawa, King's Printer, 1951). [Articles listed separately in this bibliography.]

SANDWELL, B. K. "A Canadian Philosophy?" SAT N 67: 5–6 (July 12, 1952).

———— "The Council for Culture," SAT N 66: 7 (June 12, 1951).

———— "The Minority Culture Report," SAT N 66: 7 (June 26, 1951).

———— "On the Canadian Mind," SAT N 66: 7 (July 24, 1951).

SANGSTER, ALLAN. "On the Air," CAN FORUM 31: 81–82 (July 1951).

SCOTT, JAMES. "Professional Culture: A New Career," SAT N 67/68: 1, 31 (Jan. 31, 1953).

SEDGWICK, JOSEPH. "The Massey Report and Television," SAT N 68: 10, 30 (Feb. 28, 1953).

SMETHURST, S. E. "Towards a National Literature," QUEEN'S Q 59: 455–463 (Winter 1952–1953).

STILING, FRANK. "The Governor General's Awards Board," CAN AUTH & BKMN 30: 4–5 (Autumn 1954).

STRINGER, ARTHUR. "Canada Finds Her Voice," EMPIRE CLUB ADDRESSES (1948–1949) pp 316–326.

———— "Canada and Outside Influences," CAN AUTH 11: 12–13 (Dec. 1933).

SYMINGTON, D. F. "Business Has a Stake in Culture," CAN BUS 23: 34–36, 72+ (Feb. 1950).

THOMSON, DONALD WALTER. *The Foundation and the Man* (Toronto, privately printed, 1959). [History of the Canadian Writers' Foundation founded by Dr. Pelham Edgar.]

TOMPKINSON, GRACE. "Colonialism and Art," DAL R 11: 147–154 (July 1931).

TROTTER, R. G. "Has Canada a National Culture?" QUEEN'S Q 44: 215–227 (Summer 1937).

UNDERHILL, FRANK H. "Notes on the Massey Report," CAN FORUM 31: 100–102 (Aug. 1951). [Also in *Our Sense of Identity*, ed. Malcolm Ross (Toronto, Ryerson, 1954) pp 33–39.]

VADEBONCŒUR, PIERRE. "Break with Tradition? Political and Cultural Evolution in Quebec," QUEEN'S Q 65: 92–103 (Spring 1958).

VANDRY, F. "French Culture and Canadian Civilization," DAL R 31: 73–81 (Summer 1951).

WALLACE, W. S. "Canadian History and Biography." In *The Yearbook of Canadian Art, 1913–* , comp. by the Arts & Letters Club of Toronto (Toronto, Dent, n.d.) pp 17–24.

———— ed. *Encyclopaedia of Canada* (Toronto, University Associates of Canada Ltd., 1937).

———— *The Growth of the Canadian National Feeling* (Toronto, Macmillan, 1927).

WATSON, JOHN. "Darwinism and Morality," CAN MO & NATL R 10: 319–326 (Oct. 1876).

WHITTAKER, HERBERT. "Canada on Stage," QUEEN'S Q 60: 495–500 (Winter 1953–1954).

WOODHOUSE, A. S. P. "The Humanities—Sixty Years," QUEEN'S Q 60: 538–550 (Winter 1954).

YEDDEAU, DAVID. "Ballet," FOOD FOR THOUGHT 10: 14–15 (May 1950).

Canadian English: Language and Linguistics

(The material for this section was supplied by Dr. Walter S. Avis)

AHREND, EVELYN R. "Ontario Speech," AMER SPEECH 9: 136–139 (April 1934).

ALEXANDER, H. "Charting Canadian Speech," J EDUC NOVA SCOTIA 4th ser 10: 457–458 (April 1939).

—— "Collecting Canadian Speech," QUEEN'S R (Kingston) 15: 45–47 (Feb. 1941).

—— "The English Language in Canada." In *Royal Commission Studies* (Ottawa, King's Printer, 1951) pp 13–24.

—— "Linguistic Geography," QUEEN'S Q 47: 38–47 (Spring 1940).

—— "Is There A Canadian Language?" CBC TIMES 7: 2–3 (Feb. 27, 1955).

ALLEN, H. B. "Canadian-American Speech Differences along the Middle Border," J CAN LING 5: 17–24 (Spring 1959).

ANON. "A New Language: Canadian English," NY TIMES (Nov. 29, 1959).

—— News report on the *Dictionary of Canadian English* being compiled by C. J. Lovell and members of the Canadian Library Association's Dictionary Committee, TIME (Can. ed.) 72: 10 (July 21, 1958).

—— News report on the *Newfoundland Dialect Dictionary* being compiled by Dr. George Story at the Memorial University of Newfoundland, TIME (Can. ed.) 68: 18 (Nov. 5, 1956).

—— "'Speaking as a Canadian," CAN COUNCIL BUL 13: 1–5 (Autumn 1962).

—— "There *Must* be a Canadian Way to Speak English," CAN MO 1: 13–14 (Dec. 1961).

—— "Watch Your Language," SHELL NEWS (Montreal) (July–Aug. 1957) pp 8–11.

ARMSTRONG, G. H. *Origin and Meaning of Place Names in Canada* (Toronto, 1930).

AVIS, WALTER S. "Bibliography of Writings on Canadian English," J CAN LING ASSOC 1: 19–20 (Oct. 1955). [Appears annually as part of "Linguistica Canadiana" in J CAN LING ASSOC (since Fall 1961 called *Canadian Journal of Linguistics*).]

—— "A Canadian Dictionary," *Inside the ACD* 11: 2 (Nov. 1958).

—— "Canadian English and Native Dictionaries," EDUCATION 3: 15–19 (Jan. 1959).

—— "Canadian English Merits a Dictionary," CULTURE 18: 245–256 (sept. 1957).

—— "Canadian Lexicon in the Making," CBC TIMES 9: 2 (March 24–30, 1957).

—— *"Darn* in *The Clockmaker,"* AMER SPEECH 26: 302–303 (Dec. 1951).

—— "English in Canada Today," *Documents de l'Alliance Canadienne* (1961) pp 51–59. For a French version of this article see R DE L'UNIV LAVAL 16: 314–322 (déc. 1961).

—— "Further Lexicographical Evidence from *The Clockmaker."* AMER SPEECH 27: 16–19 (Feb. 1952).

—— "The Importance of Pronunciation in a Canadian Dictionary," TRANS-LATORS' J 3: 21–24 (Jan. 1959).

—— "Linguistics in Canada." In *Encyclopedia Canadiana,* 6: 145.

—— "The Mid-Back Vowels in the English of the Eastern United States" (Thesis, University of Michigan, 1956). [Includes some speech records of Canadian border areas.]

—— "The Past Participle *Drank*: Standard American Usage?" AMER SPEECH 28: 106–111 (May 1953).

—— "Progress Report on the Study of Canadian English," PUB AMER DIA-LECT SOC 23: 57–58 (April 1955).

—— "Speech Differences along the Ontario–United States Border, I: Voca-bulary," J CAN LING ASSOC 1: 13–18 (Oct. 1954).

—— "Speech Differences along the Ontario–United States Border, II: Gram-mar and Syntax," J CAN LING ASSOC 1: 14–19 (March 1955).

—— "Speech Differences along the Ontario–United States Border, III: Pro-nunciation," J CAN LING ASSOC 2: 41–59 (Oct. 1956).

—— "The Speech of Sam Slick" (Thesis, Queen's University 1950).

AVIS, WALTER S., R. J. GREGG, C. J. LOVELL, and M. H. SCARGILL, eds. *The Beginning Dictionary* (Toronto, Gage, 1962). [An English-language diction-ary for Grades 4 and 5, first of the *Dictionary of Canadian English* series.]

AYEARST, MORLEY. "A Note on Canadian Speech," AMER SPEECH 14: 231–233 (Oct. 1939).

AYERS, H. M. and H. C. GREET. "American Speech Records at Columbia Uni-versity," AMER SPEECH 5: 333–357 (June 1930). [Includes Canadian examples.]

BAKER, R. J. "Linguistics and Literature in Canada," CAN LIT no 1: 97–100 (Summer 1959).

BELLIVEAU, J. E. "Do You Speak Good Canadian?" STAR WEEKLY MAG (July 20, 1957) pp 10–11.

BENGTSSON, ELNA. *The Language and Vocabulary of Sam Slick* (Copenhagen, Munksgaard, 1956). [Upsala Canadian Studies no 5.]

BERTON, PIERRE. "Explaining and Expanding Our Own Canadian Glossary," TORONTO DAILY STAR (Oct. 31, 1962) p 37.

—— "A Glossary of Distinctive Canadian Terms," TORONTO DAILY STAR (Oct. 23, 1962) p 17.

BLOOMFIELD, MORTON W. "Canadian English and its Relation to Eighteenth-Century American Speech," J E & G PHILOLOGY 47: 59–67 (Jan. 1948).

CAMERON, AGNES D. "New Words with Crops of Yellow Wheat," CAN MAG 31: 141–143 (June 1908).

CAMPBELL, J. L. "Scottish Gaelic in Canada," AMER SPEECH 11: 128–136 (April 1936).

CHAMBERLAIN, A. F. "Dialect Research in Canada," DIALECT N 1: 45 (pt 2, 1890).

———— "Algonkian Words in American English," J AMER FOLKLORE 15: 240 (1902).

CHAMBERS, E. T. D. "The Philology of the Ouananiche: A Plea for the Priority of Nomenclature," ROY SOC CAN PROC & TRANS 2nd ser 2: 131 (1896).

CHICANOT, E. L. "The Polyglot Vernacular of the Canadian Northwest," MOD LANG R 10: 88–89 (Jan. 1915).

Cox, D. M. "Canadian Bilingualism," CULTURE 22: 185–190 (juin 1961).

DANIELLS, ROY. "Canadian Prose Style," MAN ARTS R 5: 3–11 (Spring 1947).

DAVIAULT, P. "L'élément canadien-français de l'anglais d'Amérique," ROY SOC CAN PROC & TRANS 3rd ser 46: sect I, 5–18 (1952).

———— "The Evolution of the English and French Languages in Canada," ROY SOC CAN PROC & TRANS 3rd ser 53: 63–72 (1959).

———— "Français et Anglais du Canada." In *Studia Varia: Royal Society of Canada—Literary and Scientific Papers*, ed. E. G. D. Murray (Toronto, the Society, 1957) pp 3–9.

DEVINE, P. K. *Folklore of Newfoundland in Old Words, Phrases, and Expressions, Their Origin and Meaning* (St. John's, Robinson, 1937).

DRYSDALE, P. D. "A First Approach to Newfoundland Phonemes," J CAN LING ASSOC 5: 25–34 (Spring 1959).

DUNBABIN, THOMAS. "Canada's Own Dictionary is Coming," LONDON FREE PRESS (Feb. 12, 1957) p 4.

ELLIOTT, A. M. "Speech Mixture in French Canada, B: English and French," AMER J PHILOLOGY 10: 133–158 (pt 2, 1889).

EMENEAU, M. B. "The Dialect of Lunenburg, N.S.," LANGUAGE 11: 140–147 (June 1925).

ENGLAND, G. A. "Newfoundland Dialect Items," DIALECT N 5: 322–346 (pt 8, 1925).

ENGLISH, L. E. F. *Historic Newfoundland* (St. John's, Tourist Development and Provincial Information Division, 1955) pp 31ff.

EVANS, MARY S. "Terms from the Labrador Coast," AMER SPEECH 6: 56–58 (Oct. 1930).

FISHER, JOHN. "English by Radio," a BBC talk summarized in *Personality, Appearance and Speech* by T. H. Pear (London, Allen & Unwin, 1957) pp 104–105.

GANONG, W. F. "The Identity of the Animals and Plants Mentioned by the Early Voyagers to Eastern Canada and Newfoundland," ROY SOC CAN PROC & TRANS 2nd ser 15: 197–242 (1909).

GEIKIE, A. C. "Canadian English," CAN J INDUSTRY n.s. 2: 344–355 (Sept. 1857).

GRAHAM, ROBERT S. "The Anglicization of German Family Names in Western Canada," AMER SPEECH 30: 260–264 (Dec. 1955).

———— "The Transition from German to English in the German Settlements of Saskatchewan," J CAN LING ASSOC 3: 9–13 (Oct. 1957).

GREENLEAF, E. B. "Newfoundland Words," AMER SPEECH 6: 306 (April 1931).

GREGG, R. J. "Neutralism and Fusion of Vocalic Phonemes in Canadian English (Vancouver)," J CAN LING ASSOC 3: 78–83 (Oct. 1957).

———— "Notes on the Pronunciation of Canadian English as Spoken in Vancouver," J CAN LING ASSOC 3: 20–26 (Oct. 1957).

HAMILTON, DONALD. "The English Spoken in Montreal: A Pilot Study" (Thesis, University of Montreal, 1958).

―――― "Notes on Montreal English," J CAN LING ASSOC 4: 70–79 (Fall 1958).

HAMILTON, ROBERT M. *Canadian Quotations and Phrases, Literary and Historical* (Toronto, McClelland & Stewart, 1952).

JOOS, MARTIN. "A Phonological Dilemma in Canadian English," LANGUAGE 18: 141–144 (April 1942).

KIRKCONNELL, W. "Canadian Toponymy and the Structural Stratification of Canada," ONOMASTICA no 7: 7–15 (1954).

KIRWIN, WM. *"Labrador, St. John's* and *Newfoundland:* Some Pronunciations," J CAN LING ASSOC 6: 115–116 (Fall 1960).

LANGENFELT, G. *"she* and *her* instead of *it* and *its"* ANGLIA 70: 90–101 (1951).

LARDNER, JOHN. "Language Here and There," NEW YORKER 35: 171–174 (Sept. 26, 1959).

LARSEN, T. and F. C. WALKER. *Pronunciation: A Practical Guide to Spoken English in Canada and the United States* (Toronto, Oxford University Press, 1930).

LEECHMAN, DOUGLAS. "Good Fences Make Good Neighbours," CAN GEOG J 47: 218–235 (Dec. 1953).

LEHN, WALTER. "Vowel Contrasts in a Saskatchewan English Dialect," J CAN LING ASSOC 5: 90–98 (Fall 1959).

LIGHTHALL, W. D. "Canadian English," THE WEEK 7: 581–583 (Aug. 16, 1889).

LOVELL, C. J. "Lexicographic Challenges of Canadian English," J CAN LING ASSOC 1: 2–5 (March 1955).

―――― "A Sampling of Materials for a Dictionary of Canadian English on Historical Principles," J CAN LING ASSOC 4: 7–33 (Spring 1958).

―――― "Whys and Hows of Collecting for the Dictionary of Canadian English; Part I," J CAN LING ASSOC 1: 3–8 (Oct. 1955).

―――― "Whys and Hows of Collecting for the Dictionary of Canadian English; Part II," J CAN LING ASSOC 2: 23–32 (March 1956).

MCAREE, J. V. "Words: British, American," GLOBE & MAIL (Toronto) (Oct. 20, 1949).

MCATEE, W. L. "Folk Etymology in North American Bird Names," AMER SPEECH 26: 90–95 (May 1951).

―――― *Folk Names of Canadian Birds* (Ottawa, Queen's Printer, 1958).

MCDAVID, R. I., JR. and A. L. DAVIS. "Shivaree: An Example of Cultural Diffusion," AMER SPEECH 24: 249–255 (Dec. 1949).

MCDAVID, R. I., JR. and VIRGINIA GLENN MCDAVID. "*h* before Semi-Vowels in the Eastern United States," LANGUAGE 28: 41–62 (Jan. 1952). [Includes material for Ontario.]

―――― "Regional Linguistic Atlases in the United States," ORBIS 5: 349–386 (pt 2, 1956). [Includes Canadian material.]

MCDAVID, RAVEN I., JR. "Linguistic Geography in Canada," J CAN LING ASSOC 1: 3–8 (Oct. 1954).

―――― "Midland and Canadian Words in Upstate New York," AMER SPEECH 26: 248–256 (Dec. 1951).

———— "The Second Round in Dialectology of North American English," J CAN LING ASSOC 6: 108–114 (Fall 1960).

———— "Tape Recording in Dialect Geography: A Cautionary Note," J CAN LING ASSOC 3: 3–8 (Oct. 1957).

———— "Two Decades of the Linguistic Atlas," J E & G PHILOLOGY 50: 101–110 (Jan. 1951).

———— "Why Do We Talk that Way?" CBC TIMES 3: 2 (Feb. 11, 1951).

McKEOWN, ROBERT. "How Do You Pronounce 'Tomato,'" WEEKEND PICTURE MAG 4, no 23: 8 (1954).

McLAY, W. S. "A Note on Canadian Speech," AMER SPEECH 5: 328–329 (April 1930).

MACODRUM, WILLIAM BOYD. "The Dialect of the Cape Breton Kelt," CAN BKMN 8: 125 (April 1926).

MACPHAIL, SIR ANDREW. "Our Canadian Speech," SAT N 50: 1–2 (June 29, 1935).

———— "Our Canadian Speech." In *Yearbook of the Arts in Canada 1936*, ed. Bertram Brooker (Toronto, Macmillan, 1936) pp 235–239.

MASSEY, B. W. A. "Canadian Fish-Names in *OED* and *DAE*," NOTES & QUERIES 199: 494–497 (Nov. 1954), 522–525 (Dec. 1954); 200: 453–454 (Oct. 1955); 201: 125–129 (March 1956); 202: 173–177 (April 1957), 203–208 (May 1957).

MENCKEN, H. L. *The American Language: An Inquiry into the Development of English in the United States*, 4th ed. (New York, Knopf, 1937) *passim*. See also *Supplement I*, 5th printing (New York, Knopf, 1952) *passim* and *Supplement II*, 2nd ed. (New York, Knopf, 1952) pp 248–255.

MOORE, WILLIAM FRANCIS. *Indian Place Names in Ontario* (Toronto, Macmillan, 1930).

MOTT, L. F. "Canada," DIALECT N 4: 332 (pt 5, 1916).

———— "Items from Newfoundland," DIALECT N 5: 406 (pt 9, 1926).

MUNROE, HELEN C. "Montreal English," AMER SPEECH 5: 21 (Oct. 1929).

———— "Bilingual Signs in Montreal and its Environs," AMER SPEECH 5: 228–231 (Feb. 1930).

O'BRIEN, R. A. "The Poverty of Canadian English," CAN COMMENT 5: 22–23 (Sept. 1961).

PALMER, P. E. "The Canadian Board on Geographical Names," NAMES 1: 79–84 (June 1953).

PARTRIDGE, E. "Canada." In his *Slang To-day and Yesterday, with a Short Historical Sketch; and Vocabularies of English, American, and Australian Slang*, 3rd ed. (London, Routledge, 1950) pp 292–294.

PATTERSON, GEO. "Notes on the Dialect of the People of Newfoundland," PROC & TRANS NOVA SCOTIA INST SCIENCE 9, n.s. vol 2: 44–77 (1894–1898). [This article summarizes several contributions (under the same title) to J AMER FOLKLORE 8: 27–40 (Jan.–March 1895); 9: 19–37 (Jan.–March 1896); 10: 203–213 (July–Sept. 1897).]

PRIESTLEY, F. E. L. "Canadian English." In *British and American English since 1900*, ed. Eric Partridge (London, Dakers, 1951) pp 72–79.

———— "Do We Talk Canadian?" SAT N 67: 13 (May 10, 1952).

———— "English Language in Canada." In *Encyclopedia Canadiana* vol 4 pp 8–11.

RAND, REV. SILAS T. *Micmac Place Names in the Maritime Provinces and Gaspé Peninsula* . . . 1852 . . . 1890 (Ottawa, Surveyor's Office, 1919).

SANDILANDS, JOHN. *Western Canadian Dictionary and Phrasebook* (Winnipeg, Telegram, 1912).

SAYRES, JEAN DE. "A Brief Glossary of Canadian Expressions," PARISH NOTES [St. John's Church, Saint John, N.B., 1889] pp 39–40.

SCARGILL, M. H. "Canadian Dictionary Projects, II: Canadian English," TRANSLATORS' J 3: 114–121 (July–Sept. 1958).

——— "Canadian English and Canadian Culture in Alberta," J CAN LING ASSOC 1: 26–29 (March 1955).

——— "Do Canadians Speak Canadian?" SAT N 71: 16–18 (Dec. 8, 1956).

——— "Eighteenth-Century English in Nova Scotia," J CAN LING ASSOC 2: 3 (March 1956).

——— "Linguistics in Canada," BUL HUMAN ASSOC CAN no 17: 2 (Jan. 1956).

——— "A Pilot Study of Alberta Speech: Vocabulary," J CAN LING ASSOC 1: 21–22 (Oct. 1954).

——— "The Sources of Canadian English," J E & G PHILOLOGY 56: 610–614 (Oct. 1957).

SCOTT, N. C. "Canadian *caught* and *cot*," LE MAÎTRE PHONETIQUE III, 66: 22 (1939).

SEALOCK, R. B. and P. A. SEELY. *Bibliography of Place Name Literature: United States, Canada, Alaska, and Newfoundland* (Chicago, American Library Assoc., 1948).

——— "Place Name Literature, United States and Canada, 1952–1954," NAMES 3: 102–116 (June 1955).

SEARY, E. R. *Toponymy of the Island of Newfoundland*, Checklist no 1 Sources (St. John's, Memorial University, 1959). [Mimeographed.]

SINCLAIR, LISTER S. "The Canadian Idiom," HERE & NOW 2: 16–18 (June 1949). [Also in *Our Sense of Identity*, ed. Malcolm Ross (Toronto, Ryerson, 1954) pp 234–240.]

SOLOMON, H. "Canada Gets Own Dictionary," TORONTO DAILY STAR (Dec. 21, 1959) p 7.

STORY, G. M. "Dialect and the Standard Language," J NFLD TCHRS ASSOC 49: 16–20 (1957).

——— "Newfoundland Dialect." In *The Story of Newfoundland*, ed. A. B. Perlin (St. John's, privately printed, 1959) pp 68–70.

——— *A Newfoundland Dialect Dictionary: A Survey of the Problems* (St. John's, Memorial University, 1956).

——— *A Newfoundland Dialect Questionnaire: The Avalon Peninsula. 1. Vocabulary* (St. John's, Memorial University, 1959).

——— "Newfoundland English Usage." In *Encyclopedia Canadiana* vol 7, pp 321–322.

——— "Research in the Language and Place-Names of Newfoundland," J CAN LING ASSOC 3: 47–55 (Oct. 1957).

STRONG, W. D. "More Labrador Survivals," AMER SPEECH 6: 290–291 (April 1931).

STURSBERG, PETER. "The Strange Place Names of Canada," SAT N 76: 17–18 (Aug. 19, 1961).

SVARTENGREN, T. HILDING.   "The Feminine Gender for Inanimate Things in Anglo-American," AMER SPEECH 3: 83–113 (Dec. 1927).

TOMKINSON, GRACE.   "Shakespeare in Newfoundland," DAL R 20: 60–70 (April 1940).

TRENT, BILL.   "They Have a Word For It," WEEKEND MAG 11: 28–29 (May 13, 1961).

TRUEBLOOD, T. C.   "Spoken English," Q J SPEECH 19: 513–521 (Nov. 1933).

TWEEDY, W. M.   "New Brunswick, Nova Scotia, and Newfoundland," DIALECT N 1: 377–381 (pt 7, 1890).

VINAY, J.-P, P. DAVIAULT, and H. ALEXANDER, eds.   *The Canadian Dictionary*, concise ed. (Toronto, McClelland & Stewart, 1962). [A translation dictionary (French-English and English-French) containing a substantial number of labelled Canadianisms, both French and English.]

WANAMAKER, M. G.   "Canadian English," J EDUC NOVA SCOTIA 5th ser 9: 22–29 (Nov. 1959).

WIGHTMAN, F. A.   "Maritime Provincialisms and Contrasts: Words, Phrases, and Expressions," CAN MAG 39: 3–7 (May 1912).

WILSON, REX.   "Dialect, an Informal Record of History," TRANS ILLINOIS STATE ACAD SCIENCE 44: 190–195 (1951).

———— *The Dialect of Lunenberg County, Nova Scotia* (Ann Arbor, University Microfilms, 1959).

———— "The Implication of Tape Recording in the Field of Dialect Geography," J CAN LING ASSOC 2: 17–21 (March 1956).

Canadian Literature – General

ALLISON, W. T. "Canadian Literature of Today," BKMN (London) 75: 270–274 (Feb. 1929).

ANON. "Canadian Literature and Book Publishing," CAN GEOG J 43: 271–273 (Dec. 1951).

———— "Canadian Literature and the Curriculum [Editorial]," ACTA VIC 46: 227ff (Feb. 1922).

———— "Canadian Writers and Their Message," WORLD WIDE 29: 1743, 1744–1745 (Nov. 2, 1929).

———— "Literature in Canada," DOM ILLUS 5: 243 (Oct. 11, 1890).

———— "A Live Problem," CAN AUTH 1: 6–9 (Nov. 1924).

———— "Where is Canadian Literature?" BC MO 12: 12–13 (April 1918).

BAILEY, A. G. "Literature and Nationalism after Confederation," UNIV TOR Q 25: 409–424 (July 1956).

BAKER, RAY PALMER. *A History of English-Canadian Literature to the Confederation: Its Relation to the Literature of Great Britain and the United States* (Cambridge, Mass., Harvard University Press, 1920).

BALLSTADT, CARL. "The Quest for Canadian Identity in Pre-Confederation English-Canadian Literature" (Thesis, University of Western Ontario, 1959).

BARNARD, LESLIE GORDON. "Distinctively Canadian," CAN AUTH 10: 33–36 (Sept. 1932).

———— "A Nation's Literature," ASSOC CAN BKMN LIT BUL 1: 11–13 (Dec. 1936).

BARNETT, ELIZABETH S. "The Memoirs of Pioneer Women Writers in Ontario" (Thesis, McGill University, 1934).

BARR, ROBERT. "Literature in Canada," CAN MAG 14: 3–7 (Nov. 1899); 14: 130–136 (Dec. 1899). [See Reply by W. J. Brown, CAN MAG 15: 170–176 (June 1900).]

BELL, LILY MAY. "English-Canadian Literature before 1867 and Its Authors" (Thesis, University of Western Ontario, 1916).

BIRNEY, EARLE. "On Being a Canadian Author," CAN LIB ASSOC BUL 9: 77–79 (Nov. 1952).

BISSELL, C. T. "A Common Ancestry: Literature in Australia and Canada," UNIV TOR Q 25: 131–142 (Jan. 1956).

———— "Literary Taste in Central Canada during the Late Nineteenth Century," CAN HIST R 31: 237–251 (Sept. 1950).

————, ed. *Our Living Tradition* (Toronto, University of Toronto Press, 1957). [A continuing serial.]

BONENFANT, J. C. "L'Influence de la littérature canadienne-anglaise au Canada français," CULTURE 17: 251–260 (sept. 1956).

BOURINOT, ARTHUR S. "A Neglected Field in Canadian Literature," CAN FORUM 34: 198–199 (Dec. 1954).

BOURINOT, SIR JOHN GEORGE. "Literature and Art in Canada," ANGLO-AMER R 3: 99–110 (Feb. 1900).

—————— "Native Literature." In his *The Intellectual Development of the Canadian People* (Toronto, Hunter Rose, 1881) pp 91–128.

BROWN, E. A. "Anglo-French Literary Relations in Canada from 1920–1950" (Thesis, University of New Brunswick, 1954).

BROWN, E. K. "The Contemporary Situation in Canadian Literature." In *Canadian Literature Today* from Canadian Broadcasting Corporation (Toronto, University of Toronto Press, 1938) pp 9–16.

—————— "The Immediate Present in Canadian Literature," SEWANEE R 41: 430–442 (Oct. 1933).

—————— "The Neglect of Canadian Literature," ECHOES (Oct. 1944) pp 12, 48.

—————— "The Problem of a Canadian Literature." In his *On Canadian Poetry*, rev. ed. (Toronto, Ryerson, 1943) pp 1–27.

BROWNE, T. A. "The National Literary Competition," CAN MAG 53: 364–367 (Sept. 1919).

BRUCHESI, JEAN. "Literature [in French]," FOOD FOR THOUGHT 10: 9–12 (May 1950).

BUGNET, G. "Nationalism and Literature," CAN BKMN 14: 91–92 (Sept. 1932).

BURNETTE, NORMAN L. "Ink in their Veins [Strickland Family]," CAN AUTH & BKMN 29: 15–16 (Winter 1954).

BURNS, DEAN KERR. "Canadian Orators and Oratory" (Thesis, McGill University, 1925).

BURPEE, LAWRENCE JOHNSTONE. *A Little Book of Canadian Essays* (Toronto, Musson, 1909).

—————— "The National Note in Canadian Literature," CAN BKMN 7: 34–35 (Feb. 1925).

BUSH, DOUGLAS. "Is There a Canadian Literature?" COMMONWEAL 11: 12–14 (Nov. 6, 1929).

—————— "Making Literature Hum," CAN FORUM 7: 72–73 (Dec. 1926).

—————— "A Plea for Original Sin," CAN FORUM 2: 589–590 (April 1922). [Discussion 2: 651–652, 714–715.]

C., W. P. "Our Literature, Present and Prospective," LIT GARLAND 6 (n.s.): 245–247 (May 1848).

CALLAGHAN, MORLEY. "Writers and Critics: a Minor League," SAT N 70: 7–8 (Nov. 6, 1954).

CANADIAN WRITERS' CONFERENCE, Queen's University, Kingston, Ont., 1955. *Writing in Canada: Proceedings of the Canadian Writers' Conference, Queen's University, 28–31 July, 1955*, ed. George Whalley, with an introduction by F. R. Scott (Toronto, Macmillan, 1956).

CHAPMAN, ETHEL. "Literature of the Land," CAN AUTH 16: 21–22 (April 1939).

CLAY, C. "Cavalcade of Canadian Literature," SAT N 62: 20 (Nov. 2, 1946).

CLYNE, ANTHONY. "Canadian Writers," UNITED EMPIRE 11: 289–291 (June 1920).

COLLIN, W. E. *The White Savannahs* (Toronto, Macmillan, 1936). [Articles listed separately in this bibliography.]

COOPER, J. A. "Should Our Literature be Canadian?" CAN MAG 8: 544–545 (June 1897).

CROSS, ETHELBERT F. H. "Genius and Patriotism." In his *Fire and Frost* (Toronto, Bryant, 1898) pp 56–62.

DANIELLS, ROY. "Poetry and the Novel." In *The Culture of Contemporary Canada*, ed. Julian Park (Ithaca, N.Y., Cornell University Press, 1957) pp 1–80.

DAVIES, ROBERTSON. "Writer in the Attic," SAT N 70: 11–12 (April 30, 1955).

DAWSON, SAMUEL EDWARD. *The Prose Writers of Canada* (Montreal, Renouf, 1901).

DEACON, W. A. "Brief Survey of Canadian Literature in the English Language." In his *Poteen, a Pot-Pourri of Canadian Essays* (Ottawa, Graphic, 1926) pp 145–184.

———— "Canada's Literary Revolution," CAN AUTH & BKMN 23: 21–25 (Dec. 1947).

———— "Canadian Literature," LIT R 4: 634 (March 29, 1924).

———— "Critic Speaks: Significance of Canadian Literature," CAN AUTH 15: 13–16 (Sept. 1937).

———— "Literature in Canada—In its Centenary Year." In *Yearbook of the Arts in Canada 1928/29*, ed. Bertram Brooker (Toronto, Macmillan, 1929) pp 21–36.

———— "The Literary Scene," CAN AUTH & BKMN 25: 34–44 (1949).

———— *Poteen, a Pot-Pourri of Canadian Essays* (Ottawa, Graphic, 1926). [Articles listed separately in this bibliography.]

DICKSON, L. W. "Call for a Leader," CAN BKMN 15: 99–100 (Aug. 1933). [Discussion: 15: 115–116 (Sept. 1933); 15: 131–132 (Oct. 1933); 15: 148–149 (Nov. 1933); 15: 171 (Dec. 1933).]

DOUGLAS, JAMES, JR. "The Present State of Literature in Canada," QUE LIT HIST SOC TRANS n.s. pt 2, pp 62–73. [Sessions of 1873–1874 and 1874–1875.]

DOYLE, SIR A. C. "Future of Canadian Literature," CAN CLUB (Montreal) (1914–1915) pp 11–15.

DUHAMEL, ROGER. "A National Literature," CAN AUTH & BKMN 26: 4, 28 (Autumn 1950).

DUNCAN, CHESTER. "Anthology on the Air," CAN LIT no 6: 90–92 (Autumn 1960).

EDGAR, PELHAM. "A Fresh View of Canadian Literature," UNIV MAG (Montreal) 11: 279–286 (Oct. 1912).

———— "Our Literary Tendencies," CAN AUTH 12: 2, 19 (June 1935).

EGGLESTON, WILFRID. *The Frontier and Canadian Letters* (Toronto, Ryerson, 1957).

ELSON, JOHN M. "Canadian Literary Scene," CAN BKMN 11: 5–11 (Jan. 1929).

FAIRLEY, BARKER. "Artists and Authors," CAN FORUM 2: 460–463 (Dec. 1921).

FAWCETT, W. M. "Whither Canadian Literature?" COMMONWEAL 14: 627–628 (Oct. 28, 1931).

FRENCH, D. G. "Canadian Writers," CAN W MO 7: 105–115 (1909).

———— *The Canadian Writers' Note Book* (Toronto, Writers' Studio, 1932).

FRYE, NORTHROP. "English Canadian Literature, 1929–1954," BKS ABROAD 29: 270–274 (Summer 1955).

———— "English Canadian Literature, 1929–1954," CAN LIB ASSOC BUL 13: 107–112 (Dec. 1956).

FULFORD, ROBERT. "The Yearning for Professionalism," TAM R no 13: 80–85 (Autumn 1959).

FULLER, MARIELLE. "Obstacle to Canadian Literature," SAT N 56: 29 (March 15, 1941).

GARNEAU, RENÉ. "La Littérature." In *Royal Commission Studies* (Ottawa, King's Printer, 1951) pp 83–97.

GARVEY, MARGARET. "The Loyalist Prose Writers of the American Revolution" (Thesis, Columbia University [1945?]).

GIBBON, J. M. "Where is Canadian Literature?" CAN MAG 50: 333–340 (Feb. 1918).

GOSNELL, R. E. "Why a Canadian Literature?" CAN BKMN 5: 147–149 (June 1923).

GREENING, W. E. "Wanted: Reciprocity in Canadian Literature," DAL R 29: 271–274 (Oct. 1949).

GREER, REGINALD THOMAS. "Influence of Canadian Literature upon the Growth of Canadian Nationality to Confederation" (Thesis, Ottawa University, 1937).

GUILLET, EDWIN CLARENCE. *Early Canadian Literature: Literary Pioneers of the Old Newcastle District*, 2 vols (Toronto, 1942).

GUSTAFSON, RALPH. "Writing and Canada," NORTHERN R 3: 17–22 (Feb.–March 1950).

HALE, KATHERINE. "Our Women Writers," CAN AUTH 11: 9–10 (Sept. 1933).

HAMILTON, L. "Some Aspects of Anglo-Canadian Literature," NEUPHILOLO-GISCHE MONATSSCHRIFT 3: 227–237 (1932).

HAMILTON, ROBERT MORRIS. *Canadian Quotations and Phrases Literary and Historical* (Toronto, McClelland & Stewart, 1952).

HARTE, W. B. "Intellectual Life and Literature in Canada," NEW ENGL MAG n.s. 1: 377ff (Dec. 1889).

——— "Some Canadian Writers of Today," NEW ENGL MAG n.s. 3: 21–40 (Sept. 1890).

HATHAWAY, E. J. "Canadian Literary Homes," CAN MAG 30: 225–232 (Jan. 1908).

——— "The Trail of the Romanticist in Canada," CAN MAG 34: 529–537 (April 1910).

HAULTAIN, ARNOLD. "A Canadian Literature," CAN MAG 32: 510–511 (April 1909).

HIGGINS, MRS. RUTH HOLWAY. "Canadian History and Canadian Biography," CAN AUTH 6: 42–46 (Dec. 1928).

HODGINS, NORRIS. "Humour in Canada," CAN AUTH 11: 2 (Sept. 1933).

——— "Our Neglect of the Light Essay," DAL R 4: 296–305 (Oct. 1924).

——— "The Status of the Familiar Essay in Canadian Literature" (Thesis, McGill University, 1929).

"Honours and Awards [Editorial]," CAN LIT no 6: 3–4 (Autumn 1960).

HOPKINS, J. CASTELL. "Canadian Literature," ANN AMER ACAD POL SOC SCI 45: 189–215 (Jan. 1913).

HORNING, L. E. "Canadian Literature," ACTA VIC 21: 97–112 (Dec. 1897); 23: 219–222 (Dec. 1899); 23: 302–306 (Jan. 1900); 27: 231–240 (Dec. 1903); 33: 183–190 (Dec. 1909).

——— "Canadian Literature," THE WEEK 11: 1038–1040 (Sept. 29, 1894).

——— "Views of Canadian Literature," THE WEEK 11: 344–346 (March 9, 1894).

INNIS, HAROLD ADAMS. *The Strategy of Culture, with Special Reference to Canadian Literature—a Footnote to the Massey Report* (Toronto, University of Toronto Press, 1952) pp 1–20.

JACOB, FRED. "Canadian Literati," AMER MERCURY 8: 216–221 (June 1926).

KENNEDY, LEO. "The Future of Canadian Literature," CAN MERCURY 1: 99–100 (April–May 1929).

KING, CARLYLE. "Literature [in English]," FOOD FOR THOUGHT 10: 1–8 (May 1950).

KIRKCONNELL, WATSON. "The Literature of the New-Canadians." In *Canadian Literature Today* from Canadian Broadcasting Corporation (Toronto, University of Toronto Press, 1938) pp 57–64.

———— "Towards a National Literature," CAN AUTH 9: 23–24 (May 1932).

KLINCK, C. F. "Salvaging our Literary Past," ONT LIB R 27: 339–341 (Aug. 1943).

———— "Some Anonymous Literature of the War of 1812," ONT HIST 49: 49–60 (Spring 1957).

KNOTT, LEONARD K. "Perilous Publishing," CAN AUTH & BKMN 27: 3–8 (1951).

KNOX, ALEXANDER. "Scots Canadian Poetry," TIMES LIT SUPP (London) no 1891 (April 30, 1938) spec sec p ii.

LEACOCK, STEPHEN. "Humor as I See It and Something about Humor in Canada," MACL MAG 29: 11–13, 111–113 (May 1916).

LEECHMAN, DOUGLAS. "The 'Red Indian' of Literature: A Study in the Perpetuation of Error" (Thesis, Ottawa University, 1941).

———— "The Popular Concept of the 'Red Indian' as Revealed in Literature" (Thesis, Ottawa University, 1940).

LOCKE, GEORGE H. "The Influence of Canadian Literature on American Literature," BC MO 26: 13–15 (Can. Authors' Convention supplementary number, 1926).

LOGAN, JOHN DANIEL and DONALD G. FRENCH. *Highways of Canadian Literature* (Toronto, McClelland, 1924).

LUCHKOVICH, MICHAEL. "Racial Integration and Canadian Literature," CAN AUTH & BKMN 36: 14–16 (Summer 1960).

LUDWIG, JACK. "Clothes in Search of an Emperor," CAN LIT no 5: 63–66 (Summer 1960).

McCOURT, EDWARD. "Canadian Letters." In *Royal Commission Studies* (Ottawa, King's Printer, 1951) pp 67–82.

McDOUGALL, ROBERT L., ed. *Our Living Tradition*, Second and Third Series (Toronto, published in association with Carleton University by University of Toronto Press, 1959). [A continuing serial.]

———— "A Study of Canadian Periodical Literature of the 19th Century" (Thesis, University of Toronto, 1950).

McDOWELL, M. "A History of Canadian Children's Literature to 1900, Together with a Checklist" (Thesis, University of New Brunswick, 1957).

MacINNES, TOM. "Canadian Writers," BC MO 26: 15 (Can. Authors' Convention supplementary number, 1926).

McINNIS, EDGAR. "Biography." In *Canadian Literature Today* from Canadian Broadcasting Corporation (Toronto, University of Toronto Press, 1938) pp 37–43.

McKENZIE, RUTH I. "Proletarian Literature in Canada," DAL R 19: 49–64 (April 1939).

MacLennan, Hugh. "'Boy Meets Girl in Winnipeg and Who Cares?" In his *Scotchman's Return and Other Essays* (Toronto, Macmillan, 1960) pp 113–124.

—— "Do We Gag Our Writers?" MACL MAG 60: 13, 50, 52, 54–55 (March 1, 1947).

—— "Literature in a New Country." In his *Scotchman's Return and Other Essays* (Toronto, Macmillan, 1960) pp 137–141.

MacMechan, Archibald. "Canadian Colleges and Canadian Literature," CAN AUTH 6: 41–42 (Dec. 1928).

—— "Canadan Literature: The Beginnings," ESSAYS & STUDIES BY MEM ENG ASSOC (London) 12: 87–99 (1926).

—— *Head-Waters of Canadian Literature* (Toronto, McClelland & Stewart, 1924).

MacMurchy, Archibald. *Handbook of Canadian Literature (English)* (Toronto, Briggs, 1906).

MacPhail, Andrew. "Canadian Writers and American Politics," UNIV MAG (Montreal) 9: 3–17 (Feb. 1910).

MacPike, E. F. "American and Canadian Diaries, Journals, and Notebooks," BUL OF BIBLIOGRAPHY 18: 156–158 (May–Aug. 1945).

Marquis, Thomas Guthrie. "English-Canadian Literature." In *Canada and Its Provinces* (Toronto, Glasgow Brook, 1913) 12: 493–589.

Martin, Elizabeth. Correspondence, CAN FORUM 31: 231–232 (Jan. 1952).

Middleton, J. E. "Scotland and Canada," CAN BKMN 2: 14–15 (July 1920). [See also discussion by Adrian Macdonald, 2: 56–57 (Dec. 1920).]

Morgan, Henry James. *Bibliotheca Canadensis; or, A Manual of Canadian Literature* (Ottawa, Desbarats, 1867).

Morgan-Powell, Samuel. *This Canadian Literature: Being an Address...* (Toronto, Macmillan, 1940).

Mowat, Farley. "How to be a Canadian Writer—and Survive," SAT N 68: 22–23 (May 16, 1953).

Muddiman, Bernard. "The Immigrant Element in Canadian Literature," QUEEN'S Q 20: 404–415 (April 1913).

O'Hagan, Thomas. *Canadian Essays, Critical and Historical* (Toronto, Briggs, 1901).

—— "Canadian Women Writers." In *Canada: An Encyclopaedia of the Country*, ed. J. C. Hopkins (Toronto, Linscott, 1899) 5: 170–176.

—— "Canadian Women Writers." In his *Canadian Essays, Critical and Historical* (Toronto, Briggs, 1901) pp 54–103.

—— *Intimacies in Canadian Life and Letters* (Ottawa, Graphic, 1927).

"On the Cultivation of Laurels [Editorial]," CAN LIT no 4: 3–6 (Spring 1960).

Otty, M. G. "Canada's Place in British Fiction," EMPIRE R 29: 164–168ff (1915).

Pacey, Desmond. "Areas of Research in Canadian Literature," UNIV TOR Q 23: 58–63 (Oct. 1953).

—— "The Canadian Writer and His Public, 1882–1952." In *Studia Varia: Royal Society of Canada Literary and Scientific Papers*, ed. E. G. D. Murray (Toronto, University of Toronto Press, 1957) pp 10–20.

—— *Creative Writing in Canada: A Short History of English Canadian Literature* (Toronto, Ryerson, 1952). [Rev. and enl. ed., 1961.]

—— "Two Accents, One Voice," SAT R 35: 15–16 (June 7, 1952).

PARK, JULIAN, ed. *The Culture of Contemporary Canada* (Ithaca, N.Y., Cornell University Press, 1957). [Articles listed separately in this bibliography.]

PAUSTIAN, SHIRLEY IRENE. "Farm Life on the Great Plains as Represented in the Literature of Western America" (Thesis, University of Saskatchewan, 1948).

PERRY, M. E. "Canadian Literature To-day," UNITED EMPIRE 22: 234–242 (1931).

PHELPS, ARTHUR LEONARD. "Canadian Literature and Canadian Society," NORTHERN R 3: 23–35 (April–May 1950).

———— *Canadian Writers* (Toronto, McClelland & Stewart, 1951).

PIERCE, LORNE ALBERT. *English Canadian Literature 1882–1932* (Ottawa, 1932).

———— "Literature of the Dominion," THINK 7: 62, 82 (Sept. 1941).

———— "To Canadian Authors, without Prejudice," CAN BKMN 20: 22–24 (Aug. 1938).

———— *An Outline of Canadian Literature (French and English)* (Toronto, Ryerson, 1927).

———— *Unexplored Fields of Canadian Literature* (Toronto, Ryerson, 1932).

PRIESTLEY, F. E. L. "Creative Scholarship." In *The Arts in Canada*, ed. Malcolm Ross ([Toronto], Macmillan, 1958) pp 97–101.

RASHLEY, RICHARD ERNEST. "Canadian Literature: A Survey and Evaluation" (Thesis, University of Saskatchewan, 1936).

RAYSON, ETHEL and F. A. HADLAND. "A Glance at the Literature of Canada," LIVING AGE 291: 284–289 (Nov. 4, 1916).

RHODENIZER, VERNON BLAIR. *A Handbook of Canadian Literature* (Ottawa, Graphic, 1930).

RICHLER, MORDECAI. "Canadian Outlook," NEW STATESMAN 60: 346–347 (Sept. 10, 1960).

ROBB, W. H. "Our Birds and Our Writers," CAN AUTH 9: 12–13 (Sept. 1931).

ROBERTS, LESLIE. "Our Talk Sells Canada Short," SAT N 67: 9, 23 (Feb. 16, 1952).

RODDAN, SAMUEL. "Writing in Canada," CAN FORUM 26: 137 (Sept. 1946).

ROYAL COMMISSION ON NATIONAL DEVELOPMENT IN THE ARTS, LETTERS, AND SCIENCES, 1949–1951. "Literature." In *Report* (Ottawa, King's Printer, 1951) pp 222–227.

ROZ, F. et E. PRÉCLIN. "L'Influence de la France sur la vie intellectuelle des Canadiens-anglais et des États-Unis," FRANCE-AMERIQUE pp 7–11 (jan. 1935) and pp 111–112 (mai-juin 1935). [Translated in QUEBEC 10: 30–32 (March 1935) and 47–48 (April 1935).]

SALMON, EDWARD. "The Literature of the Dominion." In his *The Literature of the Empire* (London, Collins, 1924) pp 175–205.

SAMPSON, HERBERT GRANT. "Modern Canadian Literature: A Growth toward Maturity" (Thesis, Bishop's University, 1954).

SANDWELL, B. K. "Canadian Writing: '52," SAT N 68: 1, 21 (Nov. 29, 1952).

———— "Imaginative Literature in the United States and Canada." In *Conference of Canadian-American Affairs*, ed. R. G. Trotter, et al. (Boston, Ginn, 1937) pp 148–161 [Discussion pp 161–168].

———— "Letters in Canada," CAN AUTH & BKMN 28: 24, 26–27 (Winter 1952–1953).

———— "Our Two Kinds of Authors," SAT N 58: 15 (Oct. 10, 1942).

———— "Professorial Conspiracy to Destroy Canadian Literature," SAT N 61: 11 (July 27, 1946).

———— "Sandwell on Humour," CAN AUTH & BKMN 28: 30–34 (Autumn 1952).

SCOTT, FRANCIS REGINALD. "Canadian Writers' Conference [1955]," UNIV TOR Q 25: 96–103 (Oct. 1955).

SCOTT, LLOYD M. "The English Gentlefolk in the Backwoods of Canada," DAL R 39: 56–69 (Spring 1959).

SEVERIN, P. "Pins for Canadian Wings," CAN FORUM 17: 211 (Sept. 1937).

SHAPIRO, L. S. B. "The Myth that's Muffling Canada's Voice," MACL MAG 68: 12–13, 43–45 (Oct. 29, 1955).

SHOOLMAN, R. "Is There a Canadian Literature?" STORY 6: 2–7, 119 (March 1931).

SINCLAIR, LISTER S. "The Canadian Idiom," HERE & NOW 2: 16–18 (June 1949). [Also in *Our Sense of Identity*, ed. Malcolm Ross (Toronto, Ryerson, 1954) pp 234–240.]

SMETHURST, S. E. "Towards a National Literature," QUEEN'S Q 59: 455–463 (Winter 1952–1953).

SMITH, A. J. M. "Canadian Literature Today and Tomorrow," PROC CAN LIB ASSOC pp 32–38 (June 1947).

STANDERWICK, EUGENE. "The Future of Canadian Literature," CAN BKMN 17: 3–4 (Jan. 1935).

STEPHEN, A. M. "Canadian Literature as a Nation Builder," BC TEACHER 7: 12–18 (June 1928).

———— "Canadian Literature in the Schools," BC TEACHER 5: 124–127 (Feb. 1926).

———— "Views on Canadian Literature," INT FORUM 1: 25–30 (May 1926).

STEPHENS, HIRAM B. "Canadian Writers," DOM ILLUS 1: 78 (Aug. 4, 1888).

STEVENSON, LIONEL. *Appraisals of Canadian Literature* (Toronto, Macmillan, 1926). [Articles listed separately in this bibliography.]

———— "Canadian Authors in the United States," SAT N 47: 2 (Aug. 27, 1932).

———— "Interpreters of the Indian." In his *Appraisals of Canadian Literature* (Toronto, Macmillan, 1926) pp 171–185.

———— "A Manifesto for a National Literature." In his *Appraisals of Canadian Literature* (Toronto, Macmillan, 1926) pp 3–25. [Reprinted from CAN BKMN 6: 35–36, 46 (Feb. 1924).]

———— "Nature in Canadian Prose." In his *Appraisals of Canadian Literature* (Toronto, Macmillan, 1926) pp 160–170.

———— "Our Writers in the States," CAN AUTH 9: 19–23 (Sept. 1931).

———— "Overseas Literature from a Canadian Point of View," ENG R 39: 876–886 (Dec. 1924).

———— "The Quality of Canadian Humour." In his *Appraisals of Canadian Literature* (Toronto, Macmillan, 1926) pp 147–159.

———— "Significance of Canadian Literature," BC MO 24: 9–12 (May 1925).

———— "The Significance of Canadian Literature." In his *Appraisals of Canadian Literature* (Toronto, Macmillan, 1926) pp 43–62.

———— "The Status of Overseas Literature." In his *Appraisals of Canadian Literature* (Toronto, Macmillan, 1926) pp 26–43.

STEVENSON, O. J. *A People's Best* (Toronto, Musson, 1927).

STOCK, MARIE L. "Les Histoires d'animaux dans la littérature canadienne-anglaise" (Thesis, McGill University, 1937).

STRANGE, K. M. "Quantity and Quality in Canadian Writing," SAT N 63: 18, 22 (Nov. 1, 1947).

STRINGER, ARTHUR. "Our Authors Get Together," MACL MAG 24: 24–25, 42 (April 15, 1921).

SUTHERLAND, JOHN, ed. *Other Canadians* (Montreal, First Statement Press, 1947).

SYLVESTRE, GUY. "French Canadian Literature Comes of Age," DAL R 30: 215–228 (1950).

TROTTER, R. G. "Historical Research in Canada," CAN HIST R 20: 251–257 (Sept. 1939).

University of Toronto Quarterly. "Letters in Canada." Published annually in UNIV TOR Q since vol. 5, 1936.

VINCENT, C. J. "Canadian Literature, I: English." In *Encyclopedia of Literature*, ed. J. T. Shipley, (New York, Philological Library, 1946) pp 120–126.

WATT, FRANK W. "The Growth of Proletarian Literature in Canada, 1872–1920," DAL R 40: 157–173 (Summer 1960).

———— "Radicalism in English Canadian Literature since Confederation" (Thesis University of Toronto, 1957).

———— "The Theme of 'Canada's Century,' 1896–1920," DAL R 38: 154–166 (Summer 1958).

WATTERS, REGINALD EYRE. "[Canada's] Unknown Literature," SAT N 70: 31–33, 35–36 (Sept. 17, 1955).

WEAVER, FINDLAY I. "Canada's Literary Crusade," PUB WKLY 129: 1071 (March 7, 1936).

WEAVER, ROBERT LEIGH. "The Economics of Our Literature," QUEEN'S Q 60: 476–485 (Winter 1954).

———— "Literature: Some Promise," SAT N 74: 34 (Aug. 29, 1959).

———— "Notes on Canadian Literature," NATION (New York) 162: 198–200 (Feb. 16, 1946).

WENDELL, W. L. "The Modern School of Canadian Literature," BKMN (New York) 11: 515–526 (Aug. 1900).

WHALLEY, GEORGE, ed. *Writing in Canada* (Toronto, Macmillan, 1956). [Articles listed separately in this bibliography.]

WILLSON, LT. COL. H. B. "Canada's Undeveloped Literary Resources," CAN CLUB (Montreal) pp 190–204 (1913–1914).

WITHROW, W. H. "Canadian Literature," CHAUTAUQUAN 8: 211–214 (Jan. 1888).

Drama and Theatre

AGAZARIAN, YVONNE. "Everyman Theatre," PM 1: 13–15 (Nov. 1951).

AIKINS, CARROLL. "The Amateur Theatre in Canada." In *Yearbook of the Arts in Canada . . . 1928/29*, ed. Bertram Brooker (Toronto, Macmillan, 1929) pp 45–48.

————— "Canadian Plays for Canadian Theatres," CAN AUTH 4: 30–32 (Dec. 1928).

ALEXANDER, MARY H. T. "Little Theatres of the West," MACL MAG 34: 52, 54 (Oct. 1, 1921).

ALFORD, W. "When Canada Has Theatres Plays Will Soon Follow," SAT N 64: 18–19 (Oct. 16, 1948).

ANON. "Canadian Drama," SAT N 53: 6 (June 11, 1938).

————— "Canadian Drama Award," CURTAIN CALL 11: 16 (Nov. 1939).

————— "Canadian History Makes Good Drama," CURTAIN CALL 10: 9 (Dec. 1938).

————— "The Hart House Theatre," CAN FORUM 2: 753–756 (Sept. 1922).

————— "The Little Theatre in Manitoba," CAN BKMN 14: 60 (May 1932).

————— "Up with the Big Ones, Woodstock Little Theatre," SAT N 65/66: 19 (Jan. 23, 1951).

————— "The Work of the B.C. Dramatic School," CAN FORUM 10: 31–33 (Oct. 1929).

————— "The Work of the Hart House Theatre," CAN BKMN 2: 30–31 (Dec. 1920).

BERAUD, JEAN. "Le Théâtre au Canada-Français." In *The Arts in Canada*, ed. Malcolm M. Ross ([Toronto], Macmillan, 1958) pp 78–82.

BISSON, MARGARET MARY. "Le Théâtre français à Montreal, 1878–1931" (Thesis McGill University, 1932).

BLAKELY, PHYLLIS R. "The Theatre and Music in Halifax," DAL R 29: 8–20 (April 1949).

BOOTH, MICHAEL R. "Pioneer Entertainment: Theatrical Taste in the Early Canadian West," CAN LIT no 4: 52–58 (Spring 1960).

BOUX, RENE. "A Note on Theatre, and the Massey Report," PM 1: 48–50 (Dec.–Jan. 1951–1952).

BRODERSEN, GEORGE L. "Gwen Pharis—Canadian Dramatist," MAN ARTS R 4: 3–20 (Spring 1944).

————— "Towards a Canadian Theatre," MAN ARTS R 5: 18–23 (Spring 1947).

BURTON, JEAN. "The Little Theatre in the Country," CAN FORUM 7: 211–212 (April 1927).

CAPLAN, RUPERT. "The Ultimate National Theatre," CAN FORUM 9: 143–144 (Jan. 1929).

CASH, GWEN. "A Community Theatre 'In the Wilds' [Naramata, B.C.]," MACL MAG 34: 52–53 (Jan. 1, 1921).

CLARK, BARRETT. "Canadian Drama," SAT N 53: 6 (June 11, 1938).

COHEN, N. "Summer Theatre Troubles," SAT N 71: 15–16 (July 21, 1956).

———— "Television and the Canadian Theatre—Another Treadmill to Futility?" QUEEN'S Q 64: 1–11 (Spring 1957).

———— "Theatre Today: English Canada," TAM R no 13: 24–37 (Autumn 1959).

CONROY, PATRICIA. "A History of the Theatre in Montreal Prior to Confederation" (Thesis, McGill University, 1936).

COULTER, J. "The Canadian Theatre and the Irish Exemplar," THEATRE ARTS MO 22: 503–509 (July 1938).

———— "Theatre and Massey Report: More than Pat on the Head," SAT N 66: 12, 28 (Sept. 11, 1951).

CROFT, FRANK. "When Show Business was All Talk," MACL MAG 73: 30–31 (May 21, 1960).

CRUIKSHANK, PATRICIA. "The Influence of the University on the Development of the Drama in the United States and Canada" (Thesis, McGill University, 1931).

DALE, E. A. and BERTRAM FORSYTHE. "Hart House Theatre and Canadian Drama," ACTA VIC 46: 212–213 (Feb. 1922).

DAVIES, ROBERTSON. *Renown at Stratford: A Record of the Shakespeare Festival in Canada 1953* [with Tyrone Guthrie and Grant Macdonald] (Toronto, Clarke Irwin, 1953).

———— "Stratford: Second Year an Air of Certainty," SAT N 69: 7–9 (July 17, 1954).

———— "The Theatre." In *Royal Commission Studies* (Ottawa, King's Printer, 1951) pp 369–392.

———— *Thrice the Brinded Cat Hath Mew'd: A Record of the Stratford Shakespearean Festival in Canada 1955* (Toronto, Clarke Irwin, 1955).

———— *Twice Have the Trumpets Sounded: A Record of the Stratford Shakespearean Festival in Canada 1954* [with Tyrone Guthrie and Grant Macdonald] (Toronto, Clarke Irwin, 1954).

DENISON, MERRILL. "Hart House Theatre," CAN BKMN 5: 61–63 (March 1923).

———— "Nationalism and Drama." In *Yearbook of the Arts in Canada . . . 1928/29*, ed. Bertram Brooker (Toronto, Macmillan, 1929) pp 51–55.

EDINBOROUGH, ARNOLD. "Stratford's Slow but Solid Start," SAT N 75: 12–14 (July 23, 1960).

EDWARDS, MARGARET CHRISTIAN. "Canadian Drama, Dramatists and Players" (Thesis, McGill University, 1926).

FARMER, HARCOURT. "Play-writing in Canada," CAN BKMN 1: 55–56 (April 1919).

FERGUSSON, C. BRUCE. "The Rise of the Theatre at Halifax," DAL R 29: 419–427 (Jan. 1950).

FERRY, ANTONY. "The Tyranny of the Stratford Stage," CAN FORUM 40: 106–108 (Aug. 1960).

GALLOWAY, MYRON. "The Canadian Play and Playwright," NORTHERN R 3: 38–40 (Dec.–Jan. 1949–1950).

———— "Robert Speaight on Canadian Theatre: An Interview," NORTHERN R 3: 48–50 (Feb.–March 1950).

———— "Scene: Canada—Time: Present," NORTHERN R 3: 35–37 (Oct.–Nov. 1949).

GARDNER, D. "Canada's Theatre: Climbing in Second Gear," SAT N 74: 12–13, 40 (May 9, 1959).

GELINAS, GRATIEN. "Credo of the Comédie-Canadienne," QUEEN'S Q 66: 18–25 (Spring 1959).

GRAHAM, FRANKLIN THOMAS. *Histrionic Montreal: Annals of the Montreal Stage, with Biographical and Critical Notices of the Plays and Players of a Century,* 2nd ed. (Montreal, Lovell, 1902).

GRANVILLE-BARKER, H. "The Canadian Theatre," QUEEN'S Q 43: 256–267 (Aug. 1936).

GUTHRIE, T. "Development of Live Drama in Canada," SAT N 68: 7–8 (June 6, 1953).

HAMELIN, JEAN. "Theatre Today: French Canada," TAM R no 13: 38–47 (Autumn 1959).

HARVEY, MARTIN. "Canadian Theatres," UNIV MAG (Montreal) 13: 212–218 (April 1914).

JACOB, FRED. "Waiting for a Dramatist," CAN MAG 43: 142–146 (June 1914).

JEWITT, A. R. "Early Halifax Theatres," DAL R 5: 444–459 (Jan. 1926).

JOHNSTON, FORREST. "All-Canadian Drama Plan Makes Hit in Kingston," SAT N 63: 19 (Sept. 25, 1948).

JONES, EMRYS MALDWYN. "The University's Duty towards Canadian Drama," CULTURE 7: 311–324 (sept. 1946).

LAWTON, ROGER. "Theatrical Situation in Canada," SAT N 47: 3 (May 26, 1931).

LEONARD, A. "Theatre." In *Encyclopaedia of Canada,* ed. W. Stewart Wallace (Toronto, University Associates of Canada Ltd., 1937) 6: 132–135.

McDOUGALL, ROBERT L. "Drama Designed for Listening: A Study of Radio Drama in Canada" (Thesis, University of Toronto, 1948).

McKAY, A. G. "Western Ontario Drama," WATERLOO R 2: 13–16 (Summer 1959).

———— "Western Ontario Drama," WATERLOO R no 5: 15–19 (Summer 1960).

MASSEY, VINCENT. "The Prospects of a Canadian Drama," QUEEN'S Q 30: 194–212 (Oct. 1922).

MICHENER, WENDY. "Towards a Popular Theatre," TAM R no 13: 63–79 (Autumn 1959).

MILNE, W. S. "Drama," in "Letters in Canada 1935," UNIV TOR Q 5: 389–395 (April 1936) and annually to vol 12, 1942–1943.

———— "Drama Festival Afterthoughts," CAN FORUM 30: 82–83 (July 1950).

MOON, B. "Why the World Wants More of the Théâtre du Nouveau Monde," MACL MAG 71: 19, 62–66 (May 24, 1958).

MOORE, JOCELYN. "The Canadian Contest Plays," NEW FRONTIER 1: 13–14 (March 1937).

———— "Theatre for Canada," UNIV TOR Q 26: 1–16 (Oct. 1956).

MOORE, MAVOR. "'The Canadian Theatre," CAN FORUM 30: 108–110 (Aug. 1950).

———— "Theatre in English-Speaking Canada." In *The Arts in Canada*, ed. Malcolm Ross ([Toronto], Macmillan, 1958) pp 67–76.

———— "Theatre: Some Backsliding," SAT N 74: 32–33 (Aug. 29, 1959).

MORLEY, MALCOLM. "The Rise of Native Drama," SAT N 51: 12 (Jan. 4, 1936).

NESS, MARGARET. "Campus Capers Have Changed," SAT N 66: 11 (Feb. 27, 1951).

———— "Now We're Writing Musical Comedies," SAT N 67: 12 (June 28, 1952).

———— "Setting the Stage," SAT N 67/68: 14 (Nov. 22, 1952).

———— "The Theatre Tips a New Straw Hat," SAT N 65: 8–9 (July 4, 1950).

NEWTON, N. "Some Dramatic Suggestions," CAN FORUM 28: 110–111 (Aug. 1948).

NOVEK, RALPH. "Radio Drama in Canada," NORTHERN R 2: 29–33 (July–Aug. 1948).

PERRAULT, ERNEST. "Dorothy Somerset Curtain Call," PM 1: 9–13 (Dec.–Jan. 1951–1952).

PHELPS, ARTHUR L. "Canadian Drama," UNIV TOR Q 9: 82–94 (Oct. 1939).

———— "Drama." In *Canadian Literature Today* from Canadian Broadcasting Corporation (Toronto, University of Toronto Press, 1938) pp 17–23.

———— "Drama in Canada," CURTAIN CALL 11: 5–6 (Sept. 1939); 11: 2–8 (Nov. 1939); 11: 17–18 (Dec. 1939).

———— "Festivals and the National Drama," CURTAIN CALL 11: 11–12 (May 1940).

PRAT, HYPERBOLE [pseud.?]. "Theatre," CAN FORUM 30: 40–41 (May 1950).

PRENDERGAST, T. " 'WLT' Origins and Influence," FOOD FOR THOUGHT 18: 267–274 (March 1958).

REANEY, JAMES. "The Stratford Festival," CAN FORUM 33: 112–113 (Aug. 1953).

ROBERTSON, GEORGE. "Drama on the Air," CAN LIT no 2: 59–65 (Autumn 1959).

ROBSON, FREDERIC. "The Drama in Canada," CAN MAG 31: 58–61 (May 1908).

ROYAL COMMISSION ON NATIONAL DEVELOPMENT IN THE ARTS, LETTERS, AND SCIENCES, 1949–1951. "The Theatre." In *Report* (Ottawa, King's Printer, 1951) pp 192–200.

SABBATH, LAWRENCE. "Comédie Canadienne's First Year," SAT N 74: 19–21 (Sept. 29, 1959).

———— "French Theatre in Quebec," CAN COMMENT 3: 10–12 (Oct. 1959).

———— "Théâtre du Nouveau Monde's Ninth Season," SAT N 74: 20–22 (Dec. 5, 1959).

SANDWELL, BERNARD K. "The Annexation of Our Stage," CAN MAG 38: 22–26 (Nov. 1911).

———— "Better Canadian Plays." In *Yearbook of the Arts in Canada 1936*, ed. Bertram Brooker (Toronto, Macmillan, 1936) pp 218–221.

———— "New Quality on the Canadian Stage," SAT N 64: 2–3 (March 22, 1949).

SKINNER, ALAN. "Drama," FOOD FOR THOUGHT 10: 25–28 (May 1950).

SMITH, HILDA M. "National Drama in Canada," CAN FORUM 10: 225–226 (March 1930).

SMITH, MARION B.   "What is the Role of the DDF?" SAT N 75: 33 (June 25, 1960).

STEVENSON, LIONEL.   "What about the Canadian Drama?" In his *Appraisals of Canadian Literature* (Toronto, Macmillan, 1926) pp 138–146.

STRATFORD, PHILIP.   "New Canadian Plays Presented," CAN LIT no 6: 49–52 (Autumn 1960).

———— "Stratford after Six Years," QUEEN'S Q 66: 2–17 (Spring 1959).

———— "Theatre Criticism To-day," CAN FORUM 39: 258–259 (Feb. 1960).

TAYLOR, DOROTHY G.   "What about Little Theatres?" CAN FORUM 9: 42–43 (Nov. 1928).

TOVELL, VINCENT.   "Native Theatre," HERE & NOW 1: 81–84 (May 1948).

———— "Theatre in Canada," HERE & NOW 1: 80–81 (Dec. 1947).

TOVELL, VINCENT and GEORGE MCCOWAN.   "A Conversation," TAM R no 13: 5–23 (Autumn 1959).

VOADEN, H. A.   "A National Drama League," CAN FORUM 9: 105–106 (Dec. 1928).

WHITTAKER, HERBERT.   "The Audience is There," SAT R 42: 25–26 (Oct. 24, 1959).

———— "Canada on Stage," QUEEN'S Q 60: 495–500 (Winter 1953–1954).

———— "Drama Festival Enters New Era," SAT N 67: 16 (June 7, 1952).

———— "Our Theatre: A Youthful Bloom," SAT N 66: 8 (Jan. 30, 1951).

———— "The Theatre." In *The Culture of Contemporary Canada*, ed. Julian Park (Ithaca, N.Y., Cornell University Press, 1957) pp 163–180.

WIGH, S.   "Theatre in Newfoundland," ATLAN ADV 48: 55, 57–59 (May 1958).

WILLIAMS, N.   "Prospects for the Canadian Dramatist," UNIV TOR Q 26: 273–283 (April 1957).

WINTER, JACK.   "The Theatre Season: Montreal," CAN FORUM 40: 201–205 (Dec. 1960).

———— "The Theatre Season: Toronto," CAN FORUM 40: 178–179 (Nov. 1960).

YOUNG, LANDON.   "The Little Theatre of Winnipeg," CAN FORUM 7: 370–372 (Sept. 1927).

Fiction

ALEXANDER, P. V. "French Canada in Fiction" (Thesis, University of Toronto, 1951).

ANON. "Canadian Novels of 1922," CAN BKMN 5: 2–3 (Feb. 1923).

——— "Favourite Canadian Fiction," ONT LIB R 14: 103–105 (May 1930).

BEYEA, G. P. "The Canadian Novel Prior to Confederation" (Thesis, University of New Brunswick, 1950).

BIRNEY, EARLE. "On the Pressing of Maple Leaves," CAN LIT no 6: 53–56 (Autumn 1960).

BISSELL, C. T. "The Novel." In *The Arts in Canada*, ed. Malcolm Ross ([Toronto], Macmillan, 1958), pp 91–96.

BLISS, ETHEL M. "Could It be Self-Conscious?" CAN AUTH & BKMN 25: 49–50 (1949).

BRODIE, A. D. "Canadian Short Story Writers," CAN MAG 4: 334–344 (Feb. 1895).

BROOKER, BERTRAM. "Future of the Novel in Canada," ASSOC CAN BKMN LIT BUL 1: 9–11 (Winter 1937–1938).

BURPEE, LAWRENCE JOHNSTONE. *Canadian Novels and Novelists* (n. pl., n. pub. [1901]).

——— "Canadian Novels and Novelists," OTTAWA LIT SCI SOC 3: 9–36 (1901–1902).

——— "Canadian Novels and Novelists," SEWANEE R 11: 385–411 (Oct. 1903).

——— "Recent Canadian Fiction," FORUM 27: 752–760 (Aug. 1899).

——— "Unexplored Fields of Canadian Fiction," CAN AUTH 6: 55–56 (Dec. 1928).

CALLAGHAN, MORLEY. "Novelist." In *Writing in Canada*, ed. George Whalley (Toronto, Macmillan, 1956) pp 24–32.

——— "The Plight of Canadian Fiction," UNIV TOR Q 7: 152–161 (Jan. 1938). [See Reply, 7: 451–467 (July 1938).]

CARNOCHAN, JANET. "Rare Canadian Books," CAN MAG 43: 236–238 (July 1914).

CHILD, PHILIP. "Fiction." In *Canadian Literature Today* from Canadian Broadcasting Corporation (Toronto, University of Toronto Press, 1938) pp 31–36.

CLARK, MARGARET L. "American Influences on the Canadian Novel" (Thesis, University of New Brunswick, 1940).

CLAY, CHARLES. "Historical Novels of 1942," CAN HIST R 24: 188–195 (June 1943).

COGSWELL, FREDERICK WILLIAM. "The Canadian Novel from Confederation to World War 1" (Thesis, University of New Brunswick, 1950).

D., C. G. "Popular Canadian Fiction," ACTA VIC 46: 268–271 (March 1922).

DANIELLS, ROY. "Poetry and the Novel." In *The Culture of Contemporary Canada*, ed. Julian Park (Toronto, Ryerson; Ithaca, Cornell University Press, 1957) pp 1–81.

DAVIS, R. "Plea for a Canadian Short Story," CAN BKMN 17: 105 (Sept. 1935).

DEACON, W. A. "The Canadian Novel Turns the Corner," CAN MAG 86: 16, 38–40 (Oct. 1936). [Reprinted in *Yearbook of the Arts in Canada 1936*, ed. Bertram Brooker (Toronto, Macmillan, 1936) pp 208–217.]

DOOLEY, D. J. "Satiric Novel in Canada Today," QUEEN'S Q 64: 576–590 (Winter 1958).

ELSON, JOHN M. "Canadian Historical Fiction," SCHOOL, SECONDARY EDITION (Toronto) 24: 851–854 (June 1936).

GARRETT, ROBERT MAX. "Canadian Short Stories from Periodicals," CAN BKMN 4: 42, 44, 46 (Feb. 1922).

GIBBON, J. M. "The Coming Canadian Novel," CAN BKM 1: 13–15 (July 1919).

GROVE, FREDERICK PHILIP. "The Plight of Canadian Fiction? A Reply," UNIV TOR Q 7: 451–467 (July 1938).

HATHAWAY, E. J. "How Canadian Novelists are Using Canadian Opportunities," CAN BKMN 1: 18–22 (July 1919).

—— "The Trail of the Romanticist in Canada," CAN MAG 34: 529–537 (April 1910).

HAYNE, DAVID M. "French Canadian Novelists on the Defensive" (Thesis, Ottawa University, 1944).

—— "The Historical Novel and French Canada" (Thesis, Ottawa University, 1945).

HAZELTON, RUTH CLEAVES. "Norms," CAN AUTH & BKMN 28: 36–38 (Summer 1952).

HICKS, GRANVILLE. "Novelists in the Fifties," SAT R 42: 18–20 (Oct. 24, 1959).

KELLER, ELLA LORRAINE. "The Development of the Canadian Short Story" (Thesis, University of Saskatchewan, 1950).

KNISTER, RAYMOND. "The Canadian Short Story," CAN BKMN 5: 203–204 (Aug. 1923).

—— "The Canadian Short Story." In his *Canadian Short Stories* (Toronto, Macmillan, 1928) pp xi–xix.

LAURISTON, VICTOR. "What's Wrong with Canadian Magazine Fiction," CAN AUTH 16: 21–22 (April 1939).

LOGAN, J. D. "Re-views of the Literary History of Canada: Canadian Fictionists and Other Creative Prose Writers," CAN MAG 48: 125–132 (Dec. 1916).

McCOURT, EDWARD ALEXANDER. "The Canadian Historical Novel," DAL R 26: 30–36 (April 1946).

—— *The Canadian West in Fiction* (Toronto, Ryerson, 1949).

McMULLEN, GRACE. "Les Canadiens français d'après les romans anglo-canadiens contemporains (1925–1945)" (Thesis, Laval University, 1951).

MacMURCHY, MARJORIE. "Fiction." In *The Yearbook of Canadian Art, 1913–* comp. by the Arts & Letters Club of Toronto (Toronto, Dent, n.d.) pp 53–59.

MAGEE, WILLIAM H. "Local Colour in Canadian Fiction," UNIV TOR Q 28: 176–189 (Jan. 1959).

────── "Trends in the Recent English-Canadian Novel," CULTURE 10: 29–42 (mars 1949).

MAINER, R. HENRY. "Canadian War Fiction," CULTURE 6: 10–14 (mars 1945).

MARKHAM, MARY. "An Index to The Literary Garland, 1838–1851, with Three Essays on Colonial Fiction" (Thesis, University of Western Ontario, 1949). [Published in part as *An Index to The Literary Garland (Montreal, 1838–1851)* by Mary Markham Brown (Toronto, Bibliographical Society of Canada, 1962).]

MARQUIS, T. G. "Fiction." In his "English-Canadian Literature," in *Canada and Its Provinces*, ed. Adam Shortt (Toronto, Glasgow Brook, 1914) 12: 534–566.

NOYES, H. H. "Some Canadian Novels," ACTA VIC 63: 3–7 (March 1939).

PACEY, DESMOND. "Introduction." In his *A Book of Canadian Stories* (Toronto, Ryerson, 1947) pp xi–xxxvii.

────── "The Novel in Canada," QUEEN'S Q 52: 322–331 (Autumn 1945).

────── "The Outlook for Canadian Fiction," ACTA VIC 70: 9–11 (March 1946).

PARKER, GILBERT. "Fiction—Its Place in the National Life," NORTH AMER R 186: 495–509 (Dec. 1907).

PATERSON, ISABEL. "The Absentee Novelists of Canada," BKMN (New York) 55: 133–138 (April 1922).

POIRIER, MICHEL. "The Animal Story in Canadian Literature," QUEEN'S Q 34: 298–312 (Jan. 1927); 34: 398–419 (April 1927).

REID, J. A. "The Canadian Novel," CAN FORUM 2: 658–660 (June 1922).

ROBINSON, PATRICIA MARIAN (MRS. T. N. ROMAN). "The English-Canadian Urban and Industrial Novel and Periodical Fiction, 1920–1955" (Thesis, University of Western Ontario, 1960).

SANDWELL, B. K. "The Social Function of Fiction," QUEEN'S Q 49: 322–332 (Nov. 1942).

SELBY, JOAN. "The Transmutation of History: Landmarks in Canadian Historical Fiction for Children," CAN LIT no 6: 32–40 (Autumn 1960).

SINCLAIR, LISTER. "The Canadian Idiom," HERE & NOW 2: 16–18 (June 1949). [Also in *Our Sense of Identity*, ed. Malcolm Ross (Toronto, Ryerson, 1954) pp 234–240.]

SPENCER, R. E. "Fate Sisters (Canada) Incorporated," CAN BKMN 17: 83–84 (July 1935).

STEVENSON, LIONEL. "The Outlook for Canadian Fiction." In his *Appraisals of Canadian Literature* (Toronto, Macmillan, 1926) pp 124–137.

────── "The Outlook for Canadian Fiction," CAN BKMN 6: 157–158 (July 1924).

TALLMAN, WARREN. "Wolf in the Snow: Part One, Four Windows on Two Landscapes," CAN LIT no 5: 7–20 (Summer 1960).

────── "Wolf in the Snow: Part Two, The House Repossessed," CAN LIT no 6: 41–48 (Autumn 1960).

THOMAS, CLARA EILEEN (McCANDLESS). *Canadian Novelists 1920–1945* (Toronto, Longmans, 1946).

University of Toronto Quarterly. "Fiction." In "Letters in Canada" published
   annually in UNIV TOR Q since vol 5, 1936.
WARD, WILLIAM CLARK. "Historical Aspects of Canadian Fiction" (Thesis,
   Acadia University, 1943).
WEAVER, ROBERT. "A Sociological Approach to Canadian Fiction," HERE &
   NOW 2: 12–15 (June 1949).
WHALLEY, GEORGE. "The Great Canadian Novel," QUEEN'S Q 55: 318–326
   (Autumn 1948).
YOUNG, SCOTT. "What's Wrong with the Canadian Novel?" SAT N 69: 16–17
   (May 29, 1954).

Poetry

ANON. "Approach to Canadian Poetry," CAN THINKER 1: 13–15 (April 1937).

———— "Canadian Broadcasting Corporation: Canadian Poets Reading Their Own Verse in Weekly Broadcasts," CAN POETRY 3: 11 (April 1939).

———— "Five Canadian Publishers Tell—Why We Publish Canadian Poetry," CAN AUTH & BKMN 34: 12, 14 (Spring 1958).

———— "Mr. Coulter and Canadian Landscape [reply to a C.B.C. talk by John Coulter]," FIRST STATEMENT vol 1 no 11: 7–8 [undated].

ASHCROFT, EDITH. "The Sonnet in Canadian Poetry" (Thesis, Queen's University, 1932).

AVISON, MARGARET. "Poets in Canada," POETRY (Chicago) 94: 182–185 (June 1959).

BAILEY, ALFRED G. "The Fredericton Poets," NORTHERN R 3: 11 (Feb.-March 1950).

BEATTIE, ALEXANDER MUNRO. *The Advent of Modernism in Canadian Poetry in English, 1912–1940* (Ann Arbor, University Microfilms, 1957).

———— "Poetry Chronicle," QUEEN'S Q 65: 313–320 (Summer 1958).

BELFORD, JAMES F. B. "The Forgotten Muse," CAN MAG 60: 550–552 (April 1923).

BENSON, NATHANIEL A. "To the Rescue of Poetry," SAT N 52: 7 (March 13, 1937).

———— "True Voice of Canadian Poetry," ONT LIB R 23: 15–16 (Feb. 1939).

BIRNEY, EARLE. "Advice to Anthologists: Some Rude Reflections on Canadian Verse," CAN FORUM 21: 338–340 (Feb. 1942).

———— "Has Poetry a Future in Canada?" MAN ARTS R 5: 7–15 (Spring 1946).

———— "New Verse," CAN FORUM 20: 221 (Oct. 1940).

———— "To Arms with Canadian Poetry," CAN FORUM 19: 322–324 (Jan. 1940).

BOURINOT, ARTHUR S. "An Editor's Note Book," CAN POETRY 14: 24–28 (Spring 1951).

———— *Five Canadian Poets: Duncan Campbell Scott, Archibald Lampman, William E. Marshall, Charles Sangster, George Frederick Cameron* (Ottawa, the Author, 1954).

BROWN, E. K. "L'Âge d'or de notre poésie," GANTS DU CIEL 11: 7–17 (printemps 1946).

———— "Canadian Nature Poetry," THINK 7: 54, 93 (Sept. 1941).

———— "Canadian Poetry." In *Yearbook of the Arts in Canada 1936*, ed. Bertram Brooker (Toronto, Macmillan, 1936) pp 201–207. [Reprinted from UNIV TOR Q 5: 362–367 (April 1936).]

——— "The Development of Poetry in Canada." In his *On Canadian Poetry*, rev. ed. (Toronto, Ryerson, 1944) pp 28–87.

——— "The Development of Poetry in Canada, 1880–1940," POETRY (Chicago) 58: 34–47 (April 1941).

——— *On Canadian Poetry* (Toronto, Ryerson, 1943; rev. ed., 1944).

——— "The Wall against Canadian Poetry," SAT R LIT 27: 9–11 (April 29, 1944).

BROWN, LILLIAN ROGERS. "The Evolution of Canadian Poetry" (Thesis, University of Manitoba, 1914).

BUSH, DOUGLAS. "Making Literature Hum," CAN FORUM 7: 72–73 (Dec. 1926).

CALMER, ALAN. "A Hope for Canadian Poetry," NEW FRONTIER 1: 28–29 (Oct. 1936).

CAMPBELL, WILLIAM. "Scottish-Canadian Poetry," CAN MAG 28: 585–592 (April 1907); 29: 169–179 (June 1907).

CIARDI, JOHN. "Sounds of the Poetic Voice," SAT R 42: 18–21 (Oct. 24, 1959).

COLLIN, W. E. "On Canadian Poetry—The Stream and the Masters," UNIV TOR Q 13: 221–229 (Jan. 1944).

——— "Poetry." In *Canadian Literature Today* from Canadian Broadcasting Corporation (Toronto, University of Toronto Press, 1938) pp 24–30.

——— *The White Savannahs* (Toronto, Macmillan, 1936). [Articles listed separately in this bibliography.]

CONDELL, ANGUS TYNDALL. "A Consideration of Canadian Verse" (Thesis, University of Manitoba, 1903).

COOPER, JOHN A. "Canadian Poetry," NAT R 29: 364–381 (May 1897).

COX, LEO. "An Outline of Canadian Poetry," EDUC RECORD (Quebec) 58: 12–16 (Jan.–March 1942); 58: 83–87 (April–June 1942).

——— "Some Thoughts on Poetry Written in Canada," CAN AUTH & BKMN 34: 4, 6+ (Spring 1958).

DALTON, MRS. ANNIE CHARLOTTE. "The Future of Our Poetry," CAN AUTH 9: 17–18 (Sept. 1931).

DANIELLS, ROY. "Poetry and the Novel." In *The Culture of Contemporary Canada*, ed. Julian Park (Toronto, Ryerson; Ithaca, Cornell University Press, 1957) pp 1–81.

DEACON, W. A. "A Guide to the Anthologies." In his *Poteen* (Ottawa, Graphic, 1930) pp 187–203.

——— "Six Canadian Anthologies," CAN BKMN 4: 11–12 (Dec. 1921).

DEHLER, C. R. "Canada's English Poetry since Thirty-Nine," CULTURE 14: 247–255 (sept. 1953).

DE MILLE, A. B. "Canadian Poetry: A Word in Vindication," CAN MAG 8: 433–438 (March 1897). [A reply to Gordon Waldron, CAN MAG 8: 101–108 (Dec. 1896).]

——— "A Sketch of Canadian Poetry." In *Canada, an Encyclopaedia of the Country*, ed. J. C. Hopkins (Toronto, Linscott, 1899) vol 5, pp 166–169.

DEWART, EDWARD HARTLEY. "Introductory Essay." In his *Selections from Canadian Poets . . .* (Montreal, Lovell, 1864) pp ix–xix.

DUDEK, LOUIS. "Academic Literature," FIRST STATEMENT 2: 17–20 (Aug. 1944).

——— "Geography, Politics and Poetry," FIRST STATEMENT vol 1 no 16: 2–3 [undated].

——— "Montreal Poets," CULTURE 18: 149–154 (juin 1957).

————— "Patterns of Recent Canadian Poetry," CULTURE 19: 399–415 (1958).

————— "Poets of Revolt . . . or Reaction," FIRST STATEMENT vol 1 no 20: 3–5 [undated].

————— "The State of Canadian Poetry: 1954," CAN FORUM 34: 153–155 (Oct. 1954).

————— "Transition in Canadian Poetry," CULTURE 20: 282–295 (sept. 1959).

DUMBRILLE, D. "Need of Poetry," CAN AUTH & BKMN 34: 19–21, 30 (Spring 1958).

EDGAR, PELHAM. "Canadian Poetry," ACTA VIC 46: 198–200 (Feb. 1922).

————— "Canadian Poetry," BKMN (New York) 49: 623–628 (July 1919).

————— "Recent Canadian Poets [an Address . . . to the Ontario Library Association, April 5, 1920]," ONT LIB R 5: 3–9 (Aug. 1920).

ENDICOTT, NORMAN JAMIESON. "Poetry Chronicle; Review Article," TAM R no 7: 96–100 (Spring 1958).

FISHER, J. "Recent Canadian Poetry in English," ACTA VIC 63: 8–11 (March 1939).

FOSTER, MRS. W. G. "The Sonnet in Canadian Literature," BRIT ANN LIT 1: 64–69 (1938).

FRASER, MISS A. ERMATINGER. "Influences and Tendencies in Modern Canadian Poetry," CAN AUTH 6: 46–52 (Dec. 1928).

FRYE, NORTHROP. "Canada and Its Poetry," CAN FORUM 23: 207–210 (Dec. 1943).

————— "La Tradition narrative dans la poésie canadienne-anglaise," GANTS DU CIEL 11: 19–30 (printemps 1946). [English version subsequently published in *Canadian Anthology*, ed. C. F. Klinck and R. E. Watters, rev. ed. (Toronto, Gage, 1966) pp 523–528.]

————— "Poetry." In *The Arts in Canada*, ed. Malcolm Ross ([Toronto], Macmillan, 1958) pp 83–90.

————— "Preface to an Uncollected Anthology," In *Studia Varia: Royal Society of Canada Literary and Scientific Papers*, ed. E. G. D. Murray (Toronto, University of Toronto Press, 1957) pp 21–36. [Also, slightly revised, in *Canadian Anthology*, ed. C. F. Klinck and R. E. Watters, rev. ed. (Toronto, Gage, 1966) pp 515–523.]

GAMMON, DONALD B. "The Concept of Nature in Nineteenth Century Canadian Poetry, with Special Reference to Goldsmith, Sangster and Roberts" (Thesis, University of New Brunswick, 1948).

GIBBON, JOHN MURRAY. "The Canadian Lyric and Music," ROY SOC CAN PROC & TRANS 3rd ser 28: Sect II, 95–102 (1934).

————— "Spring and the Canadian Poet," ASSOC CAN BKMN LIT BUL 2: 11–15 (Spring 1937).

GORDON, ALFRED. "Comments on Canadian Poetry," CAN MAG 49: 132–140 (June 1917).

GORDON, HUNTLY K. "Canadian Poetry," CAN FORUM 1: 178–180 (March 1921).

GOULD, A. H. S. "Encouraging the New Voices—Most Important Contribution to Canadian Literature since 1925, Poetry Competitions," CAN BKMN 18: 19 (Nov. 1936).

GUSTAFSON, RALPH. "Anthology and Revaluation," UNIV TOR Q 13: 229–235 (Jan. 1944).

————— "New York Letter," NORTHERN R 1: 18–21 (Dec.–Jan. 1945–1946). [Comment on article by H. W. Wells in NEW ENGL Q (March 1945).]

HANEY, C. N. "Canadian Poetry," WESTMINSTER R (Vancouver) 11: 6–8 (July 1917), 11–15 (Sept. 1917).

HATHAWAY, R. H. " 'Eighteen-Nineties' of Canadian Poetry," ONT LIB R 10: 51–55 (Feb. 1926).

HOLLIDAY, J. "Poetry Has Many Faces . . . ," CAN AUTH & BKMN 34: 15, 18 (Spring 1958).

HORWOOD, HAROLD. "Number Ten Reports," NORTHERN R 4: 16–21 (Dec.–Jan. 1950–1951).

——— "Poetry in Newfoundland," NORTHERN R 3: 11–13 (June–July 1950).

JAMES, C. C. "Notes on Some Canadian Poets," ACTA VIC 24: 387–395 (May 1901).

KENNEDY, LEO. "Direction for Canadian Poets," NEW FRONTIER 1: 21–24 (June 1936).

KENNER, HUGH. "Regional Muses," POETRY (Chicago) 86: 111–116 (May 1955).

KERR, J. "Some Canadian Poets," EMPIRE R 36: 25–29 (July 1937).

KING, AMABEL. "Toronto Poetry Group Comes of Age," CAN AUTH & BKMN 29: 19–21 (Winter 1954).

KIRKCONNELL, WATSON. "Icelandic-Canadian Poetry," DAL R 14: 331–344 (Oct. 1934).

——— "New-Canadian Poetry," CAN POETRY 5: 5–8 (Aug. 1941).

——— "Poetry and National Life," CAN POETRY 6: 5–6 (Oct. 1942).

KLINCK, CARL F. "Formative Influences upon the '1860 Group' of Canadian Poets" (Thesis, Columbia University, 1929).

LAHEY, GERALD F. "Poetry in Canada," CULTURE 3: 161–164 (juin 1942).

LAUT, A. C. "Letter from Canada," SAT R LIT 2: 466 (Jan. 2, 1926). [Discussion 2: 518 (Jan. 23, 1926), 600 (Feb. 27, 1926).]

LESPERANCE, JOHN. "American and Canadian Sonnets," ROSE-BEL CAN MO 3: 449–455 (Nov. 1879).

——— "The Poets of Canada," ROY SOC CAN PROC & TRANS 1st ser 2: 31–44 (1884).

LIGHTHALL, W. D. "Canadian Poets of the Great War," CAN BKMN 1: 14–22 (April 1, 1919).

——— "Introduction." In his *Songs of the Great Dominion* . . . (London, Scott, 1889) pp xxi–xxxii.

LIVESAY, DOROTHY. "This Canadian Poetry," CAN FORUM 24: 20–21 (April 1944). [Reply by Patrick Anderson, 24: 44 (May 1944). Rejoinder by Dorothy Livesay, 24: 89 (July 1944).]

——— "Poetry," PM 1: 61–63 (Feb. 1952).

LIVESAY, FLORENCE RANDAL. "Canadian Poetry Today," POETRY (Chicago) 27: 36–40 (Oct. 1925).

LOGAN, J. D. "Canadian Poetry of the Great War," CAN MAG 48: 412–417 (March 1917).

——— "A Decade of Canadian Poetry," CAN MAG 40: 343–352 (Feb. 1913). [Discussion, 40: 580–590 (April 1913).] [Logan's article condensed in REV OF REV 47: 368–369 (March 1913).]

——— "The Martial Verse of Canadian Poetesses," CAN MAG 40: 516–522 (April 1913).

——— "Re-views of the Literary History of Canada: III—the Second Renaissance of Canadian Nativistic Poetry," CAN MAG 48: 219–225 (Jan. 1917).

——— "Re-views of the Literary History of Canada: IV, Canadian Poets and

Poetesses as Lyrists of Romantic Love," CAN MAG 48: 373–378 (Feb.
1917).

McCorkindale, T. B.   " 'The Canadian Boat-Song': An Unsolved Literary Problem," CAN MAG 58: 81–82 (Nov. 1921).

Macdonald, E. R.   "The Genius Loci in Canadian Verse," CAN MAG 53: 236–
240 (July 1919).

——— "The Sonnet in Canadian Poetry," CAN MAG 53: 101–104 (June
1919).

Macdonald, W. L.   "Nationality in Canadian Poetry," CAN MAG 62: 299–306
(March 1924).

MacDonald, Wilson.   "Poetry in Canada," CAN AUTH 9: 16–17 (Sept. 1931).

Maclean, O.   "Canada Expects," SAT N 57: 21 (Oct. 4, 1941).

McRae, C. Fred.   "The Victorian Age in Canadian Poetry 1840–1920" (Thesis,
University of Toronto, 1953).

McTavish, Newton.   "Poetry." In *The Yearbook of Canadian Art, 1913–* ,
comp. by the Arts & Letters Club of Toronto (Toronto, Dent, n.d.) pp
45–52.

Mandel, Eli W.   "Poetry Chronicle: Giants, Beasts, and Men in Recent Canadian Poetry," QUEEN'S Q 67: 285–293 (Summer 1960).

Marquis, T. G.   "Poetry." In his "English-Canadian Literature," in *Canada and
Its Provinces*, ed. Adam Shortt (Toronto, Glasgow Brook, 1914) vol 12, pp
566–589.

Needler, George Henry.   *The Lone Shieling: Origin and Authorship of the
Blackwood "Canadian Boat-Song"* (Toronto, University of Toronto Press,
1941).

——— *Moore and His Canadian Boat Song* (Toronto, Ryerson, 1950).

Newton, Norman.   "The Vegetable Kingdom," CAN FORUM 29: 129–130
(Sept. 1949).

Nims, John Frederick.   "Five Young Canadian Poets [Dudek, Hambleton, Page,
Souster, and Wreford]," POETRY (Chicago) 66: 334–340 (Sept. 1945).

O'Hagan, Thomas.   "Canadian Poets and Poetry," THE WEEK 7: 389 (May
23, 1890).

——— "Canadian Poets and Poetry." In his *Canadian Essays, Critical and Historical* (Toronto, Briggs, 1901) pp 11–53.

——— "Looking over the Field Again," CAN BKMN 14: 21 (Feb. 1932).

——— "The Patriotic Note in Canadian Poetry." In his *Intimacies in Canadian
Life and Letters* (Ottawa, Graphic, 1927) pp 57–65.

Osborn, E. B.   "Canadian Poetry," UNITED EMPIRE 3: 879–885 (1912).

Pacey, Desmond.   "English-Canadian Poetry, 1944–1954," CULTURE 15:
255–265 (sept. 1954).

——— *Ten Canadian Poets: A Group of Biographical and Critical Essays* (Toronto, Ryerson, 1958). [Articles listed separately in this bibliography.]

Park, M. G.   "Canadian Poetry," MEANJIN [Australia] no 78: 350–352
(1959).

Percival, Walter Pilling, ed.   *Leading Canadian Poets* (Toronto, Ryerson,
1948). [Articles listed separately in this bibliography.]

——— "What is the Character of Canadian Poetry?" EDUC RECORD (Quebec) 61: 3–16 (Jan.–March 1945). [Also in his *Leading Canadian Poets*
(Toronto, Ryerson, 1948) pp 1–22.]

Pierce, Lorne Albert.   *Three Fredericton Poets: Writers of the University of
New Brunswick and the New Dominion* (Toronto, Ryerson, 1933).

PRATT, E. J. "Canadian Poetry Past and Present," UNIV TOR Q 8: 1–10 (Oct. 1938).

RASHLEY, RICHARD ERNEST. *Poetry in Canada: The First Three Steps* (Toronto, Ryerson, 1958).

REANEY, JAMES. "The Canadian Imagination," POETRY (Chicago) 94: 186–189 (June 1959).

—— "The Canadian Poet's Predicament," UNIV TOR Q 26: 284–295 (April 1957).

REID, R. L. "Canadian Poetry," BC MO 19: 5–7 (March 1922). [Continued through subsequent issues.]

RHODENIZER, V. B. "Backgrounds of English-Canadian Poetry," DAL R 33: 187–195 (1953). [Also in CAN AUTH & BKMN 30: 3–7 (Spring 1954).]

—— "Contemporary Scene in Canadian Poetry," CAN AUTH & BKMN 34: 10, 12 (Spring 1958).

—— "Introduction." In *Canadian Poetry in English*, chosen by Bliss Carman, Lorne Pierce, and V. B. Rhodenizer, rev. and enl. ed. (Toronto, Ryerson, 1954) pp xxiii–xxvi.

ROBERTS, SIR C. G. D. "Of Canadian Poetry," SPOTLIGHTS 1: 13 (Dec. 1937).

ROBINS, J. D. "Backgrounds of Future Canadian Poetry," ACTA VIC 39: 309–317 (March 1915).

ROSENBERGER, COLEMAN. "On Canadian Poetry," POETRY (Chicago) 64: 281–287 (Feb. 1944).

ROSKOLENKO, HARRY. "Post-War Poetry in Canada," HERE & NOW 2: 23–31 (June 1949).

ROSS, MALCOLM. Introduction to his *Poets of the Confederation* (Toronto, McClelland & Stewart, 1960) pp ix–xiv [New Canadian Library Original no 01].

ROSS, PHILIP DANSKEN. *Canadian Poets and the Short Word* (Ottawa, the Author, 1938).

ROSS, W. W. E. "On National Poetry," CAN FORUM 24: 88 (July 1944).

—— "Poetry and Frogs," NORTHERN R 5: 30–33 (June–July 1952).

SANDWELL, B. K. "The Deforestation of Canadian Poetry," In his *The Privacity Agent* (Toronto, Dent, 1928) pp 96–101.

—— "Fifty-Six Poets," SAT N 57: 9 (Aug. 1, 1942).

—— "Our Poets: New Anthology," SAT N 68: 7 (Dec. 20, 1952).

SAPIR, EDWARD. "The Poetry Prize Contest," CAN MAG 54: 349–352 (Feb. 1920).

SCHOCH, MRS. MARGARET AITKEN. "The Evolution of Canadian Nature Poetry" (Thesis, Bishop's University, 1945).

SCHULTZ, GREGORY PETER. "The Periodical Poetry of A. J. M. Smith, F. R. Scott, Leo Kennedy, A. M. Klein and Dorothy Livesay, 1925–1950" (Thesis, University of Western Ontario, 1957).

SCOTT, D. C. "A Decade of Canadian Poetry," CAN MAG 17: 153–158 (June 1901).

—— "Poetry and Progress," CAN MAG 60: 187–195 (Jan. 1923). [Reprinted in his *The Circle of Affection* (Toronto, McClelland & Stewart, 1947) pp 123–147.]

—— "Poetry and Progress," Presidential Address to the Royal Society of Canada, May 17, 1922. ROY SOC CAN PROC & TRANS 3rd ser 16: xlvii–lxvii (1922).

SISSONS, CONSTANCE KERR. "On Poetic Gloom," SAT N 52: 23 (May 15, 1937).

SISTER MAURA. "Canada's Catholic Poetry," COMMONWEAL 18: 467 (Sept. 15, 1933).

SKINNER, M. H. "Arthurian Legend and Canadian Poets," ACTA VIC 21: 130–137 (Dec. 1897).

SMITH, A. J. M. "Canadian Anthologies, New and Old," UNIV TOR Q 11: 457–474 (July 1942).

———— "Canadian Poetry—A Minority Report," UNIV TOR Q 8: 125–138 (Jan. 1939).

———— "Colonialism and Nationalism in Canadian Poetry before Confederation," CAN HIST ASSOC ANN REP (1944) pp 74–85.

———— "Le Nationalisme et les poètes canadiens anglais," GANTS DU CIEL 8: 87–99 (juin 1945).

———— "Nationalism and Canadian Poetry," NORTHERN R 1: 33–42 (Dec.–Jan. 1945–1946).

———— " 'Our Poets': A Sketch of Canadian Poetry in the Nineteenth Century," UNIV TOR Q 12: 75–94 (Oct. 1942).

———— "Poet." In *Writing in Canada*, ed. George Whalley (Toronto, Macmillan, 1956) pp 1–24.

STANLEY, ARTHUR. "Our Canadian Poets," LONDON MERCURY 26: 537–547 (Oct. 1932).

STEPHEN, A. M. "Canadian Poets and Critics," NEW FRONTIER 1: 20–23 (Sept. 1936).

———— "The Major Note in Canadian Poetry," DAL R 9: 54–67 (April 1929).

———— "The Western Movement in Canadian Poetry," DAL R 5: 210–217 (July 1925).

STEVENSON, LIONEL. "Canadian Poets and the New Universe [Effect of Darwinism]." In his *Appraisals of Canadian Literature* (Toronto, Macmillan, 1926) pp 72–99. [Also in QUEEN'S Q 33: 143–155 (Nov. 1925).]

———— "The Case of the Lyrical Lyric." In his *Appraisals of Canadian Literature* (Toronto, Macmillan, 1926) pp 100–123.

———— "Dominion and Empire." In his *Appraisals of Canadian Literature* (Toronto, Macmillan, 1926) pp 210–225.

———— "The Fatal Gift." In his *Appraisals of Canadian Literature* (Toronto, Macmillan, 1926) pp 63–71.

———— "The Human Touch in Canadian Poetry," CAN BKMN 10: 69–75 (March 1928).

———— "Is Canadian Poetry Modern?" CAN BKMN 9: 195–201 (July 1927).

STEWART, ALEXANDER CHARLES. *The Poetical Review: A Brief Notice of Canadian Poets and Poetry* (Toronto, Anderson, 1896).

SUTHERLAND, JOHN. "New Canadian Poetry: Reply with Rejoinder," CAN FORUM 27: 17–18 (April 1947).

———— "New Necessities." In *Other Canadians*, ed. John Sutherland (Montreal, First Statement Press, 1947) pp 12–20.

———— "The Past Decade in Canadian Poetry," NORTHERN R 4: 42–47 (Dec.–Jan. 1950–1951).

THIBODEAU, COLLEEN (MRS. JAMES REANEY). "Recent Canadian Poetry" (Thesis, University of Toronto, 1950).

THOMPSON, EILEEN B. "Rus in Urbe," DAL R 8: 87–91 (April 1928).

TOMKINSON, GRACE. "The Watched Pot of Canadian Poetry," DAL R 14: 459–470 (Jan. 1935).

University of Toronto Quarterly. "Poetry." In "Letters in Canada," published annually in UNIV TOR Q since vol 5, 1936.

W., D. "Reviews—Canadian Poetry," CAN J INDUSTRY n.s. 3: 17–27 (Jan. 1858). [Discusses Sangster, McLachlan, Ryan.]

W., E. P. "Some Canadian Poets [Campbell, Lampman, Agnes Machar, I. V. Crawford, Louis Fréchette, Roberts]," MCMASTER U MO 3: 208–211 (Feb. 1894).

WALDRON, GORDON. "Canadian Poetry, a Criticism," CAN MAG 8: 101–108 (Dec. 1896). [Reply by A. B. De Mille 8: 433–438 (March 1897).]

WEBB, PHYLLIS. "Poet and Publisher," QUEEN'S Q 61: 498–512 (Winter 1955). [Also in *Writing in Canada*, ed. George Whalley (Toronto, Macmillan, 1956) pp 78–89.]

WELLS, H. W. "The Awakening of Canadian Poetry," NEW ENGL Q 18: 3–24 (March 1945). [See Comment or Reply by Ralph Gustafson, NORTHERN R 1: 18–21 (Dec.–Jan. 1945–1946).]

WEST, PAUL. "Ethos and Epic: Aspects of Contemporary Canadian Poetry," CAN LIT no 4: 7–17 (Spring 1960).

WHITESIDE, ERNESTINE R. "Canadian Poetry and Poets," McMASTER U MO 8: 21–28 (Oct. 1898), 68–74 (Nov. 1898), 114–118 (Dec. 1898), 167–172 (Jan. 1899), 209–212 (Feb. 1899).

WILGAR, W. P. "Poetry and the Divided Mind in Canada," DAL R 24: 266–271 (Oct. 1944).

W., D. [WILSON, DANIEL]. "Reviews – Canadian Poetry," CAN J INDUSTRY n.s. 3: 17–27 (Jan. 1958). [Reviews C. Sangster's *St. Lawrence and the Saguenay* ... (1858); A. McLachlan's *Poems* (1856); C. Ryan's *Oscar and Other Poems* (1857); and E. Chapman's *A Song of Charity* (1857).]

WILSON, MILTON. "Klein's Drowned Poet: Canadian Variations on an Old Theme," CAN LIT no 6: 5–17 (Autumn 1960).

——— *"Other Canadians* and after," TAM R no 9: 77–92 (Autumn 1958). [Also in *Masks of Poetry*, ed. A. J. M. Smith (Toronto, McClelland & Stewart, 1962) pp 123–138.]

——— "Recent Canadian Verse," QUEEN'S Q 66: 268–274 (Summer 1959).

WOODCOCK, GEORGE. "Recent Canadian Poetry," QUEEN'S Q 62: 111–115 (Spring 1955).

Literary Criticism

(This section contains materials about criticism itself. For criticism of fiction, poetry, individual authors, etc. see the appropriate sections elsewhere.)

BROADUS, E. K. "Criticism—or Puffery?" CAN FORUM 3: 20, 22 (Oct. 1922).

CALLAGHAN, MORLEY. "Writers and Critics: A Minor League," SAT N 70: 7–8 (Nov. 6, 1954).

COLMAN, M. E. "Poet Speaks to the Critics," CAN POETRY 2: 5–9 (April 1938).

DUNCAN, C. "Necessity for Criticism, Part I," CAN AUTH & BKMN 33: 24–27 (Autumn 1957). ["Part II," 33: 13–14, 30 (Winter 1957–1958).]

EDGAR, PELHAM. "Literary Criticism in Canada," UNIV TOR Q 8: 420–430 (July 1939). [Also in his *Across My Path*, ed. Northrop Frye (Toronto, Ryerson, 1952) pp 118–128.]

EMERY, TONY. " 'Critically Speaking' Criticized," CAN LIT no 4: 69–71 (Spring 1960).

FRENCH, DONALD G. "When the Critic Smiles," CAN MAG 53: 509–516 (Oct. 1919).

GRANT, DOUGLAS. "Critic." In *Writing in Canada*, ed. George Whalley (Toronto, Macmillan, 1956) pp 32–40.

GROVE, FREDERICK PHILIP. "Literary Criticism." In *Canadian Literature Today* from Canadian Broadcasting Corporation (Toronto, University of Toronto Press, 1938) pp 44–49.

HORWOOD, HAROLD. "Number Ten Reports," NORTHERN R 4: 16–21 (Dec. 1950–Jan. 1951).

JACOB, FRED. "The Age of Complacency in Canadian Literature," ACTA VIC 46: 202–206 (Feb. 1922).

LOGAN, JOHN DANIEL. *Aesthetic Criticism in Canada, Its Aims, Methods and Status* (Toronto, McClelland & Stewart, 1917).

MACLURE, MILLER. "Literary Scholarship." In *The Culture of Contemporary Canada*, ed. Julian Park (Ithaca, N.Y., Cornell University Press, 1957) pp 222–241.

MARQUIS, T. G. "Crude Criticism," THE WEEK 13: 350–351 (March 6, 1896).

MOORE, J. M. "Nathan Cohen," CAN COMMENT 3: 8–9 (March 1959).

PACEY, DESMOND. "Literary Criticism in Canada," UNIV TOR Q 19: 113–119 (Jan. 1950).

PERCY, H. R. "Criticism—Its Place in Canada's Future," QUEEN'S Q 64: 591–598 (Winter 1958).

SANDWELL, B. K. "The Professorial Conspiracy to Destroy Canadian Literature," SAT N 61: 11 (July 27, 1946).

SANGSTER, ALLAN. "On Canadian Criticism," CAN FORUM 31: 63–64 (June 1951).

SMITH, A. J. M. "Wanted—Canadian Criticism," CAN FORUM 8: 600–601 (April 1928). [Also in *Our Sense of Identity*, ed. Malcolm Ross (Toronto, Ryerson, 1954) pp 217–220.]

STRATFORD, PHILIP. "Theatre Criticism To-day," CAN FORUM 39: 258–259 (Feb. 1960).

SUTHERLAND, JOHN. "Critics on the Defensive," NORTHERN R 2: 18–23 (Oct.–Nov. 1947).

VESEY, T. M. "Canadian Literature and the Lower Criticism," CAN BKMN 5: 91–93 (Aug. 1923).

WOODCOCK, G. "View of Canadian Criticism," DAL R 35: 216–223 (Autumn 1955).

Literary History

ADAM, G. M. "Outline History of Canadian Literature." In *An Abridged History of Canada*, ed. W. H. Withrow (Toronto, Briggs, 1887) pp 179–232.

ADCOCK, A. ST. JOHN. "Literature of Greater Britain—Canada," BKMN (London) 42: 241–247 (Sept. 1912).

BAILEY, A. G. "Literature and Nationalism after Confederation," UNIV TOR Q 25: 406–424 (July 1956).

BAKER, RAY PALMER. *A History of English-Canadian Literature to the Confederation* . . . (Cambridge, Mass., Harvard University Press, 1920).

BISSELL, CLAUDE. "Literary Taste in Central Canada during the Late Nineteenth Century," CAN HIST R 31: 237–251 (Sept. 1950).

BOURINOT, SIR JOHN G. *The Intellectual Development of the Canadian People: An Historical Review* (Toronto, Hunter Rose, 1881).

——— . . . *Our Intellectual Strength and Weakness: A Short Historical and Critical Review of Literature, Art, and Education in Canada* (Montreal, Brown, 1893).

[BURPEE, L. J.] "Canadian Literature in 1906," NATION (New York) 84: 77–78 (Jan. 24, 1907). [*See also* 86: 99–100 (Jan. 30, 1908); 88: 108–109 (Feb. 4, 1909); 90: 81–82 (Jan. 27, 1910); 94: 106–107 (Feb. 1, 1912); 98: 104–106 (Jan. 29, 1914); 100: 252–253 (March 4, 1915).]

DEACON, WILLIAM ARTHUR. "The First Histories of Canadian Literature," WILLISON'S MO 1: 263–264ff (Dec. 1925). [Also in his *Poteen* (Ottawa, Graphic, 1926) pp 207–217.]

——— "A Letter from Canada," SAT R LIT 3: 258 (Oct. 30, 1926); 4: 847 (May 5, 1928); 6: 780 (March 1, 1930); 7: 538 (Jan. 17, 1931).

DEHLER, C. R. "Canada's English Poetry since Thirty-Nine," CULTURE 14: 247–255 (sept. 1953).

DE LA ROCHE, MAZO, STEPHEN LEACOCK, and MORLEY CALLAGHAN. "The Past Quarter Century," MACL MAG 49: 36, 38 (March 15, 1936).

DOUGLAS, JAMES JR. "The Present State of Literature in Canada," QUE LIT HIST SOC n.s. pt 2, pp 62–73. [Sessions of 1873–74 and 1874–75.]

EDGAR, PELHAM. "English-Canadian Literature." In *Cambridge History of English Literature*, ed. A. R. Ward and A. R. Waller (London, Cambridge University Press, 1916) 14: 380–400.

EGGLESTON, WILFRID. *The Frontier and Canadian Letters* (Toronto, Ryerson, 1957).

FRYE, NORTHROP. "English Canadian Literature, 1929–1954," BOOKS ABROAD 29: 270–274 (Summer 1955).

——— "English Canadian Literature, 1929–1954," CAN LIB ASSOC BUL 13: 107–112 (Dec. 1956).

GROVE, F. P. "Peasant Poetry and Fiction from Hesiod to Hémon," ROY SOC CAN PROC & TRANS 3rd ser 38: sect II, 89–98 (1944).

HOPKINS, JOHN CASTELL. "Canadian Literature," ANN AMER ACAD POL SOC SCI 45: 189–215 (Jan. 1913).

—— "A Review of Canadian Literature." In his *Canada, an Encyclopaedia of the Country* (Toronto, Linscott, 1899) vol 5, pp 117–135.

HORNING, L. E. "Canadian Literature of 1898: A Critique of Canadian Writers," ACTA VIC 22: 107–124 (Dec. 1898).

—— "A Decade of Canadian Prose," CAN MAG 17: 150–153 (June 1901).

KING, C. A. "Literature in English," FOOD FOR THOUGHT 10: 1–8 (May 1950).

KLINCK, C. F. "Early Creative Literature of Western Ontario: Some Books of the First Fifteen Years, 1828–1843," ONT HIST 45: 155–163 (Autumn 1953).

LOGAN, J. D. "The Literary Group of '61," CAN MAG 37: 555–563 (Oct. 1911).

LOGAN, J. D., and DONALD G. FRENCH. *Highways of Canadian Literature: A Synoptic Introduction to the Literary History of Canada (English) from 1760 to 1924* (Toronto, McClelland & Stewart, 1924).

McCRACKEN, M. C. "Traditions of Pre-Confederation Canadian Literature," R DE L'UNIV D'OTTAWA 7: 449–455 (oct.–dec. 1937).

MacMECHAN, ARCHIBALD M. "Canadian Literature: The Beginnings," ESSAYS & STUDIES BY MEM ENG ASSOC (London) 12: 87–99 (1926).

—— *Head-Waters of Canadian Literature* (Toronto, McClelland & Stewart, 1924).

MacMURCHY, ARCHIBALD. *Handbook of Canadian Literature (English)* (Toronto, Briggs, 1906).

MARQUIS, T. G. "Biography." In his "English-Canadian Literature," in *Canada and Its Provinces*, ed. Adam Shortt (Toronto, Glasgow Brook, 1914) 12: 506–511.

—— "General Literature." In his "English-Canadian Literature," in *Canada and Its Provinces*, ed. Adam Shortt (Toronto, Glasgow Brook, 1914) 12: 520–534.

—— "History." In his "English-Canadian Literature," in *Canada and Its Provinces*, ed. Adam Shortt (Toronto, Glasgow Brook, 1914) 12: 496–506.

—— "A History of English-Canadian Literature." In *Canada and Its Provinces*, ed. Adam Shortt (Toronto, Glasgow Brook, 1914) 12: 493–589.

—— "Travels and Exploration." In his "English-Canadian Literature," in *Canada and Its Provinces*, ed. Adam Shortt (Toronto, Glasgow Brook, 1914) 12: 511–520.

MORGAN-POWELL, S. "A Brief Review of Canadian Literature," AMER LIB ASSOC BUL 28: 623–628 (Sept. 1934).

PACEY, DESMOND. "The Canadian Writer and His Public, 1882–1952." In *Studia Varia: Royal Society of Canada Literary and Scientific Papers*, ed. E. G. D. Murray (Toronto, the Society, 1957) pp 10–20.

—— *Creative Writing in Canada: A Short History of English Canadian Literature* (Toronto, Ryerson, 1952; rev. and enl. ed., 1961).

PIERCE, LORNE. *English Canadian Literature 1882–1932* (Ottawa, 1932).

—— "Literature, English-Canadian." In *Encyclopedia of Canada*, ed. W. S. Wallace (Toronto, University Associates of Canada, Ltd., 1936) 4: 89–106.

———— *An Outline of Canadian Literature (French and English)* (Toronto, Ryerson, 1927).

———— "A Survey of English Canadian Literature (1882–1932)." In *Fifty Years Retrospect*, Royal Society of Canada Anniversary Volume, 1882–1932 (Toronto, Ryerson, 1932) pp 55–62.

RASHLEY, RICHARD ERNEST. *Poetry in Canada: The First Three Steps* (Toronto, Ryerson, 1958).

RHODENIZER, VERNON BLAIR. *A Handbook of Canadian Literature* (Ottawa, Graphic, 1930).

University of Toronto Quarterly. "Letters in Canada," published annually in UNIV TOR Q since vol 5, 1936.

WATT, FRANK W. "The Growth of Proletarian Literature in Canada, 1872–1920," DAL R 40: 157–173 (Summer 1960).

———— "Radicalism in English Canadian Literature since Confederation" (Thesis, University of Toronto, 1957).

———— "The Theme of 'Canada's Century,' 1896–1920," DAL R 38: 154–166 (Summer 1958).

WENDELL, WINIFRED LEE. "The Modern School of Canadian Writers," BKMN (New York) 11: 515–526 (Aug. 1900).

YOUNG, GEORGE RENNY. *On Colonial Literature, Science and Education . . .* (Halifax, Crosskill, 1842).

Regionalism

ALLISON, W. T. "Authorship in Manitoba," CAN AUTH 8: 13–15 (Sept. 1930).

ANON. "Extending the Art Resources of British Columbia," CAN ART 15: 221 (Aug. 1958).

———— "Newfoundlandia [Editorial]," NFLD Q 56: 3–4 (Dec. 1957).

———— " 'The Red River Valley,' Story of Only Folk Song of the West," WESTERN HOME MO 31: 32ff (June 1930).

———— "The Work of the B.C. Dramatic School," CAN FORUM 10:31–33 (Oct. 1929).

ARMSTRONG, MAURICE W. "Henry Alline's *Hymns and Spiritual Songs*," DAL R 34: 418–425 (Winter 1955).

BAILEY, ALFRED G. "Creative Moments in the Culture of the Maritime Provinces," DAL R 29: 231–244 (Oct. 1949).

BARNETT, ELIZABETH S. "The Memoirs of Pioneer Women Writers in Ontario" (Thesis, McGill University, 1934).

BOTHWELL, AUSTIN. "The Literary Resources of Saskatchewan," CAN FORUM 4: 51–53 (Nov. 1923).

BRIERLEY, JAMES G. "A Study of Literature in English Produced in the Province of Quebec Prior to Confederation, with Its Historical Background" (Thesis, McGill University, 1929).

BUGNET, G. "French Writers of the Canadian West," CAN BKMN 13: 53–54 (Mar. 1931).

BURPEE, LAWRENCE J. "The Early West," CAN AUTH 11: 11–12 (Sept. 1933).

———— "Quebec in Books," ROY SOC CAN PROC & TRANS 3rd ser 18: sect II, 75–85 (1924).

CALL, DR. F. O. "Our History a Gold Mine [Quebec as field for the Canadian writer]," CAN AUTH 7: 12–14 (Dec. 1929).

CARELESS, J. M. S. "Mid-Victorian Liberalism in Central Canadian Newspapers," CAN HIST R 31: 221–236 (Sept. 1950).

CATLEY, ELAINE M. "Poetry and Prose from Alberta," CAN AUTH & BKMN 19: 23 (Dec. 1943).

CODY, H. A. "The Maritime Provinces [as field for the Canadian writer]," CAN AUTH 7: 14–15 (Dec. 1929).

COLLIN, W. E. "On Writing in French Canada." In *Our Sense of Identity*, ed. Malcolm Ross (Toronto, Ryerson, 1954) pp 73–84.

———— "Quebec's Changing Literature," CAN FORUM 31: 274–276 (Mar. 1952).

COULSON, F. "Alberta in Books," CAN LIB ASSOC BUL 8: 160–164 (May 1952).

Cox, Leo. "Fifty Years of Brush and Pen [a historical sketch of the Pen and Pencil Club of Montreal]," QUEEN'S Q 46: 341–347 (Autumn 1939).

CREIGHTON, H. "Nova Scotian Folk Songs," J EDUC NOVA SCOTIA 4th ser 8: 206–208 (March 1937).

DEACON, W. A. "Journalistic Prose in Newfoundland." In his *The Four Jameses,* rev. ed (Toronto, Ryerson, 1953) pp 177–190.

DOUGLAS, R. W. "Present Literary Activity in British Columbia," CAN BKMN 1: 44–46 (July 1919).

FIELD, CLARA C. "Literary Landmarks in Coburg County and Its Surrounding District," ONT HIST SOC PAPERS & RECORDS 25: 220–225 (1929).

FILION, GERARD. "A New Society Grows in French Canada," SAT N 68: 7 (May 9, 1953).

GUILLET, EDWIN CLARENCE. *Early Canadian Literature: Literary Pioneers of the Old Newcastle District* (Toronto, the Author, 1942) 2 vols.

HAGERMAN, VERNE B. "The Literature of the Maritime Provinces: Its Tendencies and Its Influence" (Thesis, McGill University, 1934).

HAMMOND, M. O. "Our Literary Landmarks," CAN AUTH 9: 25–26 (May 1932).

HARVEY, D. C. "Early Public Libraries in Nova Scotia," DAL R 14: 429–443 (Jan. 1935).

———— "Newspapers of Nova Scotia, 1840–1867," CAN HIST R 26: 279–301 (Sept. 1945).

HATHAWAY, E. J. "The Province of Ontario in Fiction: Historical Fiction," CAN MAG 64: 234, 251–253 (Sept. 1925).

———— "The Province of Ontario in Fiction: Town and Rural Life," CAN MAG 64: 262, 279–280, 283–287 (Oct. 1925).

———— "Toronto's Literary Relationships," WESTMINSTER 4: 336–342 (1904).

HIRD, M. G. "The Literature of the Niagara Frontier," ONT LIB R 16: 26–28 (Aug. 1931).

HORWOOD, H. "Newfoundland Literature Has Vigor, Character," SAT N 64: 10 (March 15, 1949).

———— "Poetry in Newfoundland," NORTHERN R 3: 11–13 (June–July 1950).

HOWAY, F. W. "The Early Literature of the Northwest Coast," ROY SOC CAN PROC & TRANS 3rd ser 18: sect II, 1–31 (1924).

JACK, DAVID RUSSELL. "Acadian Magazines," ROY SOC CAN PROC & TRANS 2nd ser 9: 173–203 (1903).

———— "Early Journalism in New Brunswick," ACADIENSIS 8: 250–265 (Oct. 1908).

JACKSON, ELVA ETHEL. "Canadian Regional Novels" (Thesis, Acadia University, 1938).

KIRKCONNELL, WATSON. "Icelandic-Canadian Poetry," DAL R 14: 331–344 (Oct. 1934).

———— "New Canadian Poetry," CAN POETRY 5: 5–8 (Aug. 1941).

———— "Writing on the Prairie," CAN AUTH 10: 26–29 (Sept. 1932).

KLINCK, C. F. "Early Creative Literature of Western Ontario," ONT HIST 44: 155–163 (Autumn 1953).

LEACOCK, STEPHEN. "Writers of Quebec," SAT R LIT 20: 10 (June 3, 1939).

LOGAN, J. D. "Re-views of the Literary History of Canada: The Significance of Nova Scotia," CAN MAG 48: 3–9 (Nov. 1916).

LORRAIN, LEON. "French-Canadian Literature." In *The Yearbook of Canadian*

Art, 1913— , comp. by the Arts & Letters Club of Toronto (Toronto, Dent, n.d.) pp 25–35.

McClung, Nellie. "Our Younger Provinces, Alberta," CAN AUTH 9: 30–32 (Sept. 1931).

McCourt, Edward A. *The Canadian West in Fiction* (Toronto, Ryerson, 1949).

McElhinney, Mark G. "The Rideau Lakes in Prose and Rhyme," DOM ILLUS 2: 343 (June 1, 1889).

MacIver, I. D. "Nova Scotia's Verse Writers," ACADIA ATHENAEUM 62: 33–40 (Dec. 1936).

——— "Prose Writers of Nova Scotia," ACADIA ATHENAEUM 62: 13–17 (Jan. 1937).

MacMechan, A. M. "Cradle of Canadian Literature," CAN CLUB (Ottawa) pp 38–42 (1924).

——— "Halifax in Books," ACADIENSIS 6: 103–122, 201–217 (April, July 1906).

——— "The Literature of Nova Scotia: an Outline," CAN MAG 25: 565–571 (Oct. 1905).

——— "Maritime Literature," CAN AUTH 7: 8–10 (Dec. 1929).

McRaye, Walter. "Ontario's Literature," CAN AUTH 8: 10–13 (Sept. 1930).

Nelson, Eda Maude. "The Literature of the Maritime Provinces of Canada and Its Bearing on the Struggle for Educational and Political Freedom" (Thesis, McGill University, 1928).

Palmer, George A. "Saskatchewan's Contribution," CAN AUTH 9: 32–34 (Sept. 1931).

Paustian, Shirley Irene. "Farm Life on the Great Plains as Represented in the Literature of Western America" (Thesis, University of Saskatchewan, 1948).

——— "Saskatchewan in Fiction," SASK HIST 1: 23–26 (Oct. 1948).

Petrowsky, Michael. "Ukrainian-Canadian Writers," CAN AUTH & BKMN 19: 18 (March 1943).

Pitts, William J. "Geography of Canadian Genius," CAN MAG 30: 41–43 (Nov. 1907).

Pound, A. M. "Literature in British Columbia," CAN AUTH 7: 7–8 (Dec. 1929).

Raddall, Thomas H. "The Literary Tradition [in Nova Scotia]," CAN AUTH & BKMN 25: 3–7 (Autumn 1949).

Reade, John. "English Literature and Journalism in Quebec." In *Canada, an Encyclopaedia of the Country*, ed. J. C. Hopkins (Toronto, Linscott, 1899) 5: 147–165.

Rhodenizer, Vernon Blair. *At the Sign of the Hand and Pen, Nova-Scotian Authors* (Canadian Authors' Association, Nova Scotia Branch, 1948).

Scadding, Henry. "Pioneer Literary Endeavours in Western Canada," CAN MAG 2: 395–398 (Feb. 1894).

Seary, V. P. "Nova Scotian Culture Fifty Years Ago," DAL R 15: 275–285 (Oct. 1935).

Sime, Jessie Georgina. *Orpheus in Quebec* (London, Allen & Unwin, 1942).

Sinclair, D. Maclean. "Gaelic in Nova Scotia," DAL R 30: 252–260 (Oct. 1950).

Sissons, C. B. "Illiteracy in the West," UNIV MAG (Montreal) 12: 440–451 (Oct. 1913).

SISTER MAURA. "Halifax Harvest," DAL R 29: 45–49 (April 1949). [On local essayists.]

STAINSBY, M. "Creative Writing in British Columbia," CAN LIB ASSOC BUL 13: 156–158 (Feb. 1957).

STEVENSON, LIONEL. "British Columbia Poets," BC MO 18: 13–16 (Oct.–Nov. 1921).

———— "Down to the Sea in Ships." In his *Appraisals of Canadian Literature* (Toronto, Macmillan, 1926) pp 226–235.

———— "Interpreters of the Habitant." In his *Appraisals of Canadian Literature* (Toronto, Macmillan, 1926) pp 186–196.

———— "Land of Open Spaces." In his *Appraisals of Canadian Literature* (Toronto, Macmillan, 1926) 236–244.

———— "Mountains and Ocean." In his *Appraisals of Canadian Literature* (Toronto, Macmillan, 1926) pp 254–267.

———— "North of Fifty-Three." In his *Appraisals of Canadian Literature* (Toronto, Macmillan, 1926) pp 245–253.

———— "Pioneer and Immigrant." In his *Appraisals of Canadian Literature* (Toronto, Macmillan, 1926) pp 197–209.

STEWART, JOHN JAMES. "Early Journalism in Nova Scotia," NS HIST SOC COLL 6: 91–122 (1888).

SYLVESTRE, GUY. "The Recent Development of the French-Canadian Novel," UNIV TOR Q 21: 167–178 (Jan. 1952).

TOMKINSON, GRACE. "Shakespeare in Newfoundland," DAL R 20: 60–70 (April 1940).

WATSON, ROBERT. "Inspiration in the West," CAN AUTH 7: 15–16 (Dec. 1929).

WEAVER, EMILY P. "Fredericton and Its Literary Associations," CAN MAG 37: 517–525 (Oct. 1911).

WOODLEY, E. C. "Some Literary Associations of Montreal," CAN AUTH & BKMN 26: 6–8 (Spring 1950).

WOOLLACOTT, ARTHUR P. "Writers of the Western Front," CAN AUTH 10: 39–41 (Sept. 1932).

Songs, Folksongs, and Folklore

ANON. "The 'Lone Shieling' Mystery," SAT N 46: 11 (Jan. 11, 1930).

———— " 'The Red River Valley,' Story of Only Folk Song of the West," WESTERN HOME MO 31: 32ff (June 1930).

AXFORD, P. "Ballads of Newfoundland Give Clues to Its Life," SAT N 64: 22 (April 12, 1949).

———— "Saga of Newfoundland," CAN FORUM 27: 205+ (Dec. 1947).

BARBEAU, CHARLES MARIUS. "Blind Folk Singer," DAL R 33: 177–186 (Autumn 1953).

———— "Canadian Folk-Songs," UNIV TOR Q 16: 183–187 (Jan. 1947).

———— "Canadian Legends," DAL R 26: 207–226 (July 1946).

———— "How the Folk Songs of French Canada were Discovered," CAN GEOG J 49: 58–65 (Aug. 1954).

———— "Indian Songs of the North-west," CAN MUS J 2: 16–25 (Autumn 1957).

———— "La Chanson populaire française en Amérique du Nord," R DE L'UNIV LAVAL 10: 833–840 (mai 1956).

———— "Totems and Songs," CAN GEOG J 50: 176–181 (May 1955).

———— "Voyageur Songs: With Score," BEAVER 273: 15–19 (June 1942).

BARBEAU, MARIUS, ARTHUR LISMER, and ARTHUR BOURINOT. Come A-Singing! (Ottawa, National Museum, 1947).

BEAUGRAND, HONORÉ. "The Goblin Lore of French Canada." In his New Studies of Canadian Folk Lore (Montreal, Renouf, 1904) pp 9–22.

———— New Studies of Canadian Folk Lore (Montreal, Renouf, 1904).

BLUE, CHARLES S. "The Canadian Boat Song," CAN MAG 50: 367–374 (March 1918).

BURCHILL, GEORGE S. "Miramichi Folklore," DAL R 30: 237–243 (Oct. 1950).

CODY, H. A. " 'My Own Canadian Home,' " MACL MAG 26: 52–56 (Aug. 1913).

COOPER, J. A. "Canada's National Song," CAN MAG 6: 176–179 (Dec. 1895).

COYNE, J. H. " 'The Bold Canadian': A Ballad of the War of 1812," ONT HIST SOC PAPERS 23: 237–242 (1926).

CREIGHTON, HELEN. "Fiddles, Folk-Songs and Fisherman's Yarns [Nova Scotia]," CAN GEOG J 51: 212–221 (Dec. 1955).

———— Folklore of Lunenberg County, Nova Scotia (Ottawa, Queen's Printer, 1959).

———— "Folklore of Victoria Beach, Nova Scotia," J AMER FOLKLORE 63: 131–146 (April 1950).

———— "Folk-Singers of Nova Scotia," CAN FORUM 32: 86–87 (July 1952).

———— "Nova Scotian Folk Songs," J EDUC NOVA SCOTIA 4th ser 8: 206–208 (March 1937).

———— *Songs and Ballads from Nova Scotia* (Toronto, Dent, 1932).

———— "The Songs of Nathan Hatt," DAL R 32: 59–66 (Winter 1953).

CREIGHTON, HELEN and DOREEN SENIOR. *Traditional Songs from Nova Scotia* (Toronto, Ryerson, 1950).

DAVIES, ROBERTSON. "Toward a Long Perspective," SAT N 68: 30 (Feb. 21, 1953).

DEVINE, P. K. *Folklore of Newfoundland in Old Words, Phrases, and Expressions, Their Origin and Meaning* (St. John's, Robinson, 1937).

DOERING, J. F. and E. E. DOERING. "Some Western Ontario Folk Beliefs and Practices," J AMER FOLKLORE 51: 60–68 (Jan. 1938).

DOYLE, GERALD S. *Old-Time Songs of Newfoundland*, 3rd ed. (St. John's, the Author, 1955). [See also his *Old Time Poetry and Songs of Newfoundland*, 2nd ed. (1940).]

FOWKE, EDITH. "Canadian Folk Songs," CAN FORUM 29: 177–179 (Nov. 1949); 29: 201–202 (Dec. 1949).

———— "Canadian Folk Song Records," FOOD FOR THOUGHT 18: 57–61 (Nov. 1957).

———— "Guide to Canadian Folksong Records," CAN FORUM 37: 131–133 (Sept. 1957).

FOWKE, EDITH and RICHARD JOHNSTON. *Folk Songs of Canada* (Waterloo, Ont., Waterloo Music Co., 1954).

FOWKE, EDITH, ALAN MILLS, and HELMUT BLUME. *Canada's Story in Song* (Toronto, Gage [1960]).

FRASER, ALEXANDER. "The Gaelic Folk-Songs of Canada," ROY SOC CAN PROC & TRANS 2nd ser 9: 49–60 (1903).

GAETZ, ANNIE LOUISE. *Trails of Yesterday: Folk Lore of the Red Deer District* (Red Deer, Alta., privately printed, 1952).

GIBBON, JOHN MURRAY. "The Canadian Lyric and Music," ROY SOC CAN PROC & TRANS 3rd ser 28: sect II, 95–102 (1934).

———— *Canadian Folk Songs, Old and New* (Toronto, Dent, 1927).

GREEN, ERNEST. " 'The Song of the Battle of the Windmill,' " ONT HIST SOC PAPERS 34: 43–45 (1942).

GREENLEAF, ELIZABETH and GRACE MANSFIELD. *Ballads and Sea-Songs of Newfoundland* (Cambridge, Mass., Harvard University Press, 1933).

HAYWOOD, CHARLES. *A Bibliography of North American Folklore and Folksong* (New York, Greenberg, 1951). [Includes Canada.]

HEIDT, E. "Folklore in Saskatchewan," SASK HIST 7: 18–21 (Winter 1954).

HORWOOD, J. A. "Newfoundland Folk Music," CAN LIB ASSOC BUL 9: 127–129 (March 1953). [Also in FOOD FOR THOUGHT 13: 13–16 (May–June 1953).]

KARPELES, MAUD. *Folk Songs from Newfoundland*, 2 vols (Oxford, Oxford University Press, 1934).

McCORKINDALE, T. B. " 'The Canadian Boat Song': An Unsolved Literary Problem," CAN MAG 58: 81–82 (Nov. 1921).

MACKENZIE, WILLIAM ROY. *Ballads and Sea-Songs from Nova Scotia* (Cambridge, Mass., Harvard University Press, 1928).

———— *The Quest of the Ballad* (Princeton, N.J., Princeton University Press, 1919).

MacLeod, M. A. "Songs of the Insurrection," BEAVER 287: 18–23 (Spring 1957).

MacOdrum, Murdoch Maxwell. "Survival of the English and Scottish Popular Ballads in Nova Scotia: A Study of Folk Song in Canada" (Thesis, McGill University, 1924).

Mahon, Rev. Alexander Wylie. *Canadian Hymns and Hymn Writers* (Saint John, Globe, 1908).

Mathewson, Dorothy Ruth. "French-Canadian Folk Songs" (Thesis, McGill University, 1924).

Middleton, Jesse Edgar. *The First Canadian Christmas Carol* (Toronto, Rous, 1927).

Needler, George Henry. *The Lone Shieling: Origin and Authorship of the Blackwood "Canadian Boat-Song"* (Toronto, University of Toronto Press, 1941).

—— *Moore and His Canadian Boat Song* (Toronto, Ryerson, 1950).

Patterson, Rev. George. *Newfoundland Folk-Lore and Dialect* (Boston, American Folk-Lore Society, 1895).

—— *Notes on the Folk-Lore of Newfoundland* [no title-page].

Roberts, Helen H. and D. Jenness. "Songs of the Copper Eskimos," in *Report of the Canadian Arctic Expedition, 1913–1918*, vol 14 (Ottawa, King's Printer, 1925).

Royal Commission on National Development in the Arts, Letters, and Sciences, 1949–1951. "Folklore." In *Report* (Ottawa, King's Printer, 1951) pp 232–234.

Sclanders, Ian. "She's Collecting Long Lost Songs [about Helen Creighton]," MACL MAG 65: 14–15, 54–57 (Sept. 15, 1952).

Sewal, Hettie. "Songs and Song Writers," CAN AUTH 9: 30 (May 1932).

Smith, D. B. "Music in the Furthest West a Hundred Years Ago," CAN MUS J 2: 3–14 (Summer 1958).

Sullivan, Alan. "O Canada!" MACL MAG 37: 20, 47, 48 (July 1, 1924).

White, A. C. "Canada's Most Loved Patriotic Songs," ETUDE 61: 266ff (April 1943).

Zieman, M. K. "Canadians, New and Old, are Contributors to Music, Arts and Crafts in Dominion," SAT N 61: 4–5 (Sept. 22, 1945).

Journalism, Publishing,

and Periodicals

ALLEN, RALPH. "The Magazine." In *Writing in Canada*, ed. George Whalley (Toronto, Macmillan, 1956) pp 65–73.

ANDERSON, JEAN RITCHIE. "We Boast about Our Ancestors: A Brief History of *The Canadian Magazine* from its Inception over One Hundred Years Ago," CAN MAG 79: 3, 42 (Jan. 1933).

ANON. "Canadian Literary Review," CAN FORUM 39: 125 (Sept. 1959).

——— "Journalism and Literature." In *The Times Book of Canada* (London, The Times, 1920) pp 264–287.

——— "The Role of the Magazines," FIRST STATEMENT vol 1 no 15: 1–2 [undated].

——— "The Twenty-First Year [of the *Canadian Forum*]," CAN FORUM 21: 5–7 (April 1941).

AYRE, R. H. "15 Years of *Canadian Art*," CAN ART 15: 12–15; French summary 74 (Jan. 1958).

BALLANTYNE, M. G. "Religion and Journalism in Canada," CULTURE 6: 162–169 (juin 1945).

BEATTIE, EARLE. "The Last of the Angry Editors," MACL MAG 66: 22, 23, 24, 26–30 (Aug. 1, 1953).

BENSON, N. A. "*Canadian Poetry Magazine*—A Resumé of Its History," CAN POETRY 3: 5–8 (Oct. 1938).

BERTON, PIERRE. "The Greatest Three-Cent Show on Earth," MACL MAG 65: 7–9, 57–60 (March 15, 1952); 65: 16–17, 37–42 (April 1, 1952).

BLACK, ROBSON [FREDERIC ROBSON]. "Canadian Journalism," CAN MAG 32: 434–440 (March 1909).

BLISSETT, W. F. "*Explorations*," CAN FORUM 38: 106–107 (Aug. 1958).

BOURINOT, JOHN GEORGE. "Journalism." In his *The Intellectual Development of the Canadian People* (Toronto, Hunter Rose, 1881) pp 52–90.

BROWN, MARY MARKHAM. *An Index to The Literary Garland (Montreal 1838–1851)* (Toronto, Bibliographical Society of Canada, 1962).

BROWN, YVONNE. "The Origin of French-Canadian Journalism" (Thesis, Queen's University, 1955).

CALLWOOD, JUNE. "*MacLean's*," CAN FORUM 39: 199–200 (Dec. 1959).

CALVIN, D. D. "*Queen's Quarterly*, 1893–1943," QUEEN'S Q 50: 117–129 (1943).

CAMPBELL, WILFRED. "Four Early Canadian Journalists," CAN MAG 43: 551–558 (Oct. 1914).

CANADIAN PRESS ASSOCIATION. *A History of Canadian Journalism in the Several Portions of the Dominion* (Toronto, Murray Print., 1908).

CARD, RAYMOND. "The Daltons and the *Patriot*," CAN HIST R 16: 176–178 (June 1935).

CARELESS, J. M. S. "Mid-Victorian Liberalism in Central Canadian Newspapers," CAN HIST R 31: 221–236 (Sept. 1945).

COLQUHOUN, ARTHUR H. U. "After Twenty-One Years [first 21 years of the *Canadian Magazine*]," CAN MAG 42: 362–364 (Feb. 1914).

———— "A Century of Canadian Magazines," CAN MAG 17: 141–149 (June 1901).

———— "Journalism and the University," CAN MAG 21: 209–219 (July 1903). [Reprinted as "Canadian Universities and the Press," QUEEN'S Q 11: 85–100 (July 1903).]

CONACHER, W. M. "A Chronicle of QQ," QUEEN'S Q 60: 554–557 (Winter 1954).

COOPER, JOHN A. "The Editors of Leading Canadian Dailies," CAN MAG 12: 336–352 (Feb. 1899).

CRAICK, WILLIAM ARNOT. *A History of Canadian Journalism, II: Last Years of the Canadian Press Association, 1908–1919, with a Continuing Record of the Canadian Daily Newspaper Publishers Association, 1919–1959* (Toronto, Ontario Publishing Co., 1959). [Sequel to *A History of Canadian Journalism in the Several Portions of the Dominion*, by the Association (Toronto, 1908).]

DAFOE, JOHN WESLEY. *Sixty Years in Journalism* (Toronto, Royal Alexandra Hotel, 1943).

D'ALBERTANSON, LEONARD. *The Story of Alberta Division, Canadian Weekly Newspapers Association* [cover title: *The Printed Word, 1904–1955*] (Wainwright, Alta., [1955?]).

DEACON, W. A. "Journalistic Prose in Newfoundland." In his *The Four Jameses*, rev. ed. (Toronto, Ryerson, 1953) pp 177–190.

DE BRUYN, JAN. "Birth of a Little Magazine [*Prism*]," CAN FORUM 39: 116 (Aug. 1959).

DUDEK, L. "Role of Little Magazines in Canada," CAN FORUM 38: 76–78 (July 1958).

EGGLESTON, WILFRID. "Journalism, English-Language." In *Encyclopedia Canadiana* 5: 362–372.

———— "The Press." In *The Culture of Contemporary Canada*, ed. Julian Park (Ithaca, N.Y., Cornell University Press, 1957) pp 81–94.

———— "The Press of Canada." In *Royal Commission Studies* (Ottawa, King's Printer, 1951) pp 41–53.

EVANS, J. A. S. "Little Magazines in Canada," CAN AUTH & BKMN 35: 10–12 (Winter 1959–1960).

FALLE, G. G. "Canadian Music Journal," CAN FORUM 38: 130–132 (Sept. 1958).

FARQUHARSON, R. A. "Billy Buchanan and his *Herald*," SAT N 67: 11 (Aug. 9, 1952).

———— "Hearst's Influence on Canada," SAT N 66: 7 (Aug. 28, 1951).

———— "The Late George McCullagh," SAT N 67: 4, 18 (Aug. 23, 1952).

FAUTEUX, AEGIDIUS. *The Introduction of Printing into Canada* (Montreal, 1929).

FORD, ARTHUR R. "B. K. Sandwell," CAN AUTH & BKMN 30: 1–3 (Autumn 1954).

FRÉMONT, DONATIEN. "La Presse de langue française au Canada." In *Royal Commission Studies* (Ottawa, King's Printer, 1951) pp 55–66.

FRIEDSON, ANTHONY. "Let's Pan a Magazine," CAN LIT no 3: 86–89 (Winter 1960). [Reply to a review of *Prism* by Tony Emery in CAN LIT no 2: 94–96 (Autumn 1959).]

FULFORD, ROBERT. "Saturday Night," CAN FORUM 39: 52–53 (June 1959).

GRAY, JOHN. "Book Publishing." In *Writing in Canada,* ed. George Whalley (Toronto, Macmillan, 1956) pp 53–65.

GUNDY, H. PEARSON. *Early Printers and Printing in the Canadas* (Toronto, Bibliographical Soc. of Canada, 1957).

HAMILTON, C. F. "Canadian Journalism," UNIV MAG (Montreal) 16: 17–40 (Feb. 1917).

HARTE, W. B. "Canadian Journalists and Journalism," NEW ENGL MAG n.s. 5: 411–441 (Dec. 1891).

HARVEY, D. C. "Newspapers of Nova Scotia, 1840–1867," CAN HIST R 26: 279–301 (Sept. 1945).

HEISLER, JOHN. "The Halifax Press and B.N.A. Union 1856–1864," DAL R 30: 188–195 (July 1950).

HERBERT, WALTER. "Periodical Literature in Canada: The Humanities," CAN LIB ASSOC BUL 16: 289–290 (May 1960).

HOPKINS, J. C. "A Review of Canadian Journalism." In his *Canada, an Encyclopaedia of the Country* (Toronto, Linscott, 1899) 5: 220–237.

JACK, D. R. "Acadian Magazines," ROY SOC CAN PROC & TRANS 2nd ser 9: 173–203 (1903).

———— "Early Journalism in New Brunswick," ACADIENSIS 8: 250–265 (Oct. 1908).

LIVESAY, JOHN FREDERICK BLIGH. *The Canadian Press, Its Birth and Development* (Quebec, Chronicle-Telegraph, 1939).

LOGGIE, L. J. *"The Literary Garland:* A Critical and Historical Study of a Pioneer Canadian Literary Periodical" (Thesis, University of New Brunswick, 1948).

LUNN, A. J. E. "Bibliography of the History of the Canadian Press," CAN HIST R 22: 416–433 (Dec. 1941).

MACDADE, J. "Three Dollars, Please," CAN COMMENT 4: 22 (Feb. 1960).

MACDONALD, DWIGHT. "Landscape through a Peephole," CAN LIT no 1: 93–97 (Summer 1959).

McDOUGALL, R. L. "University Quarterlies," CAN FORUM 38: 253–255 (Feb. 1959).

———— "Literary Periodicals, English." In *Encyclopedia Canadiana* 6: 150–152.

MACKINTOSH, W. A. "Queen's Quarterly, 1893–1954," QUEEN'S Q 60: 460–461 (Winter 1953).

McNAUGHT, CARLTON. "Volume Thirty: In Retrospect: Pt I," CAN FORUM 30: 4–6 (April 1950); Pt II, 30: 33–34 (May 1950); Pt III, 30: 57–58 (June 1950).

FRÈRE MARIE-GERMAIN [GÉRARD ANGERS]. "Un Siècle de journalisme canadien" (Thesis, Ottawa University, 1941).

MARTIN, PETER. "A Household Word," CAN READER vol 2 no 2: 2–3 (Dec. 1960).

MOODIE, SUSANNA. Introduction to her *Mark Hurdlestone, The Gold Worshipper* (London, Bentley, 1853). [Reprinted in part in *Canadian Anthology*, ed. C. F. Klinck and R. E. Watters (Toronto, Gage, 1966) pp 63–66.]

NAIRN, JAMES R. and KATHLEEN NAIRN. "The Paper That Likes to Argue," SAT N 67: 11, 26 (July 26, 1952).

NICHOLS, MARK EDGAR. *The Story of the Canadian Press* (Toronto, Ryerson, 1948).

PENSE, E. J. B. "Canadian Journalism," EMP CLUB CAN 3: 213–218 (1905–1906).

PIERCE, LORNE. *An Editor's Creed* (Toronto, Ryerson, 1960).

—— *The House of Ryerson* (Toronto, Ryerson, 1954).

—— *On Publishers and Publishing* (Toronto, Ryerson, 1951).

—— "The Ryerson Press," CAN LIB ASSOC BUL 9: 135–137 (March 1953).

PORTER, MCKENZIE. "The Pulse of French Canada," MACL MAG 67: 18–19, 63, 64, 66, 68 (March 15, 1954).

READ, STANLEY MERRITT ELLERY. "An Account of English Journalism in Canada from the Middle of the Eighteenth Century to the Beginning of the Twentieth with Special Emphasis being given to the Periods Prior to Confederation" (Thesis, McGill University, 1925).

READE, JOHN. "English Literature and Journalism in Quebec." In *Canada, an Encyclopaedia of the Country*, ed. J. C. Hopkins (Toronto, Linscott, 1899) 5: 147–165.

RIDLEY, HILDA M. "My Experience as Editor of *Canadiana*," CAN AUTH & BKMN 30: 15–16 (Spring 1954).

ROYAL COMMISSION ON NATIONAL DEVELOPMENT IN THE ARTS, LETTERS AND SCIENCES 1949–1951. "The Press and Periodical Literature." In *Report* (Ottawa, King's Printer, 1951) pp 60–65.

SANDWELL, B. K. "Fourth Estate: Power or Pressure?" SAT N 66: 12 (Aug. 28, 1951).

—— "Help for Student Editors," SAT N 66: 7 (Feb. 6, 1951).

—— "The National Periodicals," SAT N 66: 7 (June 5, 1951).

SELBY, JOAN. "New Departures: *Canadian Literature* and *Prism*." BC LIB Q 23: 29–32 (Jan. 1960).

SISSONS, CONSTANCE KERR. "A Pioneer Periodical of the Canadas" [On *The Literary Garland*]," WILLISON'S MO 2: 312–315 (Jan. 1927).

SMITH, GLADYS LUCY HAMILTON. "The Regional Basis of News Distribution in the Prairie Provinces of Canada" (Thesis, McGill University, 1930).

STEWART, JOHN JAMES. "Early Journalism in Nova Scotia," NS HIST SOC COLL 6: 91–122 (1888).

TAYLOR, J. C. "Enter *Canadian Poetry Magazine* [Editorial]," ACTA VIC 60: 20–22 (Jan. 1936).

TREMAINE, MARIE, ed. *Canadian Book of Printing: How Printing Came to Canada and the Story of the Graphic Arts* (Toronto, Public Libraries, 1940).

—— *Early Printing in Canada* (Toronto, Golden Dog Press, 1934).

WADDINGTON, M. "*Canadian Art Magazine*," CAN FORUM 39: 103–105 (Aug. 1959).

WALLACE, W. S. "*The Bystander* and Canadian Journalism," CAN MAG 35: 553–558 (Oct. 1910).

—— "The First Journalists in Upper Canada," CAN HIST R 26: 372–381 Dec. 1945).

———— "Periodical Literature of Upper Canada," CAN HIST R 12: 4–22 (March 1931); 12: 182–184 (June 1931).

WALLIS, ARTHUR F.   "Historical Sketch of Canadian Journalism." In *Canada, an Encyclopaedia of the Country*, ed. J. C. Hopkins (Toronto, Linscott, 1899) 5: 182–190.

WHITE, THOMAS.   *Newspapers, Their Development in the Province of Quebec* [Lecture] (Montreal, n.p., 1883).

WILLISON, J. S.   "Journalism and Public Life in Canada," CAN MAG 25: 554–558 (Oct. 1905).

WOLFE, J. N.   "The Market for Books in Canada," CAN J ECON 24: 541–553 (1958).

WOODCOCK, GEORGE.   "The Tentative Confessions of a Prospective Editor," BC LIB Q 23: 17–21 (July 1959).

———— "Venture on the Verge," CAN LIT no 5: 73–75 (Summer 1960).

Libraries and Reading

L'AMI, C. E. "Priceless Books from Old Fur Trade Libraries," BEAVER 266: 26–29, 66 (Dec. 1935).

ANON. "National Library in Canada," LIB J 79: 1460 (Sept. 1, 1954).

———— "Public Libraries in Canada," DOM ILLUS 2: 227 (April 13, 1889).

———— "Reading for What?" CAN BKMN 21: 3–4 (April 1939).

BAIN, JAMES, JR. "Canadian Libraries," CAN MAG 16: 28–32 (Nov. 1900).

BARBEAU, CHARLES MARIUS. "Librarians' Contribution to Canadian Culture," ONT LIB R 32: 183–187 (Aug. 1948).

BASSAM, B. "Library Service for Canada," CAN FORUM 24: 257–258 (Feb. 1945).

BREEN, MELWYN. "Is Your Community Well-Read?" SAT N 66: 10, 22 (June 12, 1951).

CALLAGHAN, MORLEY. "It was News in Paris—Not in Toronto," SAT N 66: 8, 17, 18 (June 5, 1951).

CARNOCHAN, JANET. "Rare Canadian Books," CAN MAG 43: 236–238 (July 1914).

CLARKE, WILLIAM HENRY. *William Henry Clarke, 1902–1955: A Memorial Volume, Containing Some Recent Speeches and Writings Chiefly Concerned with Publishing and Education in Canada over Thirty Years* (Toronto, Clarke Irwin, 1956).

DAFOE, E. "National Library," ONT LIB R 28: 419–423 (Nov. 1944).

DAVIES, ROBERTSON. "Why Not be a Collector?" SAT N 68: 22, 24 (June 20, 1953).

DIXON, R. F. "Some Old Books on Canada," CAN BKMN 2: 49–51 (July 1920).

DOUGHTY, ARTHUR GEORGE. *The Canadian Archives and Its Activities* (Ottawa, Acland, 1924).

DROLET, A. "Early Canadiana in Laval University Library," CAN LIB ASSOC BUL 14: 107–108 (Dec. 1957).

DUFF, DOROTHY JAMES. *Bequest of Wings: A Family's Pleasure with Books* (Toronto, Macmillan, 1944).

———— "Cloud Capp'd Towers," ONT LIB R 41: 250–255 (Nov. 1957).

DUFF, LOUIS BLAKE. "Consumer Demand for Books," CAN AUTH & BKMN 27: 36–38 (1951).

———— "The Earliest Canadian Travel Books," PHILOBIBLON, ZEITSCHRIFT FÜR BÜCHERLIEBHABER, 8 Jahrgang, Heft Nr 7 (1935), pp 317–324 in German; pp 325–333 in English.

EAYRS, H. S. "Discovering Canada in Literature," PUB WKLY 117: 2990–2992 (June 21, 1930).

EGGLESTON, WILFRID. "Canadians and Canadian Books," QUEEN'S Q 52: 208–213 (May 1945).

EUSTACE, C. J. "Reading Culture Crisis," SAT N 67: 1, 29, 30 (Sept. 6, 1952).

FARQUHARSON, R. A. "Librarians: The Forgotten Profession," SAT N 67: 11, 28 (Aug. 30, 1952).

FAWCETT, WILLIAM McRAE. "Canada Looks at the Book Clubs," QUEEN'S Q 37: 656-665 (Autumn 1930).

GRAHAM, G. "Why Books Cost Too Much," MACL MAG 60: 22, 39–43 (Sept. 15, 1947). [See also rejoinder by J. M. Gray, MACL MAG 60: 46–47 (Dec. 1, 1947).]

GUNDY, HENRY PEARSON. *Early Printers and Printing in the Canadas* (Toronto, Bibliographical Soc. of Canada, 1957).

HAIG-BROWN, RODERICK LANGMERE HAIG. "How Important is Reading?" CAN LIB ASSOC BUL 12: 24–28 (Aug. 1955).

HARVEY, D. C. "Early Public Libraries in Nova Scotia," DAL R 14: 429–443 (Jan. 1935).

HOLMGREN, E. J. "Literary and Historical Society of Quebec," CAN LIB ASSOC BUL 14: 109–111 (Dec. 1957).

HOOD, DORA. *The Side Door: Twenty-Six Years in My Book Room* (Toronto, Ryerson, 1958).

JENKINS, K. R. "Inter-Relations: The Library and Its Community: National Aspects," CAN LIB ASSOC BUL 7: 47–49 (Sept. 1950).

LAMB, W. KAYE. "Library for all Canada," SAT N 67: 1 (Sept. 13, 1952).

———— " 'List Your Books, Sir?' " CAN AUTH & BKMN 26: 3–5 (Spring 1950).

LEWIS, G. "Books with a Canadian Accent," CAN LIB ASSOC BUL 6: 147–149 (Jan. 1, 1950).

LOCKE, GEORGE H. "Canadian Libraries and the War," CAN MAG 52: 588–591 (Nov. 1918).

MACBETH, MADGE HAMILTON. *Canada's Library of Parliament* (Ottawa, the Author, 1950).

MARTIN, PETER G. "Reader's Club of Canada," CAN LIB ASSOC BUL 17: 80–81 (Sept. 1960).

Montreal Gazette. "An Inventory of National Knowledge," CAN AUTH & BKMN 30: 28 (Summer 1954).

MULLENS, A. RAYMOND. "Bringing Books to Brains," MACL MAG 40: 22, 81–83 (June 1, 1927).

MULLINS, S. G. "Interesting Libraries of Ontario," CULTURE 11: 339–341 (1950).

NESS, MARGARET. "French Canada Buys Words," SAT N 66: 32–33 (Dec. 26, 1950).

OWENS, NOEL. "F. W. Howay and R. L. Reid Collection of Canadiana at the University of British Columbia," BC LIB Q 23: 9–13 (Oct. 1959).

PATRICK, A. W. "Reading in the Life of the Young Canadian," ONT LIB R 31: 396–398 (Nov. 1947).

PAYNTER, SIMON. "The Economics of Culture: The Book Trade," CAN FORUM 33: 1, 4–7 (April 1953).

PEEL, B. B. "Shortt Collection of Canadiana," CAN LIB ASSOC BUL 11: 146 (Feb. 1955).

PIERCE, LORNE ALBERT. *On Publishers and Publishing* (Toronto, Ryerson Press, Press, 1951).

RIDINGTON, JOHN. *Libraries in Canada* (Toronto, Ryerson, 1933).

ROBERTSON, K. "Young People and Reading," CAN LIB ASSOC BUL 15: 205–208 (March 1959).

ROBINSON, E. S. "Where's Our Centre of Culture," SAT N 66: 12, 36 (July 31, 1951).

ROYAL COMMISSION ON NATIONAL DEVELOPMENT IN THE ARTS, LETTERS AND SCIENCES, 1949–1951. "Book Publishing in Canada." In *Report* (Ottawa, King's Printer, 1951) pp 228–231.

—— "Federal Libraries." In *Report* (Ottawa, King's Printer, 1951) pp 327–334.

—— "Libraries." In *Report* (Ottawa, King's Printer, 1951) pp 101–110.

RUTLEDGE, JOSEPH LISTER. "Our Reading Does a Somersault," CAN MAG 83: 14, 45 (June 7, 1935).

SANDWELL, B. K. "Pocket Books by the Millions," SAT N 66: 7 (Jan. 16, 1951).

SANDWELL, B. K. and ERIC DUTHIE. "Canada—an Illiterate Nation?" QUEEN'S Q 43: 38–50 (Spring 1936).

SMITH, ELSPETH. *Recording Toronto* (Toronto, Public Libraries, 1960).

SMITH, HILTON. "Libraries." In *Writing in Canada*, ed. George Whalley (Toronto Macmillan, 1956) pp 115–127.

SRIGLEY, MRS. EVALYN. "Canadian Books for Adolescent Boys," CAN AUTH 6: 38–40 (Dec. 1928).

THOMSON, GEORGINA H. "Canadian Books for Adolescent Girls," CAN AUTH 6: 33–38 (Dec. 1928).

TOYE, W. "Children's Book Publishing in Canada," CAN LIB ASSOC BUL 16: 11–14 (July 1959).

TULLOCK, C. "Pioneer Reading," SASK HIST 12: 97–99 (Autumn 1959).

TYRRELL, WILLIAM. "The Canadian Books Canadians Read." In *Canadian Literature Today* from Canadian Broadcasting Corporation (Toronto, University of Toronto Press, 1938) pp 65–70.

WEAVER, ROBERT. "The Economics of Our Literature," QUEEN'S Q 60: 476–485 (Winter 1953–1954).

WILLISON, LADY. "Reading Canadian Books," SAT N 52: 7 (Nov. 7, 1936).

WOLFENDEN, M. "Books and Libraries in Fur Trading and Colonial Days," BC HIST Q 11: 159–185 (July 1947).

—— "Libraries in Colonial British Columbia," BC LIB Q 22: 3–8 (July 1958).

Censorship and Copyright

ADAM, G. M. "New Aspects of the Copyright Question," ROSE-BEL CAN MO 1: 369–376 (Sept. 1878).

ALEXANDER, HENRY. "Obscenity and the Law," QUEEN'S Q 60: 161–169 (1953–1954).

ANON. "Advice to Censors: Hire a Lawyer [Editorial]," MACL MAG 69: 2 (Feb. 18, 1956).

———— "Canadian Copyright," DOM ILLUS 1: 275 (Nov. 3, 1888).

———— "CLA Letter to Ilsley Commission," CAN LIB ASSOC BUL 12: 75–76 (Oct. 1955).

———— "Confiscation of Copyright," CAN AUTH 9: 27 (May 1932).

———— "Copyright," CAN AUTH 1: 11–12 (Nov. 1924).

———— "Copyright in Canada," DOM ILLUS 1: 307 (Nov. 17, 1888).

———— "Fulton Censorship: Editorial," SAT N 65: 5 (Jan. 3, 1950).

———— "Government Defines Obscenity," QUILL & QUIRE 25: 14–26 (Aug.– Sept. 1959).

———— "Let's Not Import 'Lynch Law'—Even against Books [Editorial]," MACL MAG 68: 2 (Dec. 24, 1955).

———— " 'Obscenity' in Canada," CAN FORUM 30: 99–100 (Aug. 1950).

———— "Penalizing Literature," CAN FORUM 32: 74–75 (July 1952).

———— "A Thoroughly Dangerous Law," QUILL & QUIRE 25: 12–13 (Aug.– Sept. 1959).

BANKS, WILLIAM. "The Press Censorship," CAN MAG 46: 152–155 (Dec. 1915).

CALLAGHAN, M. E. "Censorship: The Amateurs and the Law," SAT N 70: 9–10 (Feb. 4, 1956).

CRAICK, W. ARNOT. "Canada's Proposed Copyright Legislation," CAN MAG 37: 215–220 (July 1911).

DAWSON, SAMUEL EDWARD. Copyright in Books.... (Montreal, Dawson, 1882).

DEACON, WILLIAM ARTHUR. Sh-h-h ... Here Comes the Censor! An Address ... (Toronto, Macmillan, 1940).

EGGLESTON, W. "Censorship Grows in Quebec," SAT N 65: 3 (April 4, 1950).

FARRELL, JAMES T. "Canada Bans Another Book," CAN FORUM 26: 176–178 (Nov. 1946).

FRASER, BLAIR. "Our Hush-Hush Censorship: How Books are Banned," MACL MAG 62: 24–25, 44 (Dec. 15, 1949).

FRENCH, DONALD G. "Copyright Simplified," CAN BKMN 14: 31–32 (March 1932).

FULTON. E. D. "Problem of the Publication and Distribution of Obscene and

Salacious Literature," CAN LIB ASSOC BUL 15: 111–113 (Nov. 1958).

GREAT BRITAIN. Colonial Office. Canada. *Correspondence on the Subject of the Law of Copyright in Canada.* (London, H. M. Stationery Office, 1895).

HASKINS, DOUG. "The Many Faces of Censorship," CAN FORUM 33: 57–58 (June 1953).

LAMB, W. K. "Copyright and the Canadian Book Market [address]," CAN LIB ASSOC BUL 12: 69–74 (Oct. 1955).

LANCEFIELD, RICHARD T. *Notes on Copyright ... Domestic and International* (Hamilton, Canadian Literary Bureau, 1896; 2nd ed. enl. 1897).

LOVELL, JOHN and G. M. ADAM. *A Letter to Sir John Rose ... on the Canadian Copyright Question.* By Two Members of the Native Book Trade [pseud]. (London, 1872).

MCCLELLAND, JOHN G. "Reprinting of Canadian Books," ONT LIB R 40: 188–192 (Aug. 1957).

MCDOUGALL, ROBERT L. "Reprinting of Canadian Books," ONT LIB R 40: 183–188 (Aug. 1957).

MCLEAN, J. ROSS. "Bad Books in Canada," SAT N 50: 10 (April 6, 1935).

MACLENNAN, HUGH. "Do We Gag Our Writers?" MACL MAG 60: 13, 50–55 (March 1, 1947).

MORANG, GEORGE N. *The Copyright Question: A Letter to the Toronto Board of Trade.* (Toronto, Morang, 1902).

MOSS, JOHN H. "Copyright in Canada," UNIV MAG (Montreal) 13: 194–211 (April 1914).

O'BRIEN, R. A. "There's No Way to Control Censorship!" CAN AUTH & BKMN 36: 11–12 (Summer 1960).

RIDDELL, WILLIAM RENWICK. "The First Copyrighted Book in the Province of Canada," ONT HIST SOC PAPERS 25: 405–414 (1929).

[ROBERTSON, JOHN ROSS]. *Copyright in Canada: The Question Discussed Practically and Constitutionally.* (Toronto, Robertson, 1879).

ROPER, GORDON. "Mark Twain and his Canadian Publishers," AMER BOOK COLLECTOR 10: 13–29 (June 1960). [Rev. and reprinted as "Mark Twain and his Canadian Publishers: A Second Look," PAPERS, BIBLIOG SOC CAN 5: 30–89 (1966).]

ROSE, DAN A. "The Copyright Question," CAN MAG 6: 81–84 (Nov. 1895).

SANDWELL, B. K. "The Canadian Copyright Act," QUEEN'S Q 29: 182–188 (Oct. 1921).

——— "The Copyright Situation," QUEEN'S Q 38: 335–347 (Spring 1931).

——— "The New Copyright Act," CAN AUTH 9: 35–37 (Sept. 1931).

SMITH, GOLDWIN. "The Canadian Copyright Bill," CAN MAG 5: 551–553 (Oct. 1895).

[———] "Copyright Legislation," BYSTANDER n.s. 68–71 (Nov. 1889).

STEWART, J. "Censorship in Canada," FOOD FOR THOUGHT 10: 4–8 (March 1950).

SWAYZE, J. F. "The Problem of Book Censorship," SAT N 67: 19 (July 19, 1952).

TUMPANE, F. "I'm in Favor of Censorship," MACL MAG 69: 4, 83–84 (Nov. 24, 1956).

WISE, FRANK. "Canadian Copyright," UNIV MAG (Montreal) 10: 404–413 (Oct. 1911).

PART TWO

Works on Individual Authors

ADAMS, Levi, –1832

KLINCK, C. F. *"The Charivari* and Levi Adams," DAL R 40: 34–42 (Spring 1960).

LANDE, LAWRENCE M. "Levi Adams," "The Charivari," [and] "Tecumthé." In his *Old Lamps Aglow* (Montreal, the Author, 1957) pp 108–112, 130–143.

ALEXANDER, William John, 1855–1944

WALLACE, M. W. and A. S. P. WOODHOUSE. "In Memoriam: William John Alexander," UNIV TOR Q 14: 1–33 (Oct. 1944).

ALLAN, Andrew Edward Fairbairn, 1907–

LE COCQ, THELMA. "On Stage with Allan," MACL MAG 60: 21–24 (Feb. 1, 1947).

SINCLAIR, LISTER. "Andrew Allan," CAN FORUM 30: 35 (May 1950).

ALLEN, Grant, 1848–1899

CLARKE, G. H. "Grant Allen," QUEEN'S Q 45: 487–496 (Nov. 1938).

CLODD, EDWARD. *Grant Allen: A Memoir* (London, Richards, 1900).

ALLEN, Joseph Antisell, 1814–1900

MACHAR, AGNES MAULE. "Canadian Celebrities: XXIII, The Late J. A. Allen," CAN MAG 17: 13–17 (May 1901).

ALLINE, Rev. Henry, 1748–1784

ALLINE, REV. HENRY. *Life and Journals of the Rev. Mr. Henry Alline* (Boston, Gilbert & Dean, 1806).

ARMSTRONG, MAURICE W. *The Great Awakening in Nova Scotia, 1776–1809* (Hartford, Conn., Amer. Soc. of Church History, 1947).

——— "Henry Alline's 'Hymns and Spiritual Songs,'" DAL R 34: 418–425 (Winter 1955).

——— "Jonathan Scott's Brief View, Published in Nova Scotia in 1784," HARVARD THEOL R 40: 121–136 (April 1947).

BEZANSON, REV. W. B. *The Romance of Religion: A Sketch of the Life of Henry Alline, in the Pioneer Days of the Maritime Provinces* (Kentville, N.S., Kentville Publishing Co., 1927).

——— *Stories of Acadia* (Halifax, Nova Print., 1941).

CALNEK, WILLIAM A. *History of the County of Annapolis...: With Memoirs of Its Representatives in the Provincial Parliament, and Biographical and Genealogical Sketches of Its Early English Settlers and Their Families*, ed. and completed by A. W. Savary (Toronto, Briggs, 1897). [Also *A Supplement to the History...* by A. W. Savary (Toronto, Briggs, 1913).]

EATON, ARTHUR W. H. *The Church of England in Nova Scotia and the Tory Clergy of the Revolution* (New York, Whittaker, 1891) *passim*.

LANDE, LAWRENCE M. "Henry Alline." In his *Old Lamps Aglow* (Montreal, the Author, 1957) pp 3–6.

MURRAY, J. LOVELL. "Alline of the New Lights." In his *Nation Builders* (Toronto, Can. Council of the Missionary Education Movement, 1925) pp 26–29.

PERKINS, SIMEON. *The Diary of Simeon Perkins*, ed. with intro. and notes by Harold A. Innis (Toronto, Champlain Society, 1948).

SAUNDERS, REV. EDWARD M. *History of the Baptists of the Maritime Provinces* (Halifax, Burgoyne, 1902).

SCOTT, REV. JONATHAN. *A Brief View of the Religious Tenets and Sentiments, Lately Published and Spread in . . . "Two Mites" . . . Publications of Mr. Henry Alline* (Halifax, Howe, 1784).

SULLIVAN, KENNETH GEORGE. "New England Puritanism and Its Disintegration in Nova Scotia" (Thesis, Dalhousie University, 1934).

ALLISON, William Talbot, 1874–1941

STEAD, R. J. C. "William Talbot Allison," CAN AUTH & BKMN 17: 4–5 (Feb. 1941).

ANDERSON, Patrick, 1915–

ANDERSON, PATRICK. *Search Me: An Autobiography—The Black Country, Canada and Spain* (London, Chatto & Windus, 1957).

———— *Snake Wine: A Singapore Episode* (London, Chatto & Windus, 1955).

ANON. "Biographical Note," CAN AUTH & BKMN 34: 5 (Spring 1958).

FRYE, NORTHROP. Review of *The Colour as Naked* by Patrick Anderson, UNIV TOR Q 23: 254–256 (April 1954).

NORTH, JESSICA NELSON. "Mercurial," POETRY (Chicago) 69: 284–286 (Feb. 1947).

SMITH, A. J. M. "New Canadian Poetry," CAN FORUM 26: 252 (Feb. 1947).

SUTHERLAND, JOHN. "The Poetry of Patrick Anderson," NORTHERN R 2:8–20, 25–34 (April–May 1949).

———— "The Writing of Patrick Anderson," FIRST STATEMENT vol 1 no 19: 3–6 (May 14, 1943).

WREFORD, JAMES. "Canadian Background," INDEX 1: 6–10 (July 1946).

AVISON, Margaret, 1918–

GHISELIN, BREWSTER. "The Architecture of Vision," POETRY (Chicago) 70: 324–328 (Sept. 1947).

WILSON, MILTON. "The Poetry of Margaret Avison," CAN LIT no 2: 47–58 (Autumn 1959).

BAILEY, Rev. Jacob, 1731–1808

ALLEN, CHARLES E. *Rev. Jacob Bailey: His Character and Works.* Read before the Lincoln County Historical Society (pub. by the Society, 1895).

BAKER, RAY PALMER. "The Poetry of Jacob Bailey, Loyalist," NEW ENGL Q 2: 58–92 (Jan. 1929). [*See also* his *History of English Canadian*

Literature to the Confederation (Cambridge, Mass., Harvard University Press, 1920) pp 22, 26–27, 37–41.]

BARTLET, WILLIAM S. *The Frontier Missionary: A Memoir of the Life of the Rev. Jacob Bailey* (Boston, Ide & Dutton, 1853).

EATON, ARTHUR W. H. *History of King's County, Nova Scotia* (Salem, Mass., Salem Press, 1910) pp 178–179, 243–246.

GRANGER, BRUCE INGHAM. [Bailey's satire.] In his *Political Satire in the American Revolution 1763–1783* (Ithaca, Cornell University Press, 1960) *passim.*

SARGENT, WINTHROP. *The Loyalist Poetry of the Revolution* (Philadelphia, Collins, 1857) *passim.*

STARR, H. E. "Jacob Bailey," *Dictionary of American Biography* (New York, Scribner's, 1928) vol 1, pp 497–498.

BAIRD, Irene
COX, C. "A Novelist Goes to the Films," SAT N 58: 2 (Jan. 9, 1943).
MARRIOTT, ANNE. "Irene Baird, New Voice from the West," CAN AUTH & BKMN 18: 6 (April 1941).

BAKER, Ida Emma (Fitch), 1858–1948
BAKER, RAY PALMER. Introduction to *Selected Poems of Ida Emma Fitch Baker* (Toronto, Ryerson, 1951) pp ix–xvii.

BARBEAU, Charles Marius, 1883–1969

BARBEAU, Charles Marius, 1883–
CARDIN, C. "Bio-bibliographie de Marius Barbeau," ARCHIVES DE FOLKLORE 2: 17–96 (1947).
GARDINER, P. "Outdoor Man of the Month: Marius Barbeau," FOR & OUTDOORS 46: 17, 29–30 (April 1950).
HITSCHMANOVA, L. "Marius Barbeau, ami de l'habitant et du sauvage," CULTURE 7: 66–71 (mars 1946).
KEMP, HUGH. "Top Man in Totem Poles," MACL MAG 61: 7–8, 56–59 (May 1, 1948).
LACOURCIÈRE, L. "Hommage à Marius Barbeau," ARCHIVES DE FOLKLORE 2: 7–8 (1947).
SAVARD, F. A. "Eloge de Marius Barbeau," ARCHIVES DE FOLKLORE 2: 9–16 (1947).

BARR, Robert, 1850–1912 [pseud: "Luke Sharp"]
ALLAN, C. S. "A Glimpse of Robert Barr," CAN MAG 4: 545–550 (April 1895).
BROWN, W. J. "Robert Barr and Literature in Canada," CAN MAG 15: 170–176 (June 1900).
C., J. A. "Canadian Celebrities: IX, Robert Barr," CAN MAG 14: 181–182 (Dec. 1899).

BARRINGTON, E. [pseud]. *See* BECK, Mrs. Lily Adams

BAXTER, Arthur Beverley, 1891–1964
ANON. "Beaver's Bax," TIME 36: 60–61 (Nov. 11, 1940).

BECK, Mrs. Lily Adams (Moresby), –1931 [pseud: "E. Barrington"]
ANON. "Mrs. L. Adams Beck," WILSON LIB BUL 5: 164 (Nov. 1930).
——— Obituary, PUB WKLY 119: 206 (Jan. 10, 1931).
——— Obituary, WILSON LIB BUL 5: 396 (Feb. 1931).

FAWCETT, WILLIAM McRAE. "Who's Who in Canadian Literature: Mrs. L. Adams Beck (E. Barrington)," CAN BKMN 11: 275–277 (Dec. 1929).

LUGRIN, N. DE BERTRAND. "L. Adams Beck—The Lady with the Mask," MACL MAG 38: 72–74 (Nov. 1, 1925).

BECKWITH, Julia Catherine. *See* HART, Mrs. Julia Catherine

BELANEY, George Stansfeld, 1888–1938 [pseud: "Grey Owl"]
ANAHAREO, *My Life with Grey Owl* (London, Davies, 1940).
ANON. "The Adventurous Career of Grey Owl," FOR & OUTDOORS 27: 118 (March 1931).
———— "Beaver Man," TIME 28: 63 (Dec. 21, 1936).
———— "Grey Owl Hushed," TIME 31: 17 (Jan. 3, 1938).
———— "Grey Owl's Ghost," NEWSWEEK 11: 18 (May 9, 1938).
———— "Grey Owl's Silencing," SAT N 53: 2 (Jan. 29, 1938).
———— Obituary, PUB WKLY 133: 1683 (April 23, 1938).
———— "Salute a Great Canadian," CAN MAG 86: 1 (Dec. 1936).
BANKS, W. J. "Grey Owl, Big Brother of the Beavers," UNITED EMPIRE 27: 429–431 (Aug. 1936).
CARLISLE, N. "Most Incredible Indian," CORONET 36: 135–140 (Aug. 1954).
CORY, HARPER. *Grey Owl and the Beaver* (London, Nelson, 1935).
DEXTER, G. "Introducing Grey Owl," CAN MAG 76: 20, 31 (Aug. 1931).
DICKSON, LOVAT, ed. *The Green Leaf: A Tribute to Grey Owl* (London, Lovat Dickson, 1938).
———— *Half-Breed: The Story of Grey Owl (Wa-Sha-Quon-Asin)* (London, Davies, 1939).
EAYRS, HUGH. "Bookman Profiles: Grey Owl," CAN BKMN 20: 14–15 (June 1938).
FRAYNE, T. G. "Grey Owl, the Magnificent Fraud," MACL MAG 64: 14–15, 36–39 (Aug. 1, 1951).
GASKELL, E. F. "Grey Owl: Pathfinder and Artist," CAN BKMN 8: 1–5 (June 1936).
"WIYOT." "Work of Grey Owl," BRIT ANN LIT 1: 47–49 (1938).

BELL, Charles William, 1876–1938
PERRY, ANNE ANDERSON. "Is Versatility an Asset?" CAN MAG 68: 16–17, 41 (Oct. 1927).

BENGOUGH, John Wilson, 1851–1923
CHARLESWORTH, HECTOR. "A Pioneer Canadian Cartoonist." In his *The Canadian Scene* (Toronto, Macmillan, 1927) pp 125–131.
KEYES, D. P. "Bengough and Carlyle," UNIV TOR Q 2: 49–73 (Oct. 1932).

BERNARD, Lally [pseud]. *See* FITZGIBBON, Mrs. Mary Agnes

BERNHARDT, Clara Mae, 1911–
GRAY, LILLIAN COLLIER. "A Poetess, a Poem, and a Voluntary Mission of Comfort and Sympathy," SAT N 59: 22 (Aug. 19, 1944).

BIRD, Will R., 1891–
BIRD, WILL R. "My First Book," CAN AUTH & BKMN 29: 5–8, 12 (Spring 1953).

BIRNEY, (Alfred) Earle, 1904–

BAILEY, A. G. [Review article on *The Strait of Anian*], DAL R 30: 205–208 (July 1950).

BROWN, E. K. "To the North: A Wall against Canadian Poetry," SAT R LIT 27: 9–11 (April 29, 1944).

CLAY, CHARLES. "Earle Birney, Canadian Spokesman," EDUC RECORD (Quebec) 61: 83–87 (April–June 1945). [Also in *Leading Canadian Poets*, ed. W. P. Percival (Toronto, Ryerson, 1948) pp 23–29.]

DANIELLS, ROY. "Earle Birney et Robert Finch," GANTS DU CIEL 11: 83–96 (printemps 1946).

——— "Lorne Pierce Medal," ROY SOC CAN PROC & TRANS 3rd ser 47: 37–38 (1953).

ELLIOTT, BRIAN. "Earle Birney: Canadian Poet," MEANJIN (Australia) no 78 vol 18, no 3: 338–347 (1959).

FREDEMAN, WILLIAM E. "Earle Birney: Poet," BC LIB Q 23: 8–15 (Jan. 1960).

FRYE, NORTHROP. [Review of *David and Other Poems*], CAN FORUM 22: 278–279 (Dec. 1942).

LIVESAY, DOROTHY. "Earle Birney—Author, Poet," UBC ALUMNI CHRONICLE pp 9, 28 (March 1950).

PACEY, DESMOND. "Earle Birney." In his *Ten Canadian Poets* (Toronto, Ryerson, 1958) pp 293–326.

PHELPS, ARTHUR L. "Two Poets: Klein & Birney." In his *Canadian Writers* (Toronto, McClelland & Stewart, 1951) pp 111–119.

PRATT, E. J. [Review of *David and Other Poems*], CAN POETRY 6: 34–35 (March 1943).

SUTHERLAND, JOHN. "Earle Birney's *David*," FIRST STATEMENT vol 1 no 9: 6–8 [undated].

BLENNERHASSET, Margaret (Agnew), 1778?–1842

LANDE, LAWRENCE M. "Margaret Blennerhasset." In his *Old Lamps Aglow* (Montreal, the Author, 1957) pp 115–123.

BLEWETT, Mrs. Jean (McKishnie), 1862–1934

MACKLEM, JOHN. "Who's Who in Canadian Literature: Jean Blewett," CAN BKMN 9: 99–100 (April 1927).

MIDDLETON, J. E. "Writing-Lady," EDUC RECORD (Quebec) 62: 98–100 (April–June 1946).

BORDEN, Sir Robert Laird, 1854–1937

BORDEN, ROBERT LAIRD. *Robert Laird Borden: His Memoirs,* ed. with a preface by Henry Borden, and with an intro. by Arthur Meighen (Toronto, Macmillan, 1938).

BRADY, A. "Robert Laird Borden: His Memoirs," UNIV TOR Q 8: 227–234 (Jan. 1939).

DAWSON, R. M. "Robert Laird Borden: His Memoirs," CAN J ECON 5: 89–97 (Feb. 1939).

GIBSON, JAMES A. "Sir Robert Borden." In *Our Living Tradition*, Second and Third Series, ed. Robert L. McDougall (Toronto, published in association with Carleton University by University of Toronto Press, 1959) pp 95–122.

MACQUARRIE, H. N. "Robert Borden—Party Leader," CAN FORUM 37: 14–17 (April 1957).

O'LEARY, M. GRATTAN. "Robert Borden: Canadian," MACL MAG 51: 12–13, 41–42, 47 (Dec. 15, 1938).

TROTTER, REGINALD G. "Sir Robert Borden," QUEEN'S Q 46: 334–340 (Autumn 1939).

BOURINOT, Arthur Stanley, 1893–1969

KING, AMABEL. "New Editor for *Poetry Magazine*," CAN AUTH & BKMN 24: 16–17 (June 1948).

MACDONALD, GOODRIDGE. "The Poetry of Arthur S. Bourinot," CAN BKMN 3: 41–42 (June 1921).

MARTIN, BURNS. "Arthur S. Bourinot," EDUC RECORD (Quebec) 63: 225–231 (Oct.–Dec. 1947).

POMEROY, ELSIE. "The Sonnets of Arthur S. Bourinot," DAL R 29: 310–313 (Oct. 1949).

THOMSON, D. W. "Arthur S. Bourinot: Poet of the Hills." CAN AUTH & BKMN 34: 8–9 (Fall 1958).

BOURINOT, Sir John George, 1837–1902

ANON. "John George Bourinot [Bibliography]," ROY SOC CAN PROC & TRANS 1st ser 12: 16–18 (1894).

———— Obituary, ROY SOC CAN PROC & TRANS 2nd ser 9: vii–viii (1903).

DAVIN, NICHOLAS FLOOD. *The Secretary of the Royal Society of Canada (J. G. Bourinot): A Literary Fraud* (Ottawa, n.p., 1882).

MACBETH, MADGE. "A Great Canadian: Sir John Bourinot," DAL R 34: 173–180 (Summer 1954).

BRAY, Horace Edgar Kingsmill, 1895–1917

BLACKBURN, GRACE. "The Poems of Horace Bray," CAN BKMN 1: 9–12 (July 1919).

BRETT, George Sidney, 1879–1944

IRVING, JOHN A. "The Achievement of George Sidney Brett," UNIV TOR Q 14: 329–365 (July 1945).

BROOKE, Mrs. Frances (Moore), 1724–1789

BAKER, ERNEST A. "Mrs. Frances Brooke." In his *The History of the English Novel* (London, Witherby, 1934) vol 5, pp 144–146.

BLUE, CHARLES S. "Canada's First Novelist," CAN MAG 58: 3–12 (Nov. 1921).

BURPEE, LAWRENCE J. Introduction to *The History of Emily Montague* by Frances Brooke . . . , with an Appendix by F. P. Grove (Ottawa, Graphic, 1931) pp iii–vi, 327–333.

BURWASH, IDA. "An Old Time Novel," CAN MAG 28: 252–256 (Jan. 1907).

CHATEAUCLAIR, WILFRID. "The First Canadian Novel," DOM ILLUS 4: 31 (Jan. 11, 1890).

HUMPHREYS, J. "Mrs. Frances Brooke," *Dictionary of National Biography* (London, Oxford, 1921) 2: 1328–1329.

KLINCK, CARL F. Introduction to *The History of Emily Montague* by Frances Brooke (Toronto, McClelland & Stewart, 1961) pp v–xiv. [New Canadian Library no 27.]

MORGAN, H. R. "Frances Brooke: A Canadian Pioneer," Supplement to the McGILL NEWS (June 1930).

PACEY, DESMOND. "The First Canadian Novel," DAL R 26: 143–150 (July 1946).

WOODLEY, E. C. "The First Canadian Novel and Its Author," EDUC RECORD (Quebec) 57: 31–36 (Jan. 1941).

BROOKER, Bertram, 1888–1955
LeBourdais, D. M. "Protean," SAT N 65: 20 (May 2, 1950).
Lee, T. R. "Bertram Brooker 1888–1955," CAN ART 13: 286–291 (Spring 1956).
Salinger, J. B. "The Work of Bertram Brooker," CAN FORUM 10: 327, 331–332 (June 1930).

BROWN, Audrey Alexandra, 1904–
Brown, Audrey Alexandra. *The Log of a Lame Duck* (Toronto, Macmillan, 1938).
Burrell, Martin. "Audrey Alexandra Brown." In his *Crumbs are Also Bread* (Toronto, Macmillan, 1934) pp 313–327.
Clarke, George Herbert. "Audrey Alexandra Brown," EDUC RECORD (Quebec) 60: 230–233 (Oct.–Dec. 1944). [Also in *Leading Canadian Poets,* ed. W. P. Percival (Toronto, Ryerson, 1948) pp 30–36.]
Hannan, A. A. "The Most Important Contribution to Canadian Literature since 1925: Audrey Alexandra Brown's Poem 'Laodamia,'" CAN BKMN 17: 26 (Feb. 1935).
Lloyd, C. F. "Audrey Brown," SAT N 51: 23 (April 25, 1936).
MacKay, L. A. "Audrey Alexandra Brown," CAN FORUM 12: 342–343 (June 1932).

BROWN, Edward Killoran, 1905–1951
Anon. "Posthumously Awarded Lorne Pierce Medal of the Royal Society of Canada," ROY SOC CAN PROC & TRANS 3rd ser 45: 41–42 (1951).
Breen, M. "Man of Letters," SAT N 65: 12 (Dec. 27, 1949).
Bugnet, Georges. "Où l'encontre un Canadien," CANADIEN-FRANÇAIS 33: 325–332, 438–446 (jan.–fév. 1946).
Sandwell, B. K. "The Late E. K. Brown," SAT N 66: 7 (May 8, 1951).

BROWN, James, 1790–1870
Maxwell, D. F. "Hon. James Brown," ACADIENSIS 3: 184–191 (July 1903).

BRUCE, Charles Tory, 1906–1971
Anon. Biographical Note, CAN AUTH & BKMN 34: 54 (Spring 1958).
———— "The Writer Reviewed," CAN AUTH & BKMN 24: 23–24 (June 1948).

BRYMNER, Douglas, 1823–1902
Anon. "Douglas Brymner, Archivist," DOM ILLUS 5: 127 (Aug. 23, 1890).
Harvey, D. C. "Douglas Brymner, 1823–1902," CAN HIST R 24: 249–252 (Sept. 1943).
Scott, M. O. "Canadian Celebrities: XIX, Douglas Brymner, Archivist," CAN MAG 16: 206–208 (Jan. 1901).

BUCKE, Richard Maurice, 1837–1902
Berry, Edmund G. "Dr. Bucke, Whitman's Canadian Friend," MANITOBA ARTS R 4: 5–13 (Winter 1944). [Also in DAL R 24: 77–82 (April 1944).]

COYNE, JAMES HENRY. *Richard Maurice Bucke: A Sketch* (Toronto, Saunders, 1923).

MACKALL, L. L. "Whitman and Bucke," NY HERALD-TRIB BK R 12: 23 (April 12, 1936).

STEVENSON, G. H. "The Life and Work of Richard Maurice Bucke," AMER J PSYCHIATRY 93: 1127–1150 (March 1937).

BUCKLER, Ernest, 1908–

ANON. Biographical Note, MACL MAG 62: 2–3 (Jan. 1, 1949).

BISSELL, CLAUDE. Introduction to *The Mountain and the Valley* by Ernest Buckler (Toronto, McClelland & Stewart, 1961) pp vii–xii. [New Canadian Library no 23.]

BURRELL, Martin, 1858–1938

ANON. "Martin Burrell," ONT LIB R 22: 88 (May 1938).

———— Obituary, ONT LIB R 22: 97 (May 1938).

———— Obituary, SAT N 53: 3 (March 26, 1938).

———— "Hon Martin Burrell, 1858–1938," CAN AUTH 15: 15–16 (April 1938).

BURROWS, C. Acton, 1853–1948

ALLAN, HOWARD. "Burrows, the Indefatigable," MACL MAG 42: 14, 82–85 (June 15, 1929).

BURWELL, Adam Hood (1790?–1849)

LANDE, LAWRENCE M. "Adam Hood Burwell." In his *Old Lamps Aglow* (Montreal, the Author, 1957) pp 242–253.

BUTLER, Suzanne, 1919–

BUTLER, SUZANNE. "The First Lesson in Hard Work," SAT N 68: 30–31 (Sept. 12, 1953).

CALLAGHAN, Morley Edward, 1903–

ANON. Biographical Note, SCHOLASTIC 30: 4 (March 13, 1937).

———— Biographical Sketch, LIT DIGEST 120: 25 (Sept. 28, 1935).

———— Biographical Sketch, WILSON LIB BUL 3: 618 (May 1929).

———— "Prodigal Who Stayed Home," SAT N 70: 1, 21–22 (May 12, 1956).

AVISON, MARGARET. "Callaghan Revisited," CAN FORUM 39: 276–277 (March 1960).

BROWN, E. K. "The Immediate Present in Canadian Literature," SEWANEE R 41: 430–442 (Oct. 1933).

DAVIS, H. J. "Morley Callaghan," CAN FORUM 15: 398–399 (Dec. 1935).

KOCH, E. A. "Callaghan: Lend-Lease from the Bohemians," SAT N 60: 16–17 (Oct. 21, 1944).

LEWIS, WYNDHAM. "What Books for Total War," SAT N 38: 16 (Oct. 1942). [A review of *Now That April's Here.*]

McCARVELL, JOAN. "Morley Callaghan as a Short Story Writer" (Thesis, Laval University, 1957).

McPHERSON, HUGO. Introduction to *More Joy in Heaven* by Morley Callaghan (Toronto, McClelland & Stewart, 1960) pp v–x. [New Canadian Library no 17.]

———— "The Two Worlds of Morley Callaghan," QUEEN'S Q 64: 350–365 (Autumn 1957). [Also in *Canadian Anthology*, ed. C. F. Klinck and R. E. Watters, rev. ed. (Toronto, Gage, 1966) pp 507–515.]

MOON, BARBARA. "The Second Coming of Morley Callaghan," MACL MAG 73: 19, 62–64 (Dec. 3, 1960).

PHELPS, ARTHUR L. "Morley Callaghan." In his *Canadian Writers* (Toronto, McClelland & Stewart, 1951) pp 10–18.

PRATT, HYPERBOLE. "Theatre," CAN FORUM 30: 40–41 (May 1950).

PRESTON, BERNARD. "Toronto's Callaghan," SAT N 51: 12 (Jan. 18, 1936).

RIPLEY, J. D. "A Critical Study of Morley Callaghan" (Thesis, University of New Brunswick, 1959).

ROSS, MALCOLM. Introduction to *Such is My Beloved* by Morley Callaghan (Toronto, McClelland & Stewart, 1957) pp v–xiii. [New Canadian Library no 2.]

SANDWELL, B. K. "Hurt without Help," SAT N 66: 7 (March 27, 1951).

STEINHAUER, H. "Canadian Writers of Today," CAN FORUM 12: 177–178 (Feb. 1932).

WATT, FRANK W. "Morley Callaghan as Thinker," DAL R 39: 305–313 (Autumn 1959).

WEAVER, ROBERT. "Stories by Callaghan," CAN LIT no 2: 67–70 (Autumn 1959).

———— "A Talk with Morley Callaghan," TAM R no 7: 3–29 (Spring 1958).

WILSON, EDMUND. "Morley Callaghan of Toronto," NEW YORKER 36: 224–236 (Nov. 26, 1960).

CAMERON, George Frederick, 1854–1885

BOURINOT, ARTHUR S. "George Frederick Cameron," CAN AUTH & BKMN 29: 3–5 (Winter 1954). [Includes bibliography.]

———— "George Frederick Cameron (Some Notes on His Opera and His Life)." In his *Five Canadian Poets* (Montreal, Quality Press, 1956) pp 22–26.

BURPEE, LAWRENCE J. "George Frederick Cameron." In his *A Little Book of Canadian Essays* (Toronto, Musson, 1909) pp 73–87.

DYDE, S. W. "The Two Camerons," QUEEN'S R 3: 196–198 (Aug. 1929).

KYTE, E. C. "George Frederick Cameron," EDUC RECORD (Quebec) 63: 117–122 (April–June 1947).

LAMPMAN, ARCHIBALD. "Two Canadian Poets [C. G. D. Roberts and G. F. Cameron]," with a prefatory note by E. K. Brown. UNIV TOR Q 13: 406–423 (July 1944).

M., J. "Who's Who in Canadian Literature: George Frederick Cameron," CAN BKMN 13: 179–180 (Sept. 1931).

VIVIEN, GEOFFREY. "A Forgotten Canadian Poet," CAN AUTH & BKMN 23: 57 (Dec. 1947).

CAMPBELL, William Wilfred, 1858–1918

ALLISON, W. T. "William Wilfred Campbell," CAN BKMN 1: 65–66 (April 1919).

BARNETT, E. S. "The Poetry of William Wilfred Campbell," CAN BKMN 17: 93–94 (Aug. 1935).

BURPEE, L. J. "Canadian Poet: W. W. Campbell," SEWANEE R 8: 425–436 (Oct. 1900).

CHARLESWORTH, HECTOR. "Poets and Women Writers of the Past." In his *Candid Chronicles* (Toronto, Macmillan, 1925) pp 87–104.

GRAHAM, JEAN. "Canadian Celebrities: 66, Mr. Wilfred Campbell," CAN MAG 26: 109–111 (Dec. 1905).

KLINCK, CARL F. *Wilfred Campbell: A Study in Late Provincial Victorianism* (Toronto, Ryerson, 1942).

—— "Wilfred Campbell: A Study in Late Provincial Victorianism" (Thesis, Columbia University, 1942).

—— "William Wilfred Campbell." In *A Standard Dictionary of Canadian Biography, Canadian Who Was Who*, ed. C. G. D. Roberts and A. L. Tunnell (Toronto, Trans-Canada Press, 1934) vol 1, pp 88–93.

—— "William Wilfred Campbell: Poet of Lakes," CAN BKMN 21: 34–37 (Aug. 1939).

KNISTER, RAYMOND. "The Poetical Works of Wilfred Campbell," QUEEN'S Q 31: 435–449 (May 1924).

MACKAY, L. A. "W. W. Campbell," CAN FORUM 14: 66–67 (Nov. 1933).

MUDDIMAN, BERNARD. "William Wilfred Campbell," QUEEN'S Q 27: 201–210 (Oct. 1919).

SCOTT, COLIN A. "William Wilfred Campbell," CAN MAG 2: 270–274 (Jan. 1894).

STEVENSON, O. J. "A Pre-War Message." In his *A People's Best* (Toronto, Musson, 1927) pp 241–248.

—— "Who's Who in Canadian Literature: William Wilfred Campbell," CAN BKMN 9: 67–71 (March 1927).

SUTHERLAND, M. H. "William Wilfred Campbell," ACTA VIC 17: 181–185 (March 1894).

SYKES, W. J. "Wilfred Campbell," EDUC RECORD (Quebec) 62: 93–97 (April–June 1946). [Also in *Leading Canadian Poets*, ed. W. P. Percival (Toronto, Ryerson, 1948) pp 37–44.]

TUCKER, J. A. "The Poems of William Wilfred Campbell," UNIV TOR Q 1: 140–145 (May 1895).

[WHITESIDE, ERNESTINE R.] "Canadian Poetry and Poets, II [Lampman, Carman, and Campbell]," McMASTER U MO 8: 68–74 (Nov. 1898).

YEIGH, FRANK. "William Wilfred Campbell, a Scotch-Canadian Poet," BK NEWS MTHLY (Philadelphia) (Aug. 1910) pp 897–900.

CANUCK, Janey [pseud.]. *See* MURPHY, Mrs. Emily Cowan.

CAPE, Judith [pseud.]. *See* PAGE, Patricia Kathleen.

CARMAN, Bliss, 1861–1929

ANON. "Bliss Carman," LIT DIGEST 102: 21 (July 6, 1929).

—— "In memory of Bliss Carman," CAN HOME J 27: 14 (June 1930).

—— "Poems to Remember: *Vagabond Song*," with biographical note, SCHOLASTIC 41: 20 (Oct. 5, 1942).

—— "Poet Laureate of Canada Passes Away," OVERLAND n.s. 87: 219 (July 1929).

—— "When Bliss Carman Wrote 'Advertising,' " WESTERN HOME MO 31: 30, 61 (April 1930).

ARCHER, WILLIAM. "Bliss Carman." In his *Poets of the Younger Generation* (London, Lane, 1902) pp 66–82.

BRAITHWAITE, W. S. "The Imaginative Vision of Bliss Carman," BOSTON TRANSCRIPT (May 10, 1916).

BROWN, HARRY W. "Bliss Carman's Latest Books of Poems," CAN MAG 6: 477–481 (March 1896).

CAPPON, JAMES. "Bliss Carman's Beginnings," QUEEN'S Q 36: 637–665 (Oct. 1929).

———— Bliss Carman and the Literary Currents and Influences of His Time (Toronto, Ryerson, 1930).

CARMAN, BLISS. Bliss Carman's Scrap Book, ed. with a postscript by Lorne Pierce (Toronto, Ryerson, 1931).

———— "A Letter about Himself to Editor," CRITIC n.s. 26: 164–165 (Sept. 12, 1896).

CLARKE, G. F. "April on the St. John," ACADIE 1: 11–12 (April 15, 1930).

COLUM, P. "Bliss Carman's Sanctuary," COMMONWEAL 11: 225 (Dec. 25, 1929).

DE LA MARE, WALTER. "The Poetry of Life," BKMN (London) 30: 72 (May 1906).

DOUGLAS, R. W. "Canada's Poet Laureate—Bliss Carman," BC MO 19: 5–6, 12 (July 1922); 19: 3–4, 14–16 (Aug. 1922).

EDGAR, PELHAM. "Bliss Carman," EDUC RECORD (Quebec) 57: 140–143 (May 1941). [Also in Leading Canadian Poets, ed. W. P. Percival (Toronto, Ryerson, 1948) pp 45–50.]

FEWSTER, ERNEST. "Bliss Carman at Vancouver," ACADIE 1: 25–27 (July 1930).

GARVIN, J. W. "Bliss Carman," CAN BKMN 14: 34–35 (March 1932).

GRAY, C. "The Mystery of Bliss Carman's Ashes," MACL MAG 64: 40 (Aug. 1, 1951).

HATHAWAY, R. H. "Bliss Carman: an Appreciation," CAN MAG 56: 521–536 (April 1921). [Also in Later Poems by Bliss Carman (Toronto, McClelland & Stewart, 1921) pp vii–xxii.]

———— "Bliss Carman's First Editions," CAN BKMN 6: 8–9 (Jan. 1924).

———— "Bliss Carman: Poet of the Sea," THE SAILOR 2: 19–20 (July 1920).

———— "Bliss Carman's Rare Editions," CAN BKMN 1: 16–17 (Oct. 1919).

———— "Carman Memorial Unveiling," CAN BKMN 12: 222–223 (Dec. 1930).

———— "Carman's Books: A Bibliographical Essay," ACADIE 1: 4–6 (April 15, 1930).

———— "The Poetry of Bliss Carman," SEWANEE R 33: 467–483 (Oct. 1925).

———— "Vale! Bliss Carman," CAN BKMN 11: 155–159 (July 1929).

———— "Who's Who in Canadian Literature: Bliss Carman," CAN BKMN 8: 299–302 (Oct. 1926).

HAWTHORNE, JULIAN. Bliss Carman, 1861–1929 (Palo Alto, Calif., the Author, 1929). [Reprint from the San Francisco Chronicle, June 16, 1929.]

HIND, C. LEWIS. "Bliss Carman." In his More Authors and I (N.Y., Dodd, Mead, 1922), pp 65–70.

HUTCHINSON, P. "Carman, Singer of the Open Road," WORLD WIDE 31: 347 (Feb. 28, 1931).

LEE, H. D. C. *Bliss Carman: a Study in Canadian Poetry* (Buxton, Eng., "Herald" Print. Co., 1912).

LIVESAY, F. H. R. "Bliss Carman at Nassau," SAT N 59: 27 (Nov. 20, 1943).

McCRACKEN, M. S. "Bliss Carman: His Status in the Annals of Canadian Literature" (Thesis, Ottawa University, 1936).

MACDONALD, ALLAN H. *Richard Hovey: Man and Craftsman* (Durham, N.C., Duke University Press, 1957) *passim.*

MACFARLAND, KENNETH. "The Poetry of Bliss Carman," LITERARY MIS-CELLANY 2: 35–39 (Summer 1909).

MACKAY, L. A. "Bliss Carman," CAN FORUM 13: 182–183 (Feb. 1933).

McPHERSON, HUGO. "The Literary Reputation of Bliss Carman: A Study in the Development of Canadan Taste in Poetry" (Thesis, University of Western Ontario, 1950).

MARQUIS, T. G. "Crude Criticism," THE WEEK 13: 350–351 (March 6, 1896).

MARSHALL, J. "Pipes of Pan," QUEEN'S Q 11: 203–208 (Oct. 1903).

MARTIN, MARY C. "The Early Development of Bliss Carman" (Thesis, University of New Brunswick, 1957).

MASSEY, VINCENT. "Roberts, Carman, Sherman: Canadian Poets," CAN AUTH & BKMN 23: 29–32 (Fall 1947).

MILLER, MURIEL. *Bliss Carman, a Portrait* (Toronto, Ryerson, 1935).

———— "A Mental Biography of Bliss Carman in a Creative Interpretation of His Poetry" (Thesis, University of Toronto, 1933).

MORSE, WILLIAM INGLIS. *Bliss Carman: Bibliography, Letters, Fugitive Verses, and Other Data* (Windham, Conn., Hawthorne House, 1941).

MUDDIMAN, BERNARD. "A Vignette in Canadian Literature," CAN MAG 40: 451–458 (March 1913).

MUNDAY, DON. "The Faith of Bliss Carman," WESTMINSTER HALL 6: 9–12 (Sept. 1914).

PACEY, DESMOND. "Bliss Carman." In his *Ten Canadian Poets* (Toronto, Ryerson, 1958) pp 59–113.

———— "Bliss Carman: A Reappraisal," NORTHERN R 3: 2–10 (Feb.–March 1950).

PIERCE, LORNE. "Bliss Carman." In his *Three Fredericton Poets: Writers of the University of New Brunswick and the New Dominion* (Toronto, Ryerson, 1933) pp 18–24.

———— ed. *Bliss Carman's Scrap-Book* (Toronto, Ryerson, 1931).

———— Introduction to *The Selected Poems of Bliss Carman* (Toronto, McClelland & Stewart, 1954) pp 17–30.

POLLOCK, F. L. "Canadian Writers in New York," ACTA VIC 22: 434–439 (April 1899).

POUND, A. M. "My First and Last Days with Bliss Carman," ACADIE 1: 19–20 (May 1, 1930).

R., N. "Bliss Carman and the Tribute of Youth," BC MO 24: 5 (May 1925).

RHODENIZER, V. B. "Carman's Last Visit to Wolfville," ACADIE 1: 9–10 (April 15, 1930).

RITTENHOUSE, JESSIE B. "Bliss Carman." In her *Younger American Poets* (Boston, Little Brown, 1904) pp 46–74.

ROBERTS, C. G. D. "Bliss Carman," DAL R 9: 409–417 (Jan. 1930).

————— "Carman and His Own Country," ACADIE 1: 2–4 (April 15, 1930).

————— "Mr. Bliss Carman's Poems," CHAP-BOOK 1: 53–57 (June 15, 1894).

————— "More Reminiscences of Bliss Carman," DAL R 10: 1–9 (April 1930).

————— "Some Reminiscences of Bliss Carman in New York," CAN POETRY 5: 5–10 (Dec. 1940).

ROBERTS, LLOYD. "Bliss Carman: A Memory," CAN BKMN 21: 42–46 (April 1939).

ROBERTS, T. G. "The Writing of the Red Wolf," CAN BKMN 15: 103–104 (Aug. 1933).

ROSS, M. M. "Carman by the Sea," DAL R 27: 294–298 (Oct. 1947).

————— "A Symbolic Approach to Carman," CAN BKMN 14: 140–144 (Dec. 1932).

SHEPARD, ODELL. *Bliss Carman* (Toronto, McClelland & Stewart, 1923).

SHERMAN, F. F. *A Check List of First Editions of Bliss Carman* (New York, the Author, 1915).

SLADEN, DOUGLAS. "A July Holiday with Bliss Carman," THE WEEK 11: 973–974 (Sept. 7, 1894).

STEPHENS, D. G. "The Influence of English Poets upon the Poetry of Bliss Carman" (Thesis, University of New Brunswick, 1955).

STEVENSON, O. J. "The Dawning's Troubador." In his *A People's Best* (Toronto, Musson, 1927) pp 53–62.

STRINGER, ARTHUR. "Canadians in New York, America's Foremost Lyrist: Bliss Carman," NATL MO 4: 3–5 (Jan. 1904).

————— "Wild Poets I've Known: Bliss Carman," SAT N 56: 29, 36 (March 1, 1941).

VAN PATTEN, NATHAN. "Bliss Carman and the Bibliophile," QUEEN'S Q 33: 202–205 (Nov. 1925).

WADE, H. G. "Bliss Carman's Shrine," WESTERN HOME MO 32: 28ff (Feb. 1931).

WALDRON, GORDON. "Canadian Poetry—a Criticism," CAN MAG 8: 101–108 (Dec. 1896).

WHITE, GLEESON. "Carman Saeculare," BKMN (London) 5: 155–156 (Feb. 1894).

[WHITESIDE, ERNESTINE R.] "Canadian Poetry and Poets, II [Lampman, Carman, and Campbell]," McMASTER U MO 8: 68–74 (Nov. 1898).

WOODROW, C. D. "New Brunswick Honors Bliss Carman," CAN BKMN 11: 209 (Sept. 1929).

CARNOCHAN, Janet, 1839–1926

SMITH, F. D. L. "Hundred Years of Janet Carnochan," SAT N 55: 8a (Dec. 16, 1939).

————— "Miss Janet Carnochan," CAN MAG 38: 293–297 (Jan. 1912).

CARR, Emily, 1871–1945

ANON. "Artist Turns Writer," CURTAIN CALL 13: 19ff (Oct. 1941).

————— "B.C. Artist-Author Mourned," CULTURE 6: 221–222 (juin 1945).

AMSDEN, PHILIP. "Memories of Emily Carr," CAN FORUM 27: 206–207 (Dec. 1947).

BUCHANAN, D. W. "Emily Carr, Painter of the West Coast," CAN GEOG J 33: 186–187 (Oct. 1946).

——— "The Gentle and the Austere: A Comparison in Landscape Painting," UNIV TOR Q 11: 72–77 (Oct. 1941).

CARR, EMILY. *The Book of Small* (Toronto, Oxford University Press, 1942).

——— *Growing Pains . . . Autobiography . . .* (Toronto, Oxford University Press, 1946).

——— *The House of All Sorts* (Toronto, Oxford University Press, 1944).

——— *Pause: A Sketch Book* (Toronto, Clarke Irwin, 1953).

COBURN, K. H. "Emily Carr: In Memoriam," CAN FORUM 25: 24 (April 1945).

COLMAN, M. E. "Emily Carr and Her Sisters," DAL R 27: 29–32 (April 1947).

DALY, T. C. "To Emily Carr Art and Writing were Twins," SAT N 61: 28 (Dec. 15, 1945).

DILWORTH, IRA. "Emily Carr—Canadian Artist-Author," SAT N 57: 26 (Nov. 1, 1941).

——— "Emily Carr—Canadian Painter and Poet in Prose," SAT N 57: 26 (Nov. 8, 1941).

——— Foreword to *Klee Wyck* by Emily Carr (Toronto, Clarke Irwin, 1951) pp v–xvi. [Canadian Classics ed.]

——— Preface to *The Heart of a Peacock* by Emily Carr (Toronto, Oxford University Press, 1953) pp xi-xv.

DUVAL, PAUL. "Emily Carr's was a Growing Art," SAT N 61: 4–5 (Nov. 3, 1945).

HARRIS, L. "Emily Carr and Her Work," CAN FORUM 21: 277–278 (Dec. 1941).

HENRY, LORNE J. "Emily Carr (1871–1945)." In his *Canadians: a Book of Biographies* (Toronto, Longmans Green, 1950) pp 83–90.

HUMPHREY, R. "Emily Carr—an Appreciation," QUEEN'S Q 65: 270–276 (Summer 1958).

KEARLEY, MARK H. *A Few Hints and Suggestions about Emily Carr and Her Work* (Victoria, Federation of Canadian Artists, 1946).

LAMBERT, R. S. "Artistic Motives, Hidden and Revealed," SAT N 58: 20 (Feb. 27, 1943).

McDONALD, J. A. "Emily Carr: Painter as Writer," BC LIB Q 22, no 4: 17–23 (April 1959).

NATIONAL GALLERY OF CANADA, Ottawa. *Emily Carr, Her Paintings and Sketches* (Toronto, Oxford University Press, 1945).

NESBITT, J. K. "The Genius We Laughed At," MACL MAG 64: 12–13, 29–30 (Jan. 7, 1951).

OWEN, GLYN. "Emily Carr," FIRST STATEMENT vol 1 no 17: 3–4 [undated].

PEARSON, CAROL. *Emily Carr as I Knew Her* (Toronto, Clarke Irwin, 1954).

SANDERS, BYRNE HOPE. "Emily Carr." In her *Canadian Portraits—Famous Women* (Toronto, Clarke Irwin, 1958) pp 3–43.

STACTON, DAVID DEREK. "The Art of Emily Carr," QUEEN'S Q 57: 499–509 (Winter 1950).

STANIER, ROGER Y. "Emily Carr's Art: Rich Heritage for Canada," SAT N 60: 17 (March 10, 1945).

STINGLE, RICHARD. "The Painting of Emily Carr," ACTA VIC 70: 22–23 (Nov. 1945).

CARTWRIGHT, Sir Richard John, 1835–1912

ATKINSON, J. E. "A Quintette of Veterans," CAN MAG 6: 427–432 (March 1896).

CARMAN, FRANCIS A. "The Honourable Richard Cartwright," CAN MAG 57: 190–196 (July 1921).

GRANT, W. L. "Sir Richard Cartwright," CAN MAG 40: 289–293 (Jan. 1913).

CARY, Thomas, 1751–1823

LANDE, LAWRENCE M. "Thomas Cary." In his *Old Lamps Aglow* (Montreal, the Author, 1957) pp 97–101.

CASEY, Michael Thomas, 1900–1938

COX, LEO. "Michael Thomas Casey, a Tribute," CAN AUTH 16: 14, 23 (Autumn 1938).

———— "Tribute to the Late Michael Casey," CAN POETRY 3: 9–11 (Dec. 1938).

CAWDELL, James Martin, 1781?–1842

SHORTT, A., ed. "The Memorial of J. M. Cawdell," CAN HIST R 1: 289–301 (Sept. 1920).

CHILD, Philip, 1898–

KUPSL, LINZEY. "An Introduction to the Novels of Philip Child" (Thesis, Laval University, 1958).

CHUTE, Arthur Hunt, 1888–1929

ANON. Obituary, Can MAG 72: 1 (Oct. 1929).

———— Obituary, MACL MAG 42: 38 (Oct. 15, 1929).

O'CONNOR, J. "Victorious Wings," CAN BKMN 11: 257 (Nov. 1929).

CLARK, William Robinson, 1829–1912

CHAMPION, THOMAS E. "Canadian Celebrities: XXXIII, Professor William Clark, D.C.L." CAN MAG 18: 538–540 (April 1902).

CLARKE, George Herbert, 1873–1953

ANON. Obituary, QUEEN'S Q 60: ix–x (Spring 1953).

DEWAR, DAVID G. "George Herbert Clarke." In his *Queen's Profiles* (Kingston, Queen's University, 1951) pp 47–54.

RAYMOND, WILLIAM O. "George Herbert Clarke," EDUC RECORD (Quebec) 64: 83–89 (April–June 1948). [Also in *Leading Canadian Poets*, ed. W. P. Percival (Toronto, Ryerson, 1948) pp 51–62; and in ROY SOC CAN PROC & TRANS 3rd ser 47: 69–74 (1953).]

CLAY, Charles, 1906–

CLAY, CHARLES. "How and Why I Write Historical Novels," ONT LIB R 25: 245–249 (Aug. 1941).

CODY, Hiram Alfred, 1872–1948
> ANON. "A Craftsman Passes," CAN AUTH & BKMN 24: 28 (March 1948).
> FLETT, MARY. "Hiram Alfred Cody: Priest, Patriot and Poet," CAN AUTH & BKMN 17: 5, 13 (July 1940).

COHEN, Nathan
> MOORE, J. M., "Nathan Cohen," CAN COMMENT 3: 8–9 (March 1959).

COLEMAN, Helena, 1860–1953
> ALLISON, W. T. "A New Canadian Poet," CAN MAG 28: 404–408 (Feb. 1907).

COLEMAN, Mrs. Kathleen (Blake), 1864–1915
> SANFORD, J. "Queen of the Sob Sisters," MACL MAG 66: 16–17, 43–46, (Jan. 15, 1953).
> WEAVER, EMILY P. "Pioneer Canadian Women: VII, 'Kit' the Journalist," CAN MAG 49: 275–279 (Aug. 1917).

CONIBEAR, Frank, 1907–
> CONIBEAR, FRANK. "My First Book," CAN AUTH & BKMN 30: 6–7 (Autumn 1954).

CONNOR, Ralph [pseud]. *See* GORDON, Charles William

CORNISH, John, 1914–
> STEINBERG, M. W. "John Cornish, Satirist in a Provincial Landscape," BC LIB Q 23: 22–26 (Oct. 1959).

COSTAIN, Thomas Bertram, 1885–1965
> ANON. "Return of a Native," MACL MAG 67: 79 (March 15, 1954).
> DENISON, MERRILL. "Prodigy at Sixty," MACL MAG 59: 18, 24 (Jan. 15, 1946).

COTES, Mrs. Everard. *See* DUNCAN, Sara Jeannette

COULTER, John William, 1888–
> ANON. "Deirdre of the Sorrows," NEWSWEEK 27: 84 (April 29, 1946).
> MOSDELL, D. "Theatre," CAN FORUM 30: 15 (April 1950).

CRAGG, Kenneth C., 1904–1948
> ANON. "Brave Beginning was Also the End," CAN AUTH & BKMN 24: 18 (March 1948).

CRAWFORD, Alexander Wellington, 1866–1933
> ANON. "A Loss to Canadian Literature," CAN BKMN 15: 104 (Aug. 1933).

CRAWFORD, Isabella Valancy, 1850–1887
> ANON. Editorial, ARCTURUS vol 1 no 6: 94 (Feb. 19, 1887).
> BURPEE, L. J. "Isabella Valancy Crawford, a Canadian Poet," POET LORE 13: 575–586 (Oct. 1901). [Also in his *A Little Book of Canadian Essays* (Toronto, Musson, 1909) pp 1–16.]
> GARVIN, JOHN W. "Who's Who in Canadian Literature: Isabella Valancy Crawford," CAN BKMN 9: 131–133 (May 1927).
> HALE, KATHERINE. "Isabella Valancy Crawford," EDUC RECORD (Quebec) 59: 83–88 (April–June 1943). [Also in *Leading Canadian Poets*, ed. W. P. Percival (Toronto, Ryerson, 1948) pp 63–70.]
> ——— *Isabella Valancy Crawford* (Toronto, Ryerson, 1923).

HATHAWAY, E. J. "Isabella Valancy Crawford," CAN MAG 5: 569–572 (Oct. 1895).

POMEROY, E. M. "Isabella Valancy Crawford," CAN POETRY 7: 36–38 (June 1944).

REANEY, JAMES. "Isabella Valancy Crawford." In *Our Living Tradition*, Second and Third Series, ed. Robert L. McDougall (Toronto, published in association with Carleton University by University of Toronto Press, 1959) pp 268–286.

"SERANUS" [MRS. J. W. F. HARRISON]. "Isabella Valancy Crawford," THE WEEK 4: 202–203 (Feb. 24, 1887).

WETHERALD, ETHELWYN. Introduction to *The Collected Poems of Isabella Valancy Crawford*, ed. J. W. Garvin (Toronto, Briggs, 1905) pp 15–29.

CRAWLEY, Alan
LIVESAY, DOROTHY. "Pioneer for Poetry," SAT N 67: 35 (Dec. 1, 1951).

CREIGHTON, Mary Helen, 1899–
SCLANDERS, IAN. "She's Collecting Long Lost Songs," MACL MAG 65: 14–15, 54–57 (Sept. 15, 1952).

CRICHTON, John [pseud]. *See* GUTHRIE, Norman Gregor

DAFOE, John Wesley, 1866–1944
ANON. Obituary, CAN FORUM 23: 244 (Feb. 1944).

——— Obituary. "John W. Dafoe, 1866–1944," CAN J ECON 10: 79–82 (Feb. 1944).

BEATTIE, EARLE. "The Last of the Angry Editors," MACL MAG 66: 22–24, 26–30 (Aug. 1, 1953).

COOK, RAMSAY. *The Politics of John W. Dafoe and the* Free Press (Toronto, University of Toronto Press, 1963).

DOMINO. "Dafoe, Political Pivot," MACL MAG 34: 16, 50–51 (Oct. 1, 1921).

FERGUSON, GEORGE VICTOR. *John W. Dafoe* (Toronto, Ryerson, 1948).

HARWOOD, H. "Embarrassed Editor," CAN FORUM 18: 232–233 (Nov. 1938).

HUTCHISON, BRUCE. "The Greatest Man in Canada," FORTUNE 25: 106–111+ (June 1942).

L., R. T. "Mr. Dafoe," MACL MAG 46: 8, 47 (Oct. 1, 1933).

MACGIBBON, D. A. "John Wesley Dafoe (1866–1944)," ROY SOC CAN PROC & TRANS 3rd ser 38: 93–96 (1944).

O'LEARY, M. GRATTAN. "Dafoe of the Free Press," MACL MAG 42: 5, 79–81 (April 1, 1929).

THOMSON, I. and M. DAFOE. "J. W. Dafoe: Bibliography," CAN J ECON 10: 213–215 (May 1944).

UNDERHILL, FRANK H. "J. W. Dafoe," CAN FORUM 13: 23–24 (Oct. 1932). [Also in *Our Sense of Identity*, ed. Malcolm Ross (Toronto, Ryerson, 1954) pp 156–160.]

WINNIPEG FREE PRESS. *John Wesley Dafoe, Editor-in-Chief, Winnipeg Free Press, 1901–1944* (Winnipeg, Winnipeg Free Press, 1944).

DALTON, Mrs. Annie Charlotte (Armitage), 1865–1938
    ANON. "Annie Charlotte Dalton, 1865–1938," CAN AUTH 15: 14, 16 (April 1938).
    —— Obituary, CAN POETRY 2: 41 (April 1938).
    DAVIES-WOODROW, CONSTANCE. "Two Vancouver Poets," CAN BKMN 9: 83–84 (March 1927).
    FRASER, A. ERMATINGER. "The Poetry of Annie Charlotte Dalton: An Appreciative Study," CAN BKMN 11: 179–184 (Aug. 1929).
    JOYNES, A. "The Neighing North: An Appreciation of Annie Charlotte Dalton," CAN BKMN 14: 45–46 (April 1932).
    PRATT, E. J. "Bookman Profiles: Annie Charlotte Dalton," CAN BKMN 20: 11 (April 1938).
    STEVENSON, LIONEL. "Annie Charlotte Dalton: A Personal Impression," CAN BKMN 6: 242 (Nov. 1924).
    —— "Two Vancouver Poets," CAN BKMN 18: 4–7 (Jan. 25, 1936).

DANIELLS, Roy, 1902–
    ANON. Biographical Note, CAN AUTH & BKMN 34: 5 (Spring 1958).
    McPHERSON, HUGO. "Roy Daniells: Humanist," BC LIB Q 24: 29–35 (July 1960).

DAVIES, Blodwen, 1897–1966
    DAVIES, BLODWEN. "The Author Herself," CAN AUTH & BKMN 24: 41 (Sept. 1948).

DAVIES, Robertson, 1913–
    CALLWOOD, JUNE. "The Beard," MACL MAG 65: 16–17, 30–33 (March 15, 1952).
    KIRKWOOD, HILDA. "Robertson Davies," CAN FORUM 30: 59–60 (June 1950).
    McINNES, GRAHAM. "An Editor from Skunk's Misery is Winning Fame for Peterboro," SAT N 62: 14–15 (April 26, 1947).
    McPHERSON, HUGO. "The Mask of Satire: Character and Symbolic Pattern in Robertson Davies' Fiction," CAN LIT no 4: 18–30 (Spring 1960).
    MARCHBANKS, SAMUEL [pseud]. "The Double Life of Robertson Davies," LIBERTY pp 18–19, 53–58 (April 1954). [Reprinted in *Canadian Anthology* ed. by C. F. Klinck and R. E. Watters, rev. ed. (Toronto, Gage, 1966) pp 393–400.]
    OWEN, IVAN. "The Salterton Novels," TAM R no 9: 56–63 (Autumn 1958).
    TURNER, JAMES OGDEN FREEMAN. "Robertson Davies: Critic and Author" (Thesis, University of Manitoba, 1958).

DAVIN, Nicholas Flood, 1843–1901
    CHARLESWORTH, HECTOR W. "Patriots and the Poets of the West." In his *More Candid Chronicles* (Toronto, Macmillan, 1928) pp 18–36.
    HASSARD, ALBERT R. "Great Canadian Orators: III, Nicholas Flood Davin," CAN MAG 53: 455–463 (Oct. 1919).
    STUBBS, ROY ST. G. *Lawyers and Laymen of Western Canada* (Toronto, Ryerson, 1939).
    WARD, N. M. "Davin and the Founding of the *Leader*," SASK HIST 6: 13–16 (Winter 1953).

DAWSON, George Mercer, 1849–1901
  HARRINGTON, B. J. "George Mercer Dawson," McGILL U MAG 1: 123–133 (Dec. 1901).

DAWSON, Sir John William, 1820–1899
  ADAMS, FRANK D. "Memoir of Sir J. William Dawson," McGILL U PAPERS DEPT GEOLOGY no 10 (1900). [Articles by same author in SCIENCE n.s. 10: 905–910 (Dec. 22, 1899) and CAN RECORD SCI 8: 137–148 (Jan. 1900).]
  AMI, HENRY M. "Sir John William Dawson: A Brief Biographical Sketch," AMER GEOLOGIST 26: 1–14 (July 1900). [Bibliography 26: 15–48.]
  ANON. "Bibliography of Sir John William Dawson," ROY SOC CAN PROC & TRANS 2nd ser 7: 15–44 (1901).
  DAWSON, SIR JOHN WILLIAM. Fifty Years of Work in Canada, Scientific and Educational: Being autobiographical notes . . . , ed. Rankine Dawson (London, Ballantyne, 1901).
  MACKINNON, IAN F. "Sir William Dawson: The Church and Science," DAL R 28: 246–256 (Oct. 1948).
  MACPHAIL, ANDREW. "Sir William Dawson," McGILL U MAG 5: 12–29 (Dec. 1905).
  MURRAY, J. LOVELL. "Linking Science with Religion." In his Nation Builders (Toronto, Can. Council of the Missionary Education Movement, 1925) pp 85–91.
  TAYLOR, FENNINGS. "J. William Dawson, LL.D." In Portraits of British Americans by W. Notman . . . with Biographical Sketches by Fennings Taylor, vol. 1: pp 143–157 (Montreal, Notman, 1865).
  YEIGH, FRANK. "Canadian Celebrities: VI, Sir William Dawson," CAN MAG 13: 343–346 (Aug. 1899).

DEACON, William Arthur, 1890–
  ANON. "New Canadian Literature," ACTA VIC 48: 27 (Nov. 1923).

DE LA ROCHE, Mazo, 1885–1961
  ANON. Biographical Note, SCHOLASTIC 36: 32 (May 13, 1940).
  BROWN, E. K. "The Whiteoaks Saga," CAN FORUM 12: 23 (Oct. 1931).
  DE LA ROCHE, MAZO. "My First Book," CAN AUTH & BKMN 28: 3–4 (Spring 1952).
  ——— Ringing the Changes: An Autobiography (Toronto, Macmillan, 1957).
  EAYRS, HUGH. "Bookman Profiles: Mazo de la Roche," CAN BKMN 20: 17–22 (Oct. 1938).
  EDGAR, PELHAM. "The Cult of Primitivism." In Yearbook of the Arts in Canada 1928/29, ed. Bertram Brooker (Toronto, Macmillan, 1929) pp 39–42.
  MACKLEM, JOHN. "Who's Who in Canadian Literature: Mazo de la Roche," CAN BKMN 9: 259–260 (Sept. 1927).
  MOORE, JOCELYN. "Mazo de la Roche," CAN FORUM 12: 380–381 (July 1932).
  PRINGLE, GERTRUDE. "World Fame to Canadian Author, Mazo de la Roche," CAN MAG 67: 19, 31–32 (May 1927).

SANDWELL, B. K. "The Work of Mazo de la Roche," SAT N 68: 7 (Nov. 8, 1952).

WEEKS, EDWARD. "Mazo de la Roche." In his *In Friendly Candor* (Boston, Little Brown, 1959) pp 86–97.

WUORIO, EVA-LIS. "Mazo of Jalna," MACL MAG 62: 19, 39–41 (Feb. 1, 1949).

DE MILLE, James, 1833–1880

BEVAN, A. R. "James De Mille and Archibald MacMechan," DAL R 35: 201–215 (Autumn 1955).

BURPEE, L. J. "James De Mille," CAN BKMN 8: 203–206 (July 1926).

CROCKETT, A. J. and GEORGE PATTERSON. "Concerning James De Mille." In Patterson's *More Studies in Nova Scotia History* (Halifax, Imperial Pub. Co., 1941) pp 120–148.

DOUGLAS, R. W. "James De Mille," CAN BKMN 4: 39–44 (Jan. 1922).

KOOPMAN, HARRY LYMAN. "Literary Men of Brown [University] III: James De Mille," BROWN ALUMNI MO 8: 27–30 (July 1907).

MACMECHAN, ARCHIBALD. "Concerning James De Mille," CAN BKMN 4: 125–126 (April 1922).

——— "De Mille, the Man and the Writer," CAN MAG 27: 404–416 (Sept. 1906).

MAHON, A. WYLIE. "James De Mille," WESTMINSTER 7 (n.s.): 320–323 (Nov. 1905).

DENISON, George Taylor, 1839–1925

DENISON, GEORGE TAYLOR. *Recollections of a Police Magistrate* (Toronto, Musson, 1920).

——— *Soldiering in Canada: Recollections and Experiences...* (Toronto, Morang, 1901).

——— *The Struggle for Imperial Unity: Recollections and Experiences* (London, Macmillan, 1909).

DENISON, RICHARD L. *The Canadian Pioneer Family of County York, England and County York, Ontario: A History, Genealogy and Biography* (Toronto, the Author, 1951–1952), 4 vols. [Mimeographed.]

FLEMING, JAMES GRANVILLE. "The Fighting Denisons: A Military Instinct that Runs in the Blood of Five Generations," MACL MAG 27: 5–10, 136–137 (Dec. 1913).

V., E. Q. "Canadian Celebrities: XXXVII, Lieutenant-Colonel Denison," CAN MAG 19: 398–400 (Sept. 1902).

DENISON, Merrill, 1893–

CHAMBERLAIN, FRANK. "Merrill Denison is a Big Shot," SAT N 58: 19 (March 27, 1943).

GRAHAM, JEAN. "Among Those Present," SAT N 13: 27 (Oct. 8, 1932).

MILNE, W. "Merrill Denison," CAN FORUM 13: 63–64 (Nov. 1932).

PHELPS, ARTHUR L. "Merrill Denison." In his *Canadian Writers* (Toronto, McClelland & Stewart, 1951) pp 43–50.

DICKIE, Francis, 1890–

P., A. M. "Francis Dickie," CAN BKMN 8: 110 (April 1926).

DONOVAN, Peter, 1884–   [pseud: P. O'D.]

ANON. "Part-time Canuck," SAT N 56: 16 (Nov. 2, 1940).

DOUGALL, Lily, 1858–1923
MACPHERSON, KATHERINE L. "Lily Dougall and Her Work," CAN MAG 27: 478–480 (Sept. 1906).

DOUGHTY, Sir Arthur George, 1860–1936
ANON. Obituary, AMER HIST R 42: 627 (April 1937).
MCARTHUR, D. "Sir Arthur Doughty," CAN HIST R 2: 86–87 (March 1937).

DOUGLAS, James, 1837–1918
ANON. "Dr. James Douglas," QUEEN'S Q 23: 239–247 (March 1916).
GRANT, W. L. and W. L. GOODWIN. "The Late Chancellor Douglas," QUEEN'S Q 26: 1–6 (Sept. 1918).
LANGTON, HUGH H. *James Douglas: A Memoir* (Toronto, University of Toronto Press, 1940).

DRUMMOND, William Henry, 1854–1907
ANON. "Two Canadian Poets: Fréchette and Drummond," EDINBURGH R 209: 474–499 (April 1909).
BURPEE, LAWRENCE J. "William Henry Drummond," NATION (New York) 84: 334–336 (April 11, 1907).
—— "William Henry Drummond," EDUC RECORD (Quebec) 61: 208–212 (Oct.–Dec. 1945). [Also in *Leading Canadian Poets*, ed. W. P. Percival (Toronto, Ryerson, 1948) pp 71–78.]
CRAIG, ROBERT H. "Reminiscences of W. H. Drummond," DAL R 5: 161–169 (July 1925).
DUSTAN, WILLIAM GORDON. "The Interpreter of the Habitant, William Henry Drummond" (Thesis, Dalhousie University, 1928).
DRUMMOND, MARY HARVEY. "Preface" and "William Henry Drummond [A Biographical Sketch]." In *The Great Fight: Poems and Sketches* by William Henry Drummond (New York, Putnam's, 1908) pp vii–xviii, 3–48.
FRÉCHETTE, LOUIS. Introduction to *The Poetical Works of William Henry Drummond* (New York, Putnam's, 1912) pp xxi–xxv.
GIBBON, JOHN MURRAY. "William Henry Drummond," EDUC RECORD (Quebec) 60: 93–96 (April–June 1944).
GILMOUR-SMITH, E. "Link with the Habitant Poet [death of Mrs. Drummond]," SAT N 55: 9 (Feb. 17, 1940).
MACDONALD, JOHN FORD. *William Henry Drummond* (Toronto, Ryerson, [1923?]).
MAHON, A. W. "The Poet of the Habitant," CAN MAG 29: 56–60 (May 1907).
—— "The Poet of Les Habitants," SPECTATOR 98: 609–610 (April 20, 1907).
MUNRO, NEIL. "William Henry Drummond [an Appreciation]." In *Poetical Works of William Henry Drummond* (New York, Putnam's, 1912) pp v–xx.
O'HAGAN, THOMAS. "A Canadian Dialect Poet." In his *Intimacies in Canadian Life and Letters* (Ottawa, Graphic, 1927) pp. 83–94.
PHELPS, ARTHUR L. Introduction to *Habitant Poems* by William Henry Drummond (Toronto, McClelland & Stewart, 1959) pp 7–16. [New Canadian Library no 11.]
RASHLEY, R. E. "W. H. Drummond and the Dilemma of Style," DAL R 28: 387–396 (Jan. 1949).

RHODENIZER, V. B. "Who's Who in Canadian Literature: William Henry Drummond," CAN BKMN 9: 35–36 (Feb. 1927).

STEVENSON, O. J. "Poet, Artist, and Citizen." In his *A People's Best* (Toronto, Musson, 1927) pp 211–218.

STRINGER, ARTHUR. "Wild Poets I've Known: W. H. Drummond," SAT N 56: 33 (April 26, 1941).

V., E. Q. "Canadian Celebrities: III, Dr. W. H. Drummond," CAN MAG 13: 62–64 (May 1899).

DUDEK, Louis, 1918–

ANON. Biographical Note, CAN AUTH & BKMN 34: 7 (Spring 1958).

———— "Three New Poets," FIRST STATEMENT vol 1 no 12: 1–4 [undated].

SMITH, A. J. M. "Turning New Leaves," CAN FORUM 27: 42–43 (May 1947).

DUNCAN, Dorothy, 1903–1957

ANON. "Canada," with biographical sketch, UN WORLD 1: 77–80 (May 1947).

DUNCAN, Norman, 1871–1916

COGSWELL, F. W. *"Way of the Sea*, a Symbolic Epic," DAL R 35: 374–375, 377, 379, 381 (Winter 1956).

HATHAWAY, E. J. "Who's Who in Canadian Literature: Norman Duncan," CAN BKMN 8: 171–174 (June 1926).

NIVEN, F. "To Remember Norman Duncan," SAT N 57: 29 (June 20, 1942).

STEVENSON, O. J. "The Boy Eternal." In his *A People's Best* (Toronto, Musson, 1927) pp 249–256.

DUNCAN, Sara Jeannette (Mrs. Everard Cotes), 1861–1922

ANON. [Women Writers]. CAN MAG 25: 583–585 (Oct. 1905).

BISSELL, CLAUDE. Introduction to *The Imperialist* by Sara Jeannette Duncan (Toronto, McClelland & Stewart, 1961) pp v–ix. [New Canadian Library no 20.]

DONALDSON, F. "Mrs. Everard Cotes," BKMN (London) 14: 65–67 (June 1898).

MACCALLUM, H. R. "Sara Jeannette Duncan." In *A Standard Dictionary of Canadian Biography: The Canadian Who Was Who*, ed. C. G. D. Roberts and A. L. Tunnell (Toronto, Trans-Canada Press, 1934) 1: 168–170.

MACMURCHY, M. "Mrs. Everard Cotes," BKMN (London) 48: 39–40 (May 1915).

DUNHAM, Mabel, 1881–1957

ANON. "Pioneers! O Pioneers!" CAN LIB ASSOC BUL 10: 127 (Dec. 1953).

———— "Librarian Authors," LIBRARY J 56: 317 (April 1, 1931).

———— "Retires after 36 years of Library Work," ONT LIB R 28: 313 (Aug. 1944).

SNIDER, L. "Miss Mabel Dunham," ONT LIB R 38: 221–224 (Aug. 1954).

DUNLOP, William, 1792–1848

ANON. "Gallery of Literary Characters, no. xxxv: The Tiger," FRASER'S MAG 7: 436 (April 1833).

———— "Upper Canada, by a Backwoodsman," BLACKWOOD'S MAG 32: 238–262 (Aug. 1832).

BLUE, CHARLES S. "The Canadian Boat Song," CAN MAG 50: 367–374 (March 1918).

DUNLOP, WILLIAM. *Recollections of the American War 1812–14*, ed. with a biographical sketch of the author by A. H. U. Colquhoun (Toronto, Historical Pub. Co., 1905).

FORD, FREDERICK SAMUEL LAMPSON. "William Dunlop, 1792–1848," CAN MEDICAL J n.s. 25: 210–219 (Aug. 1931). [Reprinted as separate publication: *William Dunlop* (Toronto, Murray Print. Co., 1931; also with imprint: Toronto, Britnell, 1934).]

KLINCK, CARL F. "The Canadian Chiefs and 'Tiger' Dunlop," WATERLOO R 2: 46–51 (Summer 1959).

———— ed. *William "Tiger" Dunlop, "Blackwoodian Backwoodsman"* (Toronto, Ryerson, 1958).

LAURISTON, VICTOR. "Tiger Dunlop," SAT N 40: 3 (Sept. 26, 1925).

LIZARS, ROBINA and KATHLEEN M. LIZARS. *In the Days of the Canada Company* (Toronto, Briggs, 1896).

MCARTHUR, PETER. "The Over-Looking of Gideon," CAN MAG 36: 144–150 (Dec. 1910). [A short story.]

MORGAN, H. J. "William Dunlop." In his *Bibliotheca Canadensis* (Ottawa, Desbarats, 1867) pp 112–113.

RATTRAY, W. J. "William Dunlop." In his *The Scot in British North America* (Toronto, Maclear, 1880) vol 2, pp 445–451.

SMITH, W. H. "William Dunlop," CAN MEDICAL J n.s. 25: 737 (Dec. 1931).

STEVENSON, J. A. "Among Unusual Canadians He is Near the Top," SAT N 64: 20–21 (April 26, 1949).

DURHAM, Julian [pseud]. *See* HENSHAW, Mrs. Julia Wilmotte

DURKIN, Douglas Leader, 1884–1968
ANON. ["Douglas Durkin"], CAN BKMN 1: 65 (Oct. 1919).

DUVAR, John Hunter. *See* HUNTER-DUVAR, John

EATON, Arthur Wentworth, 1849–1937
WASSON, JAMES B. "Poet and Priest," CAN MAG 29: 252–257 (Aug. 1907).

EDGAR, (Oscar) Pelham, 1871–1948
DEACON, WILLIAM ARTHUR. "A Leader Passes," CAN AUTH & BKMN 24: 10–11 (Dec. 1948).

EDGAR, PELHAM. *Across My Path*, ed. with intro. by Northrop Frye (Toronto, Ryerson, 1952). [Includes an autobiography and also a bibliography of Edgar's writings comp. by Margaret Ray.]

FRYE, NORTHROP. "Dean of Critics," CAN FORUM 28: 169–170 (Nov. 1948).

SANDWELL, B. K. "Oscar Pelham Edgar (1871–1948)," ROY SOC CAN PROC & TRANS 3rd ser 43: Sect II, 107–111 (1948).

———— "Pelham Edgar's Literary Path," SAT N 68: 7 (Nov. 22, 1952).

THOMSON, DONALD WALTER. *The Foundation and the Man* by Walter Dawson (pseud.) (Toronto, privately printed, 1959). [History of Canadian Writers' Foundation, founded by Pelham Edgar.]

EDWARDS, Robert Chambers, 1864–1922

CAMERON, D. E. "Robert Chambers Edwards." In *Canadian Portraits*, ed. R. G. Riddell (Toronto, Oxford, 1940) pp 144–152.

FORD, ARTHUR R. "Bob Edwards and the Calgary Eye-Opener." In his *As the World Wags On* (Toronto, Ryerson, 1950) pp 18–26.

MACEWAN, GRANT. *Eye-Opener Bob: The Story of Bob Edwards* (Edmonton, Institute of Applied Art, 1957).

SNADDEN, ANDREW. "The Eye-Opener," MACL MAG 63: 18–19, 30–33 (Feb. 1, 1950).

STUBBS, R. S. "Edwards of the *Eye-Opener*," BEAVER 286: 34–38 (Autumn 1955).

ELSON, John Mebourne, 1880–

ANON. "Here is the Writer," CAN AUTH & BKMN 24: 23 (Dec. 1948).

ERICKSEN-BROWN, Gwethalyn McNaught. *See* GRAHAM, Gwethalyn [pseud.]

FAIRLEY, Barker, 1887–

BROWN, E. K. "The Immediate Present in Canadian Literature," SEWANEE R 41: 430–442 (Oct. 1933).

EDGAR, PELHAM. "Barker Fairley." In his *Across My Path*, ed. Northrop Frye (Toronto, Ryerson, 1952) pp 77–82.

FALCONER, Sir Robert Alexander, 1867–1943

CODY, H. J., M. W. WALLACE, W. R. TAYLOR, and KATHERINE WALES. "In Memoriam: Sir Robert Alexander Falconer, K.C.W.G.," UNIV TOR Q 13: 135–174 (Jan. 1944).

MACMECHAN, ARCHIBALD. "The President of Toronto University," CAN MAG 35: 249–250 (July 1910).

STANLEY, CARLETON. "Sir Robert Alexander Falconer (1867–1943)," ROY SOC CAN PROC & TRANS 3rd ser 38: 97–98 (1944).

THOMSON, JAMES S. "Sir Robert A. Falconer," DAL R 30: 361–368 (Jan. 1951).

FAUGHNAN, Thomas, *fl* 1835–1883

FAUGHNAN, THOMAS. *Stirring Incidents in the Life of a British Soldier: An Autobiography* (Toronto, Hunter Rose, 1879). [Several later and enlarged editions.]

FERGUSON, George Victor, 1897–

BENSON, N. A. "Ferguson of the Free Press," SAT N 58: 24 (Dec. 12, 1942).

LECOCQ, THELMA. "Editor Ferguson," MACL MAG 60: 18, 38–42 (April 1, 1947).

FINCH, Robert Duer Claydon, 1900–

ANON. Biographical Note, CAN AUTH & BKMN 34: 9 (Spring 1958).

DANIELLS, ROY. "Earle Birney et Robert Finch," GANTS DU CIEL 11: 83–96 (printemps 1946).

MATHERS, KAY. "The Triumvirate of Robert Finch as Poet, Painter and Pianist," SAT N 63: 16 (Sept. 20, 1947).

SMITH, A. J. M. "Turning New Leaves," CAN FORUM 27: 42–43 (May 1947).

FITZGIBBON, Mrs. Mary Agnes (Bernard), 1862–1933 [pseud: Lally Bernard]
STODDARD, ETHEL CODY. "An Imperial Daughter," CAN MAG 46: 513–515 (April 1916).

FONTAINE, Robert Louis, 1911–1965
DUGAN, JAMES. "The Happy Times of Robert Fontaine," MACL MAG 63: 20–21, 47–50 (May 15, 1950).

FORSYTH, Jean [pseud]. See McIlwraith, Jean Newton

FOSTER, Mrs. W. Garland. See HANLEY, Mrs. Annie Harvie

FRASER, Alexander Louis, 1870–1954
ANON. "A Canadian Poet," WESTMINSTER HALL 4: 2–3 (July 1913).
O'HAGAN, THOMAS. "Alexander Louis Fraser," CAN BKMN 9: 133–135 (May 1927).

FRASER, Annie Ermatinger, –1930
ANON. "Miss A. Ermatinger Fraser," CAN BKMN 12: 260–261 (Dec. 1930).

FRASER, Simon, 1776–1862
BANCROFT, HUBERT H. *History of the Northwest Coast* (San Francisco, Bancroft, 1884) pp 87–119.

BURPEE, LAWRENCE J. "Exploring the Canyon of the Fraser." In his *The Search for the Western Sea* (Toronto, Musson, 1908; rev. ed. 1935) pp 513–535.

DENTON, VERNON L. *Simon Fraser* (Toronto, Ryerson, 1928). [Ryerson Canadian History Readers.]

DOUGHTY, ARTHUR G. *Report of the Public Archives for . . . 1929* (Ottawa, Acland, 1930). [Contains transcript of Fraser's 1806 journal and some of his letters from New Caledonia.]

FRASER, ALEXANDER. *The Clan Fraser in Canada*. Souvenir of the First Annual Gathering (Toronto, Mail Print., 1895). [Pamphlet.]

FRASER, SIMON. "Journal of a Voyage from the Rocky Mountains to the Pacific Coast 1808." In *Les Bourgeois de la Compagnie du Nord-ouest, récits de voyages, lettres et rapports . . .*, ed. L. R. Masson (Quebec, Coté et Cie., 1889–1890) vol 1, pp 155–221.

——— *The Letters and Journals of Simon Fraser, 1806–1808*, ed. W. Kaye Lamb (Toronto, Macmillan, 1960).

MACKAY, CORDAY. "With Fraser to the Sea," BEAVER 275: 3–7 (Dec. 1944).

MACKENZIE, ALEXANDER. *History of the Frasers of Lovat* (Inverness, 1896).

MORICE, ADRIAN G. *The History of the Northern Interior of British Columbia . . . [1660–1880]* (Toronto, Briggs, 1904).

MORTON, ARTHUR S. *A History of the Canadian West to 1870–1871 ...* (Toronto, Nelson, 1939).

PARKER, ELIZABETH. "Early Explorers of the West: Simon Fraser," CAN ALPINE J 29: 30–32 (1944–1945).

SAGE, WALTER N. "Simon Fraser, Explorer and Fur Trader." In AMER HIST ASSOC PROC (Pacific Coast Branch) (1929) pp 172–186.

SCHOLEFIELD, E. O. S. "Simon Fraser," WESTWARD HO! MAG 3: 217–231 (Oct. 1908); 4: 61–76 (Jan. 1909); 4: 138–144 (Feb. 1909).

SCHOLEFIELD, E. O. S. and F. W. HOWAY. *British Columbia from the Earliest Times to the Present* (Vancouver, Clarke, 1914) vol 1, pp 235–282.

SPARGO, JOHN. *Two Bennington-Born Explorers and Makers of Modern Canada* (Bradford, Vt., Green Mountain Press, 1950).

WALLACE, W. S. "The Two Simon Frasers," CAN HIST R 13: 183–184 (June 1932).

FRASER, William Alexander, 1859–1933

ANON. "The Author of 'Mooswa,'" CAN AUTH 9: 11–12 (Sept. 1931).

———— Obituary, CAN BKMN 15: 163 (Nov. 1933).

FARAH, T. K. "Fraser—the 'Heathen Idol' of Countless Readers," CAN MAG 67: 16, 34 (Jan. 1927).

FRENCH, DONALD G. "Who's Who in Canadian Literature: W. A. Fraser," CAN BKMN 12: 27–28 (Feb. 1930).

FRÉCHETTE, Mrs. Annie (Howells)

MERRILL, ANNE. "Annie Howells Fréchette," CAN BKMN 21: 26–29 (June 1939).

FRYE, Northrop, 1912–

ANON. Biographical Note, CAN LIB ASSOC BUL 10: 18–19 (July 1953).

EDGAR, PELHAM. "Northrop Frye." In his *Across My Path*, ed. Northrop Frye (Toronto, Ryerson, 1952) pp 83–89.

SANDWELL, B. K. "Student of Pelham Edgar's Writes Epoch-Marking Volume on Blake," SAT N 62: 17 (July 19, 1947).

GALT, John, 1779–1839

ABERDEIN, JENNIE W. *John Galt* (London, Oxford University Press, 1936).

ALLISON, WILLIAM T. "John Galt, Novelist and Empire-Builder," CAN MAG 37: 172–181 (June 1911).

GALT, JOHN. *The Autobiography of John Galt*, 2 vols (London, Cochrane & M'Crone, 1833).

GORDON, ROBERT KAY. *John Galt* (Toronto, Oxford University Press, 1920).

INNIS, M. Q. "Galt Centenary," DAL R 19: 495–501 (Jan. 1940).

KERR, JAMES. "Two Ontario Cities and an Early Scots Novelist," CAN BKMN 14: 123–124 (Nov. 1932).

KLINCK, C. F. "John Galt's Canadian Novels," ONT HIST 49: 187–194 (Autumn 1957).

LIZARS, ROBINA and KATHLEEN M. LIZARS. *In the Days of the Canada Company* (Toronto, Briggs, 1896).

NEEDLER, G. H. "John Galt, Dramatist," UNIV TOR Q 11: 194–208 (Jan. 1942).

—— *John Galt's Dramas: A Brief Review* (Toronto, University of Toronto Press, 1945).

WETHERELL, J. E. "John Galt: Founder of Cities," CAN MAG 43: 39–49 (May 1914).

GARVIN, Mrs. Amelia Beers (Warnock), 1878–1956 [pseud: "Katherine Hale"]

DEMPSEY, LOTTA. "Katherine Hale," EDUC RECORD (Quebec) 62: 214–219 (Oct.–Dec. 1946). [Also in *Leading Canadian Poets*, ed. W. P. Percival (Toronto, Ryerson, 1948) pp 79–87.]

RHODENIZER, V. B. "Who's Who in Canadian Literature: 'Katherine Hale,'" CAN BKMN 11: 84–85 (April 1929).

GARVIN, John William, 1859–1935

DARE, LAWRENCE. "A Canadian Anthologist," CAN BKMN 7: 146 (Sept. 1925).

MARQUIS, T. G. "A Shepherd of Canadian Poets," CAN BKMN 17: 106 (Sept. 1935).

PIERCE, LORNE. "Foreword" to *Cap and Bells: An Anthology of Light Verse by Canadian Poets*, chosen by John W. Garvin (Toronto, Ryerson, 1936) pp v–viii.

GAY, James, 1810–1891

AYRE, ROBERT. "The Master of Poets—James Gay," CAN MAG 65: 12–13 (Feb. 1926).

DEACON, W. A. "James Gay: Poet Laureate of Canada and Master of All Poets." In his *The Four Jameses* (Ottawa, Graphic, 1927) pp 7–41.

MACKAY, L. A. "James Gay," CAN FORUM 13: 457–458 (Sept. 1933).

GIBBON, John Murray, 1875–1952

CHALMERS, D. A. "The First President of the C.A.A.—John Murray Gibbon," BC MO 19: 7, 9 (July 1922).

COMPOSERS, AUTHORS, AND PUBLISHERS ASSOCIATION OF CANADA. *Tribute to a Nation Builder* (Toronto, the Association, 1946).

GLYNN, W. "Man with a Plan but Little to Say," CAN MAG 72: 21 (Oct. 1929).

KIRKCONNELL, W. "John Murray Gibbon 1875–1952," ROY SOC CAN PROC & TRANS 3rd ser 47: 79–83 (1953).

SANDWELL, BERNARD K. "John Murray Gibbon, a British Novelist in Canada," CAN MAG 52: 598–602 (Nov. 1918).

GILLIS, James D., 1870–

DEACON, W. A. "James D. Gillis: A Man of Parts." In his *The Four Jameses* (Ottawa, Graphic, 1927) pp 89–156.

GILLIS, JAMES D. *A Little Sketch of My Life* (Halifax, Allen, n.d.).

—— *My Palestine Pilgrimage . . . 1936 A.D.* (North Sydney, N.S., Herald Print., 1936).

GODSELL, Philip Henry, 1889–1961

ANON. "Nomad of the North," CAN AUTH 16: 11 (Autumn 1938).

GOLDSMITH, Oliver, 1794–1861

GAMMON, DONALD B. "The Concept of Nature in Nineteenth Century Canadian Poetry, with Special Reference to Goldsmith, Sangster and Roberts" (Thesis, University of New Brunswick, 1948).

GOLDSMITH, OLIVER. *The Autobiography of Oliver Goldsmith...*, with intro. and notes by Wilfrid E. Myatt (Toronto, Ryerson, 1943).

———— *The Manuscript Book of Oliver Goldsmith, Author of "The Rising Village,"* with description and comment by E. Cockburn Kyte (Toronto, Bibliographical Society of Canada, 1950).

LANDE, LAWRENCE M. "Oliver Goldsmith." In his *Old Lamps Aglow* (Montreal, the Author, 1957) pp 67–74.

PACEY, DESMOND. "The Goldsmiths and Their Villages," UNIV TOR Q 21: 27–38 (Oct. 1951).

GORDON, Charles William, 1860–1937 [pseud: Ralph Connor]

ADAMS, HARRIS L. "The Career of 'Ralph Connor,'" MACL MAG 25: 109–113 (April 1913).

ANON. "Canadian Mr. Valiant for Truth," CHRISTIAN SCI MON p 10 (July 13, 1938).

———— Obituary, CHRISTIAN CENT 54: 1634 (Dec. 29, 1937).

———— Obituary, PUB WKLY 132: 1950 (Nov. 13, 1937).

———— Obituary, WILSON LIB BUL 12: 226 (Dec. 19, 1937).

BEHARRIELL, ROSS. Introduction to *The Man from Glengarry* by Ralph Connor (Toronto, McClelland & Stewart, 1960) pp vii–xii. [New Canadian Library no 14.]

DORAN, GEORGE H. "A Modern Apostle." In his *Chronicles of Barabbas 1884–1934* (Toronto, McLeod, 1935) pp 200–206.

FRENCH, D. G. "Who's Who in Canadian Literature: Ralph Connor," CAN BKMN 12: 77–79 (April 1930).

GORDON, CHARLES WILLIAM. *Postscript to Adventure: The Autobiography of Ralph Connor* (New York, Farrar, 1938).

KIRKCONNELL, W. "Passing of 'Ralph Connor,'" CAN THINKER 1: 7–9 (Dec. 1937).

McCOURT, EDWARD A. "Sky Pilot." In his *The Canadian West in Fiction* (Toronto, Ryerson, 1949) pp 18–38.

PATERSON, BETH. "Ralph Connor and His Million-Dollar Sermons," MACL MAG 66: 26, 56–60 (Nov. 15, 1953).

WATT, FRANK W. "Western Myth, the World of Ralph Connor," CAN LIT no 1: 26–36 (Summer 1959).

GOURLAY, Robert Fleming, 1778–1863

CRUIKSHANK, E. A. "The Government of Upper Canada and Robert Gourlay," ONT HIST SOC PAPERS 23: 65–179 (1926).

GOURLAY, ROBERT FLEMING. *The Banished Briton and Neptunian...: The Life...of* Robert Gourlay (Boston, Dickinson, 1843–46).

———— *Chronicles of Canada: Being a Record of Robert Gourlay...* (St. Catherine's, "Journal," 1842).

———— *Mr. Gourlay's Case before the Legislature, with His Speech* (Toronto, Globe, 1858).

LANDE, LAWRENCE M. "Robert Fleming Gourlay." In his *Old Lamps Aglow* (Montreal, the Author, 1957) pp 260–265.

RIDDELL, W. R. "Robert Gourlay," ONT HIST SOC PAPERS 14: 5–133 (1916).

SMITH, W. "Robert Gourlay," QUEEN'S Q 34: 149–168 (Oct. 1926).

GRAHAM, Gwethalyn, 1913–1965 [pseud. of ERICKSEN-BROWN, Gwethalyn McNaught]

AITKEN, MARGARET A. "Gwethalyn Graham, a Canadian Author with a Crusading Spirit," SAT N 60: 36 (Oct. 28, 1944).

ANON. [Biography]. In *Current Biography 1945* (New York, H. W. Wilson, 1946) pp 246–247.

———— "Governor-General's Awards Announced," PUB WKLY 147: 1652–1653 (April 21, 1945).

———— "S.R.L.—Anisfield-Wolf Awards," SAT R LIT 28: 18 (Feb. 24, 1945).

MANDEL, ELI. Introduction to *Earth and High Heaven* by Gwethalyn Graham (Toronto, McClelland & Stewart, 1960) pp v–xi. [New Canadian Library no 13.]

STANLEY, C. "Voices in the Wilderness," DAL R 25: 173–181 (July 1945).

GRANNAN, Mary Evelyn

BRAITHWAITE, MAX. "Just Mary," MACL MAG 60: 8, 56–57 (June 1, 1947).

GRANNAN, H. "My Sister Mary," ATLAN ADV 47: 58 (May 1957).

GRENFELL, Sir Wilfred T., 1865–1940

ANON. "Grenfell of Labrador," TIME 36: 64–65 (Oct. 21, 1940).

———— [Obituary]. In *Current Biography 1940* (New York, H. W. Wilson, 1941) p 349.

———— Obituary, NEWSWEEK 16: 6 (Oct. 21, 1940).

———— Obituary, SCHOLASTIC 37: 20 (Oct. 21, 1940).

———— Obituary, WILSON LIB BUL 15: 294 (Dec. 1940).

CARPENTER, J. H. "Grenfell Returns to Labrador," CHRISTIAN CENT 56: 1146 (Sept. 20, 1939).

COMBER, WINIFRED M. *Wilfred Grenfell, the Labrador Doctor* (London, Lutterworth Press, 1950).

FOX, G. M. *Sir Wilfred Grenfell* (Toronto, Oxford University Press, 1942).

GRENFELL, W. T. "Embarked on 'Somewhere Near' His 25th Trip to Labrador," SAT N 54:4 (July 22, 1939).

———— *Forty Years for Labrador* (Boston, Houghton, 1932).

———— *A Labrador Doctor: The Autobiography of*—(Boston, Houghton, 1919).

HALL, A. G. *Doctor Wilfred Grenfell* (New York, Doran, n.d.).

HAYES, ERNEST H. *Forty Years on the Labrador: The Life Story of Sir Wilfred Grenfell* (New York, Revell, 1930).

JOHNSTON, JAMES. *Grenfell of Labrador* (London, Partridge, 1908).

KERR, JAMES LENNOX. *Wilfred Grenfell: His Life and Work* (London, Harrap, 1959).

MACDONALD, D. "Shaggy Saint of Labrador," MACL MAG 67: 34, 38 (Nov. 15, 1954).

MATTHEWS, B. J. *Wilfred Grenfell, the Master Mariner* (New York, Doran, 1923).

PEATTIE, D. C. "Man of the Month," REV OF REV 96: 25–26ff (July 1937).

REASON, J. *Deep-Sea Doctor* (London, Edinburgh House, 1942).

WALDO, FULLERTON L. *Grenfell: Knight-Errant of the North* (Philadelphia, Jacobs, 1924).

——— *With Grenfell on the Labrador* (New York, Revell, 1920).

GREY OWL (Wa-Sha-Quon-Asin) [pseud.]. *See* BELANEY, George Stansfeld

GRIFFIN, Watson, 1860–1952
ANON. Obituary, FOREIGN TR 11: 77 (Jan. 19, 1952).
R., H. M. "Watson Griffin, F.R.G.S.," CAN BKMN 13: 244–245 (Dec. 1931).

GROVE, Frederick Philip, 1879–1948
ANON. "Canadian Dreiser," CAN FORUM 28: 121–122 (Sept. 1948).
——— "The Passing of Greatness," CAN AUTH & BKMN 24: 46–47 (Sept. 1948).
AYRE, ROBERT. "Canadian Writers of Today—Frederick Philip Grove," CAN FORUM 12: 255–257 (April 1932).
CLARKE, G. H. "A Canadian Novelist and His Critic," QUEEN'S Q 53: 362–368 (Aug. 1946).
COLLIN, W. E. "La Tragique Ironie de Frederick Philip Grove," GANTS DU CIEL 4: 15–40 (hiver 1946).
DEACON, WILLIAM ARTHUR. "The Canadian Novel Turns the Corner," CAN MAG 86: 16 (Oct. 1936).
EATON, CHARLES ERNEST. "Life and Works of Frederick Philip Grove" (Thesis, Acadia University, 1940).
EGGLESTON, WILFRID. "Frederick Philip Grove." In *Our Living Tradition*, First Series, ed. Claude T. Bissell (Toronto, University of Toronto Press, 1957) pp 105–127.
FERGUSON, MILDRED (MRS. G. M. DAVIES). "A Study of the Tragic Element in the Novels of Frederick Philip Grove" (Thesis, University of Manitoba, 1947).
GRANT, GWENDOLEN MARGARET. "Frederick Philip Grove: Birth of the Canadian Novel" (Thesis, Dalhousie University, 1946).
GROVE, F. P. "Apologia pro Vita et Opere Sua," CAN FORUM 11: 420–422 (Aug. 1931).
——— "In Search of Myself," UNIV TOR Q 10: 60–67 (Oct. 1940).
——— *In Search of Myself* (Toronto, Macmillan, 1946).
——— "A Postscript to *A Search for America*," QUEEN'S Q 49: 197–213 (Autumn 1942).
HOLLIDAY, W. B. "Frederick Philip Grove: An Impression," CAN LIT no 3: 17–22 (Winter 1960).
K., W. "Frederick Philip Grove," CAN BKMN 8: 110 (April 1926).
McCOURT, EDWARD A. "Spokesman of a Race?" In his *The Canadian West in Fiction* (Toronto, Ryerson, 1949) pp 55–70.
PACEY, DESMOND. "Frederick Philip Grove," MAN ARTS R 3: 28–41 (Spring 1943).
——— *Frederick Philip Grove* (Toronto, Ryerson, 1945).
PERRY, ANNE ANDERSON. "Who's Who in Canadian Literature: Frederick Philip Grove," CAN BKMN 12: 51–53 (March 1930).
PHELPS, ARTHUR L. "Frederick Philip Grove." In his *Canadian Writers* (Toronto, McClelland & Stewart, 1951) pp 36–42.

PIERCE, LORNE. "Frederick Philip Grove (1871–1948)," ROY SOC CAN PROC & TRANS 3rd ser 43: sect II, 113–119 (1949).

RANNA, H. O. "Notable Canadian Author," BKMN (London) 80: 9 (April 1931).

ROSS, MALCOLM. Introduction to *Over Prairie Trails* by Frederick Philip Grove (Toronto, McClelland & Stewart, 1957) pp v–x. [New Canadian Library no 1.]

ROWE, KAY M. "Here He Lies Where He Longed," MAN ARTS R 6: 62–64 (Spring 1949).

SANDWELL, B. K. "Frederick Philip Grove and the Culture of Canada," SAT N 61: 18 (Nov. 24, 1945).

SKELTON, ISOBEL. "Frederick Philip Grove," DAL R 19: 147–163 (July 1939).

STANLEY, C. "Voices in the Wilderness," DAL R 25: 173–181 (July 1945).

——— "Frederick Philip Grove," DAL R 25: 433–441 (Jan. 1946).

GUEVREMONT, Germaine
LeBOURDAIS, ISABEL. "A Canadian Worth Celebrating," SAT N 67: 14 (May 17, 1952).

GUTHRIE, Norman Gregor, 1877–1929 [pseud.: "John Crichton"]
MARQUIS, T. G. "The Poetry of John Crichton [Norman G. Guthrie]," CAN BKMN 7: 183 (Nov. 1925).

HAIG-BROWN, Roderick Langmere, 1908–
CRAMOND, M. "Outdoor Man of the Month: Rod Haig-Brown," FOR & OUTDOORS 46: 17, 32 (May 1950).

GRAHAM, JOHN. "Haig-Brown of B.C.," VAN DAILY PROV MAG (Oct. 2, 1948) p 15.

HAIG-BROWN, RODERICK L. "The Writer in Isolation," CAN LIT no 1: 5–12 (Summer 1959).

KEATE, STUART. "Boswell of the Brooks," MACL MAG 64: 21, 31–32 (June 15, 1951).

READ, S. E. "Roderick L. Haig-Brown," BC LIB Q 22: 15–22 (July 1958).

WALBRIDGE, EARLE F. "Roderick Haig-Brown," WILSON LIB BUL 24: 462 (March 1950).

HALE, Katherine [pseud.]. *See* GARVIN, Mrs. Amelia Beers (Warnock)

HALIBURTON, Robert Grant, 1831–1901
DENISON, LIEUT. COL. GEORGE T. "Robert Grant Haliburton," CAN MAG 17: 126–130 (June 1901).

HALIBURTON, Thomas Chandler, 1796–1865
ANON. "Haliburton Family," J EDUC NOVA SCOTIA 4th ser 8: 68–69 (Jan. 1937).

——— "Sam Slick in Nova Scotia," SCHOLASTIC 46: 24 (May 1945).

——— "Testi Americana: II, T. C. Haliburton (1855)," ANGLICA 1: 20–23 (April–June 1946).

AVIS, W. S. "The Speech of Sam Slick" (Thesis, Queen's University, 1950).

BAKER, E. A. Introduction to *Sam Slick the Clockmaker* [by Thomas Chandler Haliburton] (London, Routledge, 1904) pp xi–xvi.

BAKER, RAY PALMER. "Haliburton and the Loyalist Tradition in the Development of American Humor." In his *A History of English-Canadian Literature to the Confederation* (Cambridge, Harvard University Press, 1920) pp 68–97.

———— Introduction to *Sam Slick* by Thomas Chandler Haliburton (Toronto, McClelland & Stewart, 1941) pp 13–28.

BENGTSSON, ELNA. *The Language and Vocabulary of Sam Slick* (I. Upsala, A-B Lundequistoka Bokhandeln; Copenhagen, E. Munksgaard; 1956).

BOND, WILLIAM H., ed. "The Correspondence of Thomas Chandler Haliburton and Richard Bentley." In *The Canadian Collection at Harvard University*, ed. William Inglis Morse, Bulletin IV (1947) pp 48–105.

BOURINOT, SIR JOHN. "Thomas Chandler Haliburton." In his *Builders of Nova Scotia* (Toronto, Copp Clark, 1900) pp 62–65.

CALNEK, W. A. and A. W. SAVARY. "Thomas Chandler Haliburton." In their *History of the County of Annapolis* (Toronto, Briggs, 1897) pp 418–426.

CHASLES, PHILARÈTE. "Samuel Slick." In *Etudes sur la littérature et les Mœurs des Anglo-Americains au XIXᵉ siècle* (Paris, 1851) pp 389–419. [English trans.: *Anglo-American Literature and Manners*, from the French of P. Chasles (New York, 1852) pp 222–248. Pub. originally in REVUE DES DEUX MONDES 26: 306–326 (avril 15, 1841).]

CHISHOLM, M. P. F. "Sam Slick and Catholic Disabilities in Nova Scotia," CATHOLIC WORLD 64: 459–465 (Jan. 1897).

CHITTICK, V. L. O. "Books and Music in Haliburton," DAL R 38: 207–221 (Summer 1958).

———— "Haliburton on Men and Things," DAL R 38: 55–64 (Spring 1958).

———— "Haliburton Postscript I: Ring-Tailed Yankee," DAL R 37: 19–36 (Spring 1957).

———— "Haliburton's 'Wise Saws' and Homely Imagery," DAL R 38: 348–363 (Autumn 1958).

———— "The Persuasiveness of Sam Slick" DAL R 33: 88–101 (Summer 1953).

———— *Thomas Chandler Haliburton ("Sam Slick")* (New York, Columbia University Press, 1924).

CROFTON, F. BLAKE. *Haliburton, the Man and the Writer* (Winslow, N.S., Anslow, 1889).

———— "Thomas Chandler Haliburton," ATLAN MO 69: 355–363 (March 1892).

———— "Thomas Chandler Haliburton." In *Canada: An Encyclopaedia of the Country*, ed. J. C. Hopkins (Toronto, Linscott, 1899) 5: 177–181.

EATON, A. W. H. "Haliburton Genealogy," NEW ENGLAND HIST & GENEALOGICAL REGISTER 71: 57–74.

FENETY, G. E. *Life and Times of the Hon. Joseph Howe* (Saint John, Carter, 1896) pp 39–46.

FULLERTON, A. "Funny Old Go-Getter," CAN BUS 19: 66–67, 90, 92 (April 1946).

GRAY, F. W. "Pioneer Geologists of Nova Scotia," DAL R 26: 13–15 (April 1946).

HALIBURTON CLUB, KING'S COLLEGE, Windsor, N.S. *Haliburton* (Toronto, Briggs, 1897).

HARVEY, D. C. "The Centenary of Sam Slick," DAL R 16: 429–440 (Jan. 1937).

HORNING, L. E. "Judge Haliburton," ACTA VIC 20: 148–150 (Nov. 1896).

HOWELLS, W. D. "Editor's Easy Chair," HARPER'S 134: 442–445 (Feb. 1917).

JACK, DR. T. ALLEN. "Sam Slick and Old King's," DOM ILLUS 1: 351 (Dec. 1, 1888).

JEFFERYS, CHARLES W. *Sam Slick in Pictures . . .* , ed. with an intro. by Lorne Pierce (Toronto, Ryerson, 1956).

LOGAN, JOHN DANIEL. *Scott and Haliburton* (Halifax, Allen, 1921).

——— *Thomas Chandler Haliburton* (Toronto, Ryerson, 1923).

——— "Why Haliburton Has No Successor," CAN MAG 57: 362–368 (Sept. 1921).

MACDONALD, ADRIAN. "Thomas Chandler Haliburton." In his *Canadian Portraits* (Toronto, Ryerson, 1925) pp 52–63.

MACDONALD, DAVID. "Sam Slick Slept Here," MACL MAG 67: 22–23, 30, 35–36 (July 1, 1954).

MCDOUGALL, ROBERT L. Introduction to *The Clockmaker* by Thomas Chandler Haliburton (Toronto, McClelland & Stewart, 1958) pp ix–xvi. [New Canadian Library no 6.]

——— "Thomas Chandler Haliburton." In his ed., *Our Living Tradition*, Second and Third Series (Toronto, published in association with Carleton University by University of Toronto Press, 1959) pp 3–30.

MACMECHAN, ARCHIBALD. "Who's Who in Canadian Literature: Thomas Chandler Haliburton," CAN BKMN 8: 8–9 (Jan. 1926).

MAHON, A. WYLIE. "Sam Slick Letters," CAN MAG 44: 75–79 (Nov. 1914).

MARQUIS, T. G. Biographical Sketch in *Sam Slick the Clockmaker* by Thomas Chandler Haliburton, Centenary ed. (Toronto, Musson, n.d. [1936?]) pp ix–xxii.

MARTELL, J. S. "Creator of Sam Slick," J EDUC NOVA SCOTIA 4th ser 8: 63–67 (Jan. 1937).

MONTÉGUT, EMILE. "Un Humoriste Anglo-Americaine," REVUE DES DEUX MONDES 5: 731–748 (fév. 1850).

O'BRIEN, ARTHUR HENRY. *Haliburton ("Sam Slick")* (Montreal, Gazette, 1909).

——— "Thomas Chandler Haliburton, 1796–1865: A Sketch and a Bibliography," ROY SOC CAN PROC & TRANS 3rd ser 3: sect II, 43–66 (1909).

O'BRIEN, JAMES. "A Neglected Centenary," SAT N 51: 5 (Sept. 19, 1936).

PHELPS, ARTHUR L. "Thomas Haliburton." In his *Canadian Writers* (Toronto, McClelland & Stewart, 1951) pp 19–27.

REID, R. L. "Sam Slick and His Creator," BC MO 22: 3–6, 12–13 (Jan. 1924).

ROSS, EFFIE MAY. "A Sam Slick Centenary," CAN BKMN 3: 29–32 (Sept. 1921).

——— "Thomas Chandler Haliburton: Sam Slick, the Founder of American Humor," AMERICANA 16: 62–70 (Jan. 1922).

SEELEY, S. "Clifton," CAN GEOG J 48: 40–44 (Jan. 1954).

TRENT, WILLIAM P. "A Retrospect of American Humor," CENTURY n.s. 41: 45–64 (Nov. 1921).

WOOD, RUTH K. "The Creator of the First Yankee in Literature," BKMN (New York) 41: 152–160 (April 1915).

HAM, George Henry, 1847–1926

CHARLESWORTH, HECTOR. "Two Canadian Memoirists." In his *The Canadian Scene* (Toronto, Macmillan, 1927) pp 106–124. [Also discusses John Stephen Willison.]

HAMILTON, Pierce Stevens, 1826–1893

SHANNON, M. JOSEPHINE. "Two Forgotten Patriots," DAL R 14: 85–97 (April 1934).

HANLEY, Mrs. Annie Harvie (Ross), 1875–

ANON. "Editor's Note Book," CAN GEOG J 28: vii (Feb. 1944).

HARDY, William George, 1896–

HARDY, W. G. "My First Book," CAN AUTH & BKMN 30: 9–11 (Summer 1954).

HARMON, Daniel Williams, 1778–1843

BRYCE, GEORGE. *The Remarkable History of the Hudson's Bay Company* . . . (Toronto, Briggs, 1900) pp 165–167.

BURPEE, LAWRENCE J. "Nineteen Years in the West." In his *The Search for the Western Sea* (Toronto, Musson, 1908; rev. ed. 1935) pp 492–512.

HARMAN, JOHN WILLIAM, ed. *Harman-Harmon Genealogy and Biography, with Historical Notes, 19 B.C. to 1928 A.D.* . . . (Parsons, W. Va., privately printed, 1928).

HARMON, DANIEL WILLIAMS. *A Journal of Voyages and Travels in the Interior of North America . . . from Montreal nearly to the Pacific Ocean* . . . (Andover, Vt., Flagg & Gould, 1820).

———— *Sixteen Years in the Indian Country: The Journal of Daniel Williams Harmon 1800–1816*, ed. with an intro. by W. Kaye Lamb (Toronto, Macmillan, 1957).

MORICE, A. G. "Stuart and Harmon at Stuart Lake, 1809–1821." In his *History of the Northern Interior of British Columbia* . . . (London, Bodley Head, 1906) pp 84–101.

O'MEARA, WALTER. "Adventure in Local History," MINNESOTA HIST 31: 1–10 (March 1950).

———— *The Grand Portage* (Indianapolis, Bobbs-Merrill, 1951). [Fictionalized account of the romance of Daniel and Elizabeth Harmon.]

SPARGO, JOHN. *Two Bennington-Born Explorers and Makers of Modern Canada* (Bradford, Vt., Green Mountain Press, 1950).

HARRISON, Mrs. Susie Frances (Riley), 1859–1935 [pseud: "Seranus"]

WILLISON, MARJORY. "Seranus," CAN BKMN 14: 80–81 (July–Aug. 1932).

HART, Mrs. Julia Catherine (Beckwith), 1796–1867

ANON. "The Collector [First Novel by a Canadian]," CAN BKMN 12: 194–195 (Sept. 1930).

BENNET, C. L. "An Unpublished Manuscript of the First Canadian Novelist," DAL R 43: 317–332 (Autumn 1963).

CARNOCHAN, JANET. "Rare Canadian Books," CAN MAG 43: 236–238 (July 1914).

GAGNON, PHILÉAS. "Le Premier Roman Canadien [on *St. Ursula's Convent or the Nun of Canada*]," ROY SOC CAN PROC & TRANS 2nd ser 6: 121–132 (1900).

MAXWELL, LILIAN M. BECKWITH. "The First Canadian Born Novelist," DAL R 31: 59–64 (April 1951).

MORGAN, H. R. "Mrs. Julia Catherine Hart: Author of the First Canadian Novel," SAT N 40: 23 (Oct. 3, 1925).

HATHAWAY, Rufus Hawtin, 1869–1933

HATHAWAY, MAUD SNARR. "Rufus H. Hathaway," CAN BKMN 15: 45 (March 1933).

PIERCE, LORNE. "Rufus Hawtin Hathaway," CAN BKMN 21: 17–21 (Oct. 1939).

HAWLEY, William Fitz, 1804–1855

LANDE, LAWRENCE M. "William Fitz Hawley." In his *Old Lamps Aglow* (Montreal, the Author, 1957) pp 144–150.

HAYMAN, Robert, 1579?–1631?

MACKINNON, M. H. M. "Parnassus in Newfoundland," DAL R 32: 110–119 (1952).

HEARNE, Samuel, 1745–1792

BLANCHET, G. H. "Thelewey-aza-yeth," BEAVER 280: 8–11 (Sept. 1949).

BRYCE, GEORGE. *The Remarkable History of the Hudson's Bay Company* (Toronto, Briggs, 1900).

BURPEE, LAWRENCE J. *The Search for the Western Sea* (Toronto, Musson, 1908; rev. ed. 1935) pp 136–164.

GLOVER, R. G. "Note on John Richardson's Digression Concerning Hearne's Route," CAN HIST R 32: 252–263 (Sept. 1951).

——— "Sidelights on Samuel Hearne," BEAVER 277: 10–14 (March 1947).

——— "Witness of David Thompson," CAN HIST R 31: 25–38 (March 1950).

HAWKES, ARTHUR. "Hearne and Matonabbee," CAN MAG 38: 231–236 (Jan. 1912).

LAUT, AGNES. *The Pathfinders of the West* (Toronto, Macmillan, 1904).

——— *The Conquest of the Great North-west*, 2 vols (New York, Outing Pub., 1908).

LEACOCK, STEPHEN. *Adventurers of the Far North* (Toronto, Glasgow Brook, 1914).

TYRRELL, J. B., ed. *The Journals of Samuel Hearne and Philip Turnor* (Toronto, Champlain Society, 1934).

WALLACE, WILLIAM S. *By Star and Compass* (Toronto, Oxford University Press, 1922).

WILLSON, BECKLES. *The Great Company* (Toronto, Copp Clark, 1899).

WILSON, J. T. "New Light on Hearne," BEAVER 280: 14–18 (June 1949).

HEAVYSEGE, Charles, 1816–1876

ANON. "Charles Heavysege," DOM ILLUS 2: 263, 266 (April 27, 1889).

——— "The Modern British Drama," *North British Review* (August 1858). [An article attributed to Coventry Patmore.]

BAKER, RAY PALMER. "Charles Heavysege." In his *A History of English-*

Canadian Literature to the Confederation (Cambridge, Mass., Harvard University Press, 1920) pp 168–176.

BURPEE, LAWRENCE J. "Charles Heavysege," ROY SOC CAN PROC & TRANS 2nd ser 7: 19–60 (1901). [Also, greatly abridged, in his *A Little Book of Canadian Essays* (Toronto, Musson, 1909) pp 17–29.]

CLARK, DANIEL. "The Poetry of Charles Heavysege," CAN MO & NATL R 10: 127–134 (Aug. 1876).

DALE, T. R. "The Life and Works of Charles Heavysege, 1817–1876" (Thesis, University of Chicago, 1951).

————— "Our Greatest Poet—a Century Ago," CAN FORUM 37: 245–246 (Feb. 1958).

————— "The Revolt of Charles Heavysege," UNIV TOR Q 22: 35–42 (Oct. 1952).

GREENSHIELDS, E. B. "A Forgotten Poet," UNIV MAG (Montreal) 7: 343–359 (Oct. 1908).

MONTGOMERY, M. J. "Charles Heavysege," CAN POETRY 5: 5–12 (Sept. 1940).

MURRAY, LOUISA. "Heavysege's 'Saul'," CAN MO & NATL R 10: 250–254 (Sept. 1876).

HEMING, Arthur Henry Howard, 1870–1940

ANON. "Careers of Canadian Painters," CURTAIN CALL vol 9 no 7: 6 (April 1938).

————— Obituary, CURRENT BIOG (1940).

————— Obituary, WILSON LIB BUL 15: 294 (Dec. 1940).

BENEDICT, EARDLEY. "Arthur Heming—A Vignette," CAN FORUM 28: 84 (July 1948).

COLGATE, WILLIAM S. *Arthur Heming. Recorder of the North* (Toronto, Best, 1934). [Another ed. of this pamphlet appeared in 1938.]

GRAHAM, JEAN. "Mr. Arthur Heming," SAT N 47: 5 (June 25, 1932).

PHILLIPS, W. J. "The Art of Arthur Heming," BEAVER 271 no 2: 24–29 (Sept. 1940).

R., N. R. "Heming's New Drama of the Wilds," MACL MAG 38: 5 (July 1, 1925).

HENRY, Alexander, 1739–1824

ANON. "A Biographical Sketch of the Late Alexander Henry, Esquire," CAN MAG & LIT REPOSITORY 2: 289–304 (April 1824), 385–397 (May 1824).

ASKIN, JOHN. *The John Askin Papers* . . . , ed. Milo M. Quaife ([Detroit], Public Library Commission, 1928, 1931) 2 vols.

BURPEE, L. J. "Alexander Henry," CAN GEOG J 34: 199–200 (April 1947).

————— *The Search for the Western Sea: The Story of the Exploration of Northwestern America*, new and rev. ed. (Toronto, Macmillan, 1935) pp 389–414.

HENRY, ALEXANDER. *New Light on the Early History of the Greater Northwest: The Manuscript Journals of Alexander Henry . . . and of David Thompson . . . 1799–1814*, ed. Elliott Coues (New York, Harper, 1897) 3 vols.

LIVINGSTON, H. A. "Hard-Boiled Henry of the North-west Company," CAN MAG 83: 15ff (March 1935).

WALDON, FREDA F. "Alexander Henry, Esq., of Montreal, Fur Trader, Adventurer and Man of Letters" (Thesis, University of London, 1930).

[Copies are deposited in the National Library, Ottawa, and the Public Libraries in Hamilton and Toronto.]

HENSHAW, Mrs. Julia Wilmotte (Henderson) 1869–1937 [pseud: "Julian Durham"]
M., B. "Canadian Celebrities: XXX, Julia W. Henshaw," CAN MAG 18: 220–221 (Jan. 1902).

HIEBERT, Paul Gerhardt, 1892–
WHEELER, A. L. "Up from Magma and back again with Paul Hiebert," MANITOBA ARTS R vol 6 no 1: 3–14 (Spring 1948).

HIND, Ella Cora, 1861–1942
HAIG, KENNETHE M. *Brave Harvest: The Life Story of E. Cora Hind* (Toronto, Allen, 1945).
SANDERS, BYRNE HOPE. "Cora Hind." In her *Canadian Portraits—Famous Women* (Toronto, Clarke Irwin, 1958) pp 47–81.
STEINER, FLORENCE. "Cora Hind as I Remember Her," SAT N 61: 39 (April 20, 1946).

HOLLAND, Norah Mary, 1876–1925
JACOB, FRED. "A Quaint Canadian Poetess: Character Study of the Late Norah Holland, a Woman of Rare Lyric Gifts," SAT N 40: 2 (Aug. 8, 1925).

HOLMES, Abraham S.
HAMIL, FRED C. "A Pioneer Novelist of Kent County," ONT HIST SOC PAPERS 39: 101–113 (1947).
KLINCK, CARL F. "Early Creative Literature of Western Ontario," ONT HIST 45: 161–163 (Autumn 1953).

HOPKINS, John Castell, 1864–1923
GRANT, G. M. "Castell Hopkins' Life of Mr. Gladstone," CAN MAG 6: 84–87 (Nov. 1895).

HOWE, Joseph, 1804–1873
BAKER, R. P. "Joseph Howe and the 'Nova Scotian.'" In his *A History of English-Canadian Literature to the Confederation* (Cambridge, Harvard University Press, 1920) pp 57–67.
BECK, J. M. "Joseph Howe: Opportunist or Empire-Builder," CAN HIST R 41: 185–202 (Sept. 1960).
BREBNER, J. BARTLETT. "Joseph Howe and the Crimean War Enlistment Controversy between Great Britain and the United States," CAN HIST R 11: 300–327 (Dec. 1930).
BURPEE, LAWRENCE J. "Joseph Howe and the Anti-Confederation League," ROY SOC CAN PROC & TRANS 3rd ser 10: sect II, 409–473 (1916).
CARMAN, FRANCIS A. "The Howe Papers," CAN MAG 45: 365–369 (Sept. 1915).
CHISHOLM, JOSEPH ANDREW. "Hitherto Unpublished Letters of Joseph Howe," DAL R 12: 309–314 (Oct. 1932).
——— *Joseph Howe* (Halifax, Chronicle Print., 1909).
——— "More Letters of Joseph Howe," DAL R 12: 481–496 (Jan. 1933).
FENETY, GEORGE EDWARD. *Life and Times of the Hon. Joseph Howe* (Saint John, Carter, 1896).
GRANT, REV. GEORGE MONRO. *Joseph Howe* (Halifax, MacKinlay, 1904).

———— "The Late Hon. Joseph Howe," CAN MO & NATL R 7: 377–387 (May 1875); 7: 497–508 (June 1875); 8:20–25 (July 1875); 8: 115–122 (Aug. 1875). [Subsequently collected and published under title *Joseph Howe* (Halifax, MacKinlay, 1904).]

GRANT, WILLIAM LAWSON. *The Tribune of Nova Scotia: A Chronicle of Joseph Howe* (Toronto, Glasgow Brook, 1915).

HARVEY, DANIEL COBB. *Joseph Howe and Local Patriotism* (Winnipeg. 1921).

HASSARD, ALBERT R. "Great Canadian Orators: II, Joseph Howe," CAN MAG 53: 423–430 (Sept. 1919).

HENDERSON, JOHN. "Joseph Howe." In his *Great Men of Canada* (Toronto, Southam, 1928) pp 131–153.

LOGAN, J. D. "Joseph Howe," CAN MAG 62: 19–25 (Nov. 1923).

LONGLEY, THE HON. J. W. "Howe and His Times," CAN MAG 2: 207–212 (Jan. 1894).

———— "Joseph Howe," CAN MAG 3: 531–540 (Oct. 1894); 4: 77–83 (Nov. 1894).

———— *Joseph Howe* (Toronto, Morang, 1904).

MACDONALD, ADRIAN. "Joseph Howe." In his *Canadian Portraits* (Toronto, Ryerson, 1925) pp 64–81.

MACDONALD, DAVID. "Nova Scotia's Strangest Son," MACL MAG 66: 22, 30–37 (April 1, 1953).

MARTELL, L. H. "Joe Howe's Last Opponent," MACL MAG 28: 31–32 (April 1915).

MEAGHER, SIR NICHOLAS H. *The Religious Warfare in Nova Scotia, 1855–1860 . . . : Joseph Howe's Part in It and the Attitude of Catholics* (Halifax, the Author, [1927?]).

MUNROE, DAVID. "Joseph Howe as Man of Letters," DAL R 20: 451–457 (Jan. 1941).

PATTERSON, HON. JUDGE. "Joseph Howe and the Anti-Confederation League," DAL R 10: 397–402 (Oct. 1930).

RADDALL, T. H. "Joe Howe: Maritimes Gadfly," SAT N 67: 13, 49 (Dec. 8, 1951).

RHODENIZER, V. B. "Who's Who in Canadian Literature: Joseph Howe (1804–1873)," CAN BKMN 8: 139–141 (May 1926).

ROY, JAMES ALEXANDER. *Joseph Howe: A Study in Achievement and Frustration* (Toronto, Macmillan, 1935).

SAUNDERS, REV. EDWARD MANNING. *Three Premiers of Nova Scotia: The Hon. J. W. Johnstone, The Hon. Joseph Howe, The Hon. Charles Tupper* (Toronto, Briggs, 1909).

TAYLOR, F. "Hon. Joseph Howe." In *Portraits of British Americans*, ed. W. Notman (Montreal, W. Notman, 1865) pp 291–308.

THOMAS, W. K. "Canadian Political Oratory in the Nineteenth Century," DAL R 39: 377–389 (Autumn 1959).

WEAVER, EMILY P. "Homes and Haunts of Joseph Howe," CAN MAG 25: 195–202 (July 1905).

———— "Recollection of Joseph Howe and His Family," CAN MAG 28: 278–281 (Jan. 1907).

HUGHES, James Laughlin, 1846–1935

PIERCE, LORNE. "James Laughlin Hughes: Patriot, Preacher, Pedagogue, Poet," CAN MAG 58: 57–62 (Nov. 1921).

HUNTER-DUVAR, John, 1830–1899
  BURPEE, LAWRENCE J. "John Hunter-Duvar (1830–1899)." In his *A Little Book of Canadian Essays* (Toronto, Musson, 1909) pp 65–72.
  PAYZANT, J. A. "John Hunter Duvar," DOM ILLUS 5: 127 (Aug. 23, 1890).

HUTCHISON, (William) Bruce, 1901–
  ANON. Biographical Sketch, WILSON LIB BUL 19: 146 (Nov. 1944).
  BENSON, N. A. M. "Sports Editor Becomes Interpreter of Canada," SAT N 57: 19 (June 13, 1942).
  HANRAHAN, T. J. "Bruce Hutchison: Canadian Visionary," BC LIB Q 22: 45–49 (Oct. 1958).
  MACGIBBON, D. A. "Lorne Pierce Medal [awarded to] William Bruce Hutchison," ROY SOC CAN PROC & TRANS 3rd ser 49: 37–38 (1955).
  NESBITT, J. K. "Editor Bruce Hutchison Commutes between Victoria and Winnipeg," SAT N 62: 26–27 (May 10, 1947).
  UNDERHILL, FRANK H. "Turning New Leaves," CAN FORUM 32: 206–207 (Dec. 1952).

HUTTON, Maurice, 1856–1940
  ANON. Obituary, CURRENT BIOG (1940).
  FALCONER, SIR ROBERT. "Maurice Hutton 1856–1940," ROY SOC CAN PROC & TRANS 3rd ser 34: 111–114 (1940).
  WALLACE, MALCOLM W. "Principal Maurice Hutton," UNIV TOR MO 40: 172a–172d (April 1940).

INGERSOLL, Will E.
  TALLMAN, LYN. "Who's Who in Canadian Literature: Will E. Ingersoll," CAN BKMN 11: 131–132 (June 1929).

INGRAHAM, Mrs. Mary (Kinley), 1874–1949
  ELLIOTT, J. H. "Mary Kinley Ingraham," CAN LIB ASSOC BUL 10: 261 (June 1954).
  SHAW, BEATRICE M. H. "Maritime Librarian Would Not Permit Fate's Blows or Frail Physique to Stop Her," MACL MAG 37: 68–70 (Nov. 15, 1924).

INNIS, Harold Adams, 1894–1952
  ANON. Biographical Note, CAN HIST R 33: 405–406 (Dec. 1952).
  BRADY, A. "Harold Adams Innis, 1894–1952," CAN J ECON 19: 87–96 (Feb. 1953).
  BREBNER, J. B. "Tribute to Harold Innis," SAT N 67: 13 (May 24, 1952).
  CREIGHTON, DONALD GRANT. *Harold Adams Innis: Portrait of a Scholar* (Toronto, University of Toronto Press, 1957).
  EASTERBROOK, W. T. "Innis and Economics," CAN J ECON 19: 291–303 (Aug. 1953).
  GRAHAM, GERALD. "Tribute to Harold Innis," SAT N 67: 13 (May 24, 1952).
  LOWER, A. R. M. "Harold Adams Innis (1894–1952)," ROY SOC CAN PROC & TRANS 3rd ser 47: 89–91 (1953).

McLuhan, Marshall. "The Later Innis," QUEEN'S Q 60: 385–394 (1953–1954).

Nef, J. U. "Shapers of the Modern Outlook, Harold A. Innis (1894–1952)," CAN FORUM 32: 224–225 (Jan. 1953).

Sage, W. N. "Harold A. Innis, 1894–1952," BC HIST Q 17: 149–151 (Jan.–April 1953).

Ward, J. "Published Works of H. A. Innis: Bibliography," CAN J ECON 19: 233–244 (May 1953).

JAMIESON, Mrs. Nina (Moore), 1885–1932

Bernhardt, C. "Portrait of Nina Moore Jamieson," CAN BKMN 14: 139 (Dec. 1932).

JAQUES, Edna, 1891–

Jacques, Edna. "Uphill All the Way," *Chatelaine* vol 27, no 10: 24–25, 76–87, 92–93 (Oct. 1954); no 11: 24, 38–43 (Nov. 1954).

McClung, Nellie L. "The Scrap-book Poet," MACL MAG 47: 22 (Nov. 15, 1934).

Myers, L. A. "Wide Horizons," CAN BKMN 18: 9 (Jan. 25, 1936).

Tyrwhitt, Janice. "Rhymes in a Ten-Cent Scribbler," MACL MAG 65: 14–17, 46–48 (Sept. 1, 1952).

JOHNSON, Emily Pauline (Tekahionwake), 1862–1913

Ayre, Robert. "Pauline Johnson," CAN FORUM 14: 17 (Oct. 1933).

Bryan, Mary J. "The Passing of Pauline Johnson," BC DIGEST 1: 83–85 (March 1946).

Charlesworth, Hector. "Miss Pauline Johnson's Poems," CAN MAG 5: 478–480 (Sept. 1895).

———— "Poets and Women Writers of the Past." In his *Candid Chronicles* (Toronto, Macmillan, 1925) pp 87–104.

Foster, Mrs. W. G. "The Lyric Beauty of Pauline Johnson's Poetry," CAN BKMN 16: 37, 43 (March 1934).

———— *The Mohawk Princess* (Vancouver, Lion's Gate, 1931).

———— "Pauline Johnson's Gift to Vancouver," CAN BKMN 18: 6–7 (June 1936).

Grossman, Mrs. Max. "Pauline Johnson, Her Life, Legends, and Verses," JEWISH WESTERN BUL (Sept. 1936) pp 11, 16.

Hammond, M. O. "Who's Who in Canadian Literature: E. Pauline Johnson," CAN BKMN 8: 41–43 (Feb. 1926).

MacKay, Isabel Ecclestone. "Pauline Johnson: A Reminiscence," CAN MAG 41: 273–278 (July 1913).

McRaye, Walter. "East and West with Pauline Johnson," CAN MAG 60: 381–389 (March 1923), 494–502 (April 1923).

———— "Pauline Johnson," EDUC RECORD (Quebec) 58: 92–97 (April–June 1942). [Also in *Leading Canadian Poets*, ed. W. P. Percival (Toronto, Ryerson, 1948) pp 88–97.]

———— *Pauline Johnson and Her Friends* (Toronto, Ryerson, 1947).

Mair, Charles. "Pauline Johnson: An Appreciation," CAN MAG 41: 281–283 (July 1913).

Scott, Jack. "The Passionate Princess," MACL MAG 65: 12, 13, 54, 57 (April 1, 1952).

Stevenson, O. J. "Tekahionwake." In his *A People's Best* (Toronto, Musson, 1927) pp 141–152.

STRINGER, ARTHUR. "Wild Poets I Have Known—Pauline Johnson," SAT N 57: 29 (Oct. 11, 1941).

WALDIE, JEAN H. "The Iroquois Poetess, Pauline Johnson," ONT HIST SOC PAPERS 40: 65–75 (1948).

YEIGH, FRANK. "Memories of Pauline Johnson," CAN BKMN 11: 227–229 (Oct. 1929).

KENNEDY, Howard Angus, 1861–1938
ANON. "Howard Angus Kennedy, 1861–1938," CAN AUTH 15: 6–11 (April 1938).
——— Obituary, SAT N 53: 3 (Feb. 19, 1938).
BARNARD, LESLIE GORDON. "So I Shall Remember Him," CAN AUTH 15: 5 (April 1938).

KENNEDY, Leo, 1907–
COLLIN, W. E. "Leo Kennedy," CAN FORUM 14: 24–27 (Oct. 1933).
——— "The Man of April." In his *The White Savannahs* (Toronto, Macmillan, 1936), pp 267–284.
PRATT, E. J. "New Notes in Canadian Poetry," CAN COMMENT vol 3 no 2: 26–27 (Feb. 1934).
SCHULTZ, GREGORY PETER. "The Periodical Poetry of A. J. M. Smith, F. R. Scott, Leo Kennedy, A. M. Klein and Dorothy Livesay, 1925–1950" (Thesis, University of Western Ontario, 1957).

KERNIGHAN, Robert Kirkland, 1857–1926 [pseud: "The Khan"]
HASSARD, ALBERT P. "When the Khan Sang," CAN BKMN 14: 99–100 (Sept. 1932).

KIDD, Adam, 1802–1831
LANDE, LAWRENCE M. "Adam Kidd." In his *Old Lamps Aglow* (Montreal, the Author, 1957) pp 164–171.

KINGSFORD, William, 1819–1898
SHANNON, R. W. "A Canadian Historian," CAN MAG 12: 191–195 (Jan. 1899).

KIRBY, William Arthur, 1817–1906
ANON. "William Kirby," DOM ILLUS 2: 298 (May 11, 1889).
CARNOCHAN, JANET. "Reminiscences of William Kirby, F.R.S.C.," UNITED EMPIRE LOYALISTS' ASSOC TRANS 6:49–56 (Brampton, Conservator Book Dept., 1914).
DE GUTTENBERG, A. C. "William Kirby," R DE L'UNIV LAVAL 9: 337–345 (Dec. 1954).
MORGAN, H. J., ed. "William Kirby," In his *Representative Men: A Cyclopaedia of Canadian Biography* (Toronto, Rose, 1886).
PIERCE, LORNE, ed. *Alfred, Lord Tennyson and William Kirby: Unpublished Correspondence, to which are added Some Letters from Hallam, Lord Tennyson* (Toronto, Macmillan, 1929).
——— "Who's Who in Canadian Literature: William Kirby," CAN BKMN 11: 35–39 (Feb. 1929).
——— *William Kirby: The Portrait of a Tory Loyalist* (Toronto, Macmillan, 1929).

RIDDELL, WILLIAM R. *William Kirby* (Toronto, Ryerson, 1923).
SANDWELL, B. K. "Debunking *The Golden Dog*," SAT N 45: 2 (Oct. 4, 1930).

KIRKCONNELL, Watson, 1895–
ANON. Biographical Note, PUB AFFAIRS 14: II (Autumn 1951).
——— Biographical Note, CAN AUTH & BKMN 34: 5 (Spring 1958).
KING, A. [Editorial], CAN POETRY 7: 5–6 (June 1944).
LLOYD, C. F. "A New Note in Canadian Poetry: Kirkconnell's Ta Grammata," CAN BKMN 16: 75–76, 80–81 (June 1934).

KLEIN, Abraham Moses, 1909–1972
ANON. Biographical Note, CAN AUTH & BKMN 34: 13 (Spring 1958).
BROWN, E. K. "The Immediate Present in Canadian Literature," SEWANEE R 41: 430–432 (Oct. 1933).
COLLIN, W. E. "The Spirit's Palestine." In his *The White Savannahs* (Toronto, Macmillan, 1936) pp 207–231.
CRAWLEY, ALAN. "Notes on A. M. Klein," CONTEMP VERSE 28: 20 (Summer 1949).
DUDEK, LOUIS. "A. M. Klein," CAN FORUM 30: 10–12 (April 1950).
EDEL, LEON. "Abraham M. Klein," CAN FORUM 12: 300–302 (May 1932).
——— "Poetry and the Jewish Tradition," POETRY (Chicago) 58: 51–53 (April 1941).
LEWISOHN, LUDWIG. Foreword to *Hath Not a Jew* . . . by A. M. Klein (New York, Behrman's, 1940) pp v–viii.
PACEY, DESMOND. "A. M. Klein." In his *Ten Canadian Poets* (Toronto, Ryerson, 1958) pp 254–292.
PHELPS, ARTHUR L. "Two Poets: Klein and Birney." In his *Canadian Writers* (Toronto, McClelland & Stewart, 1951) pp 111–119.
RÉGIMBAL, A. "Artistes israélites au Canada français," RELATIONS 8: 184–185 (juin 1948).
SCHULTZ, GREGORY PETER. "The Periodical Poetry of A. J. M. Smith, F. R. Scott, Leo Kennedy, A. M. Klein and Dorothy Livesay, 1925–1950" (Thesis, University of Western Ontario, 1957).
SMITH, A. J. M. "Abraham Moses Klein," GANTS DU CIEL 11: 67–81 (printemps 1946).
SPURGEON, D. C. "Whither Green-Haired Poet?" SAT N 65: 12, 46 (May 23, 1950).
STEINBERG, M. W. "A Twentieth Century Pentateuch," CAN LIT no 2: 37–46 (Autumn 1959).
SUTHERLAND, JOHN. "Canadian Comment," NORTHERN R 2: 30–34 (Aug.–Sept. 1949).
——— "The Poetry of A. M. Klein," INDEX 1: 8–12 (Aug. 1946).
WILSON, MILTON. "Klein's Drowned Poet," CAN LIT no 6: 5–17 (Autumn 1960).

KNISTER, Raymond, 1900–1932
ANON. Obituary, CAN AUTH 10: 55 (Sept. 1932).
——— Obituary, CAN BKMN 14: 95 (Sept. 1932).

—— Obituary, CAN FORUM 13: 45 (Nov. 1932).

—— Obituary, CAN MAG 78: 48 (Oct. 1932).

KENNEDY, LEO. "Raymond Knister," CAN FORUM 12: 459–461 (Sept. 1932).

LIVESAY, DOROTHY. Memoir. In her ed. *Collected Poems of Raymond Knister* (Toronto, Ryerson, 1949) pp xi–xli.

RAY, MARGARET. "Raymond Knister: A Bibliography of His Works." In *Collected Poems of Raymond Knister*, ed. with a Memoir by Dorothy Livesay (Toronto, Ryerson, 1949) pp 39–45.

KNOX, Gilbert [pseud]. *See* MACBETH, Mrs. Madge Hamilton

KNOX, (William) Alexander, 1907–

MILLER, H. O. "Alexander Knox, Canadian Actor-Playwright," SAT N 55: 4 (May 25, 1940).

WILSON, E. "The Man Who Plays Wilson," MACL MAG 57: 19, 31ff (July 1, 1944).

KREISEL, Henry, 1922–

ANON. "Hurdling the English Language," CAN AUTH & BKMN 24: 40 (Dec. 1948).

STEDMOND, JOHN. Introduction to *The Rich Man* by Henry Kreisel (Toronto, McClelland & Stewart, 1961) pp v–vii. [New Canadian Library no 24.]

LAMPMAN, Archibald, 1861–1899

ANON. "The Lampman Cairn at Morpeth," SAT N 46: 8 (Sept. 27, 1930).

—— "The Lampman Memorial, Unveiling of the Cairn at Morpeth," CAN AUTH 8: 42–43 (Sept. 1930).

—— "Lampman's Birthplace," CAN MAG 28: 201 (Dec. 1906).

—— "Lampman's Memory Honored: Impressive Ceremonies at the Dedication of a Commemorative Cairn in Churchyard at Morpeth," CAN BKMN 12: 175–176 (Sept. 1930).

—— "Memorial to Lampman: Cairn at Morpeth, Ontario," COMMON-WEAL 12: 566 (Oct. 8, 1930).

BARRY, L. E. F. "Prominent Canadians: Archibald Lampman," THE WEEK 8: 298–300 (April 10, 1891).

BEATTIE, MUNRO. "Archibald Lampman." In *Our Living Tradition*, First Series, ed. Claude T. Bissell (Toronto, University of Toronto Press, 1957) pp 63–88.

BEGLEY, LUCILLE. "Harmonies canadiennes: Pamphile le May, Archibald Lampman," LECTURES 6: 296–297 (juin 1960).

BOURINOT, ARTHUR S. "Archibald Lampman and What Some Writers Have Said of Him," CAN AUTH & BKMN 26: 20–22 (1950). [Also in his *Five Canadian Poets* (Montreal, Quality Press, 1956) pp 4–7.]

—— *Some Letters of Duncan Campbell Scott, Archibald Lampman & Others* (Ottawa, 1959).

BRENNAN, M. W. "The Prosody of Archibald Lampman" (Thesis, Queen's University, 1931).

BROWN, E. K. "Archibald Lampman." In his *On Canadian Poetry*, rev. ed. (Toronto, Ryerson, 1947) pp 88–118.

───── "Archibald Lampman 1861–1899:· What We lost," SAT N 64: 15 (Feb. 8, 1949).

───── Foreword to *At the Long Sault and Other New Poems* by Archibald Lampman (Toronto, Ryerson, 1943) pp vii–xxix.

BURPEE, L. J. "Archibald Lampman." In his *A Little Book of Canadian Essays* (Toronto, Musson, 1909) pp 30–42.

BURTON, JEAN. "Archibald Lampman's Poetry of Release," WILLISON'S MO 3: 425–427 (April 1928).

CANADIAN AUTHORS' ASSOCIATION, Western Ontario Branch. *Addresses . . . at . . . Archibald Lampman Memorial Cairn* (London, Ont., the Branch, 1930).

COLGATE, WILLIAM. *Archibald Lampman: A Dedication and a Note* (Toronto, privately printed, 1957). [Reprinted from the *Canadian Forum* 36: 279–280 (March 1957).]

COLLIN, W. E. "Natural Landscape." In his *The White Savannahs* (Toronto, Macmillan, 1936) pp 3–40. [Also in UNIV TOR Q 4: 103–120 (Oct. 1934).]

CONNOR, CARL Y. *Archibald Lampman, Canadian Poet of Nature* (New York, Carrier, 1929).

CRAWFORD, A. W. "Archibald Lampman," ACTA VIC 17: 77–81 (Dec. 1895).

DUDEK, LOUIS. "The Significance of Lampman," CULTURE 18: 277–290 (sept. 1957).

ELSON, J. M. "Lampman Memorial," CAN BKMN 12: 105–106 (May 1930).

"FIDELIS" [pseud. of Agnes Maule Machar], "Among the Millet," THE WEEK 6: 251–252 (March 22, 1889).

GORDON, HUNTLEY K. "Canadian Poetry," CAN FORUM 1: 178–180 (March 1921).

GUSTAFSON, RALPH. "Among the Millet," NORTHERN R 1: 26–34 (Feb.–March 1947).

GUTHRIE, NORMAN G. *The Poetry of Archibald Lampman* (Toronto, Musson, 1927).

HOWELLS, W. D. "Editor's Study," HARPER'S MAG 78: 821–823 (April 1889).

KENNEDY, LEO. "Archibald Lampman," CAN FORUM 13: 301–303 (May 1933).

KNISTER, RAYMOND. "The Poetry of Archibald Lampman," DAL R 7: 348–361 (Oct. 1927).

LAMPMAN, ARCHIBALD. *Archibald Lampman's Letters to Edward William Thomson (1890–1898)*, ed. with an intro., annotations, a bibliography with notes, and his "Essay on Happiness," by Arthur S. Bourinot (Ottawa, 1956).

LOGAN, J. D. "Literary Group of '61," CAN MAG 37: 555–563 (Oct. 1911).

MACDONALD, ADRIAN. "Archibald Lampman." In his *Canadian Portraits* (Toronto, Ryerson, 1925) pp 220–230.

MACDONALD, E. R. "A Little Talk About Lampman," CAN MAG 52: 1012–1016 (April 1919).

MARSHALL, JOHN. "Archibald Lampman," QUEEN'S Q 9: 63–79 (July 1901)..

MUDDIMAN, BERNARD. "Archibald Lampman," QUEEN'S Q 22: 233–243 (Jan. 1915).

MUNDAY, DON. "Soul-Standards of Archibald Lampman," WESTMINSTER HALL 4: 15–17 (Oct. 1914).

PACEY, DESMOND. "Archibald Lampman." In his *Ten Canadian Poets* (Toronto, Ryerson, 1958) pp 114–140.

———— "A Reading of Lampman's 'Heat,' " CULTURE 14: 292–297 (sept. 1953).

PHELPS, ARTHUR L. "Archibald Lampman." In his *Canadian Writers* (Toronto, McClelland & Stewart, 1951) pp 51–59.

SCOTT, DUNCAN CAMPBELL. "Archibald Lampman," EDUC RECORD (Quebec) 59: 221–225 (Oct.–Dec. 1943). [Also in *Leading Canadian Poets*, ed. W. P. Percival (Toronto, Ryerson, 1948) pp 98–106.]

———— "Decade of Canadian Poetry," CAN MAG 17: 153–158 (June 1901).

———— Introduction to *Lyrics of Earth* by Archibald Lampman (Toronto, Musson, 1925) pp 3–47.

———— Letter [about Lampman] . . . to Ralph Gustafson [17 July 1945]," *Fiddlehead* no 41: 12–14 (Summer 1959).

———— Memoir. In *Selected Poems of Archibald Lampman* (Toronto, Ryerson, 1947) pp xiii–xxvii.

———— Memoir. In *The Poems of Archibald Lampman* (Toronto, Morang, 1900) pp xi–xxv.

———— "Who's Who in Canadian Literature: Archibald Lampman," CAN BKMN 8: 107–109 (April 1926).

STEVENSON, O. J. "The Song of the Spirit." In his *A People's Best* (Toronto, Musson, 1927) pp 127–134.

STRINGER, ARTHUR. "A Glance at Lampman," CAN MAG 2: 545–548 (April 1894).

———— "Wild Poets I've Known: Archibald Lampman," SAT N 56: 29 (May 24, 1941).

SUTHERLAND, JOHN. "Edgar Allan Poe in Canada," NORTHERN R 4: 22–37 (Feb.–March 1951).

SWIFT, S. C. "Lampman and Le Comte de Lisle," CAN BKMN 9: 261–264 (Sept. 1927).

UNTERMEYER, L. "Archibald Lampman and the Sonnet," POET LORE 20: 432–437 (Nov. 1909).

UNWIN, G. H. "The Poetry of Lampman," UNIV MAG (Montreal) 16: 55–73 (Feb. 1917).

VOORHIS, THE REV. ERNEST. "The Ancestry of Archibald Lampman, Poet," ROY SOC CAN PROC & TRANS 3rd ser 15: sect II, 103–121 (1921).

WATT, F. W. "The Masks of Archibald Lampman," UNIV TOR Q 27: 169–184 (Jan. 1958).

WENDELL, W. L. "Modern School of Canadian Writers," BKMN (New York) 11: 515–526 (Aug. 1900).

[WHITESIDE, ERNESTINE R.], "Canadian Poetry and Poets, II [Lampman, Carman, and Campbell]," McMASTER U MO 8: 68–74 (Nov. 1898).

LANIGAN, George Thomas, 1846?–1886

ANON. "George T. Lanigan: Wit, Humorist and Poet," CAN BKMN 2: 42–44 (Jan. 1920).

———— "Lord Athelstan's Partner," SAT N 53: 3 (Feb. 19, 1938).

BURPEE, LAWRENCE J. "George Thomas Lanigan (1845–1886)." In his *A Little Book of Canadian Essays* (Toronto, Musson, 1909) pp 43–55.
———— "Literary Piracy," QUEEN'S Q 46: 295–303 (Autumn 1939).
WESTCOTT, ALLAN. "George Thomas Lanigan." In *Dictionary of American Biography* (New York, Scribner's, 1933) 10: 605–606.

LAUT, Agnes Christina, 1871–1936
ANON. Obituary, AM HIST R 42: 417 (Jan. 1937).
———— Obituary, WILSON LIB BUL 11: 234 (Dec. 1936).
STEVENSON, O. J. "From Fort Garry, West." In his *A People's Best* (Toronto, Musson, 1927) pp 63–70.

LAYTON, Irving, 1912–
ANON. Biographical Note, CAN AUTH & BKMN 34: 11 (Spring 1958).
———— "Three New Poets," FIRST STATEMENT vol 1 no 12: 1–4 [undated].
DUDEK, LOUIS. "Layton Now and Then," QUEEN'S Q 63: 291–293 (Summer 1956).
———— "Layton on the Carpet," DELTA no 9: 17–19 (Oct.–Dec. 1959).
LAYTON, IRVING. Foreword. In his *A Red Carpet for the Sun* (Toronto, McClelland & Stewart, 1959) pp v–viii.
MARCOTTE, GILLES. "Le Poète Irving Layton, vu d'ici," LE DEVOIR (samedi, 17 octobre, 1959) p 11.
SMITH, A. J. M. "The Recent Poetry of Irving Layton: with Reply by L. Dudek," QUEEN'S Q 62: 587–591 (Winter 1956); 63: 291–293 (Summer 1956).
WILLIAMS, WILLIAM CARLOS. "A Note on Layton." In *The Improved Binoculars* by Irving Layton (Highlands, N.C., Williams, 1956) pp 9–10.

LEACOCK, Stephen Butler, 1869–1944
ANON. "American Readers Will Miss Them," SCHOLASTIC 44: 22 (May 1, 1944).
———— Biographical Note, SCHOLASTIC 43: 14 (Jan. 24, 1944).
———— Biographical Sketch, GOLDEN BOOK 21: 115 (Feb. 1935).
———— Biographical Sketch, SCHOLASTIC 25: 7 (Jan. 12, 1935).
———— Chronicle and Comment, BKMN (London) 76: 150–151 (Feb. 1933).
———— "For the Last Time He Says: 'That'll be all for Today,' " NEWSWEEK 7: 44 (May 16, 1936).
———— "Good-Night—Forever," TIME 43: 24 (April 10, 1944).
———— "Memorial to Stephen Leacock Movement Launched in Orillia," ONT LIB R 28: 405–406 (Nov. 1944).
———— Obituary, NEWSWEEK 23: 56 (April 10, 1944).
———— Obituary, SCHOOL & SOCIETY 59: 250 (April 8, 1944).
———— "Stephen Butler Leacock, Select Bibliography . . . Contributions to the Social Sciences," CAN J ECON 10: 228–230 (May 1944).
———— "Stephen Leacock," MACL MAG 55: 11 (Aug. 11, 1942).
ALLEN, C. K. *Oh, Mr. Leacock* (London, Lane, 1925).
BARTON, BRUCE. "Billionaire of Humor," COLLIER'S 69: 9 (April 15, 1922).
BRAYBROOKE, PATRICK. [On Leacock's *My Discovery of England*]. In his *Peeps at the Mighty* (London, Drane, 1927) pp 130–146.

CALDWELL, WILLIAM. "A Visit to a Canadian Author," CAN MAG 59: 55–60 (May 1922).

CANADIAN LIBRARY WEEK COUNCIL, 1959. *Meet the Authors: A Dinner Conducted in the Style and Tradition of Stephen Leacock*, Royal York Hotel, Toronto, Thursday, April 16, 1959 (Toronto 1959). [Sponsored by the Council in association with *The Telegram*; contains programme, menu, and "Humor as I See It" by Leacock.]

CLEMENTS, C. "An Evening with Stephen Leacock," CATHOLIC WORLD 159: 236–241 (June 1944).

COLLINS, J. P. "Professor Leacock, Ph.D.: Savant and Humorist," BKMN (London) 51: 39–44 (Nov. 1916). [Also in LIVING AGE 291: 800ff (Dec 30, 1916).]

CURRY, RALPH L. Introduction to *Arcadian Adventures with the Idle Rich* by Stephen Leacock (Toronto, McClelland & Stewart, 1959) pp vii–xi. [New Canadian Library no 10.]

———— "Leacock and Benchley: An Acknowledged Literary Debt," *American Book Collector* 7: 11–15 (March 1957).

———— "Stephen Butler Leacock, A Check-List," BUL OF BIBLIOGRAPHY 22: 106–109 (Jan.–April 1958). [Supplements Lomer's *Check-List.*]

———— *Stephen Leacock: Humorist and Humanist* (Garden City, N.Y., Doubleday, 1959).

———— "The Unknown Years of Stephen Leacock," MACL MAG 72: 20–21, 45–47 (July 4, 1959); 26–27, 34 (July 18, 1959).

DAVIES, ROBERTSON. Introduction to *Literary Lapses* by Stephen Leacock (Toronto, McClelland & Stewart, 1957) pp vii–ix. [New Canadian Library no 3.]

———— "Stephen Leacock." In *Our Living Tradition*, First Series, ed. Claude T. Bissell (Toronto, University of Toronto Press, 1957) pp 128–149.

DAY, J. P. "Professor Leacock at McGill," CAN J ECON 10: 226–228 (May 1944).

DUFF, LOUIS BLAKE. *Address ... on the Occasion of the Unveiling of a Bronze Bust of Stephen Leacock ... 14th September, 1951* (Orillia, privately printed, 1951).

EDGAR, PELHAM. "Stephen Leacock," QUEEN'S Q 53: 173–184 (Summer, 1946). Reprinted in his *Across My Path*, ed. Northrop Frye (Toronto, Ryerson, 1952) pp 90–98. [Also in *Our Sense of Identity*, ed. Malcolm Ross (Toronto, Ryerson, 1954) pp 136–146.]

FEIBLEMAN, JAMES KERR. "Criticism of Modern Theories of Comedy." In his *In Praise of Comedy: A Study in its Theory and Practice* (London, Allen & Unwin, 1939) pp 123–167.

FRAYNE, TRENT. "The Erudite Jester of McGill," MACL MAG 66: 19, 37–39 (Jan. 1, 1953).

GILLISS, K. E. "Stephen Leacock as a Satirist" (Thesis, University of New Brunswick, 1957).

HIND, C. LEWIS. "Stephen Leacock." In his *More Authors and I* (New York, Dodd Mead, 1922) pp 180–185.

INNIS, HAROLD. "Stephen Butler Leacock (1869–1944)," CAN J ECON 10: 216–226 (May 1944).

L., R. T. [CHARLES A. M. VINING]. "Mr. Leacock," MACL MAG 47: 10 (Aug. 1, 1934).

LARNED, WILLIAM T. "Professor Leacock and Other Professors," NEW REPUBLIC 9: 299 (Jan. 13, 1917).

LEACOCK, STEPHEN. *The Boy I Left behind Me* (New York, Doubleday, 1946).

———— *My Memories and Miseries as a Schoolmaster* (Toronto, Upper Canada College Endowment Fund, n.d.).

LOMER, GERHARD R. *Stephen Leacock: A Check-List and Index of His Writings* (Ottawa, National Library, 1954).

LOWER, ARTHUR. "The Mariposa Belle," QUEEN'S Q 58: 220–226 (Summer 1951).

MCARTHUR, PETER. *Stephen Leacock* (Toronto, Ryerson, 1923).

MCCORD, D. "Old Magic," SAT R LIT 19: 10 (Jan. 14, 1939).

MCGILL UNIVERSITY LIBRARY SCHOOL. *A Bibliography of Stephen Butler Leacock* (Montreal, McGill Library, 1935).

MACPHAIL, ANDREW. "Stephen Leacock." *In The Yearbook of Canadian Art, 1913–* , comp. by the Arts & Letters Club of Toronto (Toronto, Dent, n.d.) pp 1–7.

MASSON, T. L. "Stephen Leacock." In his *Our American Humorists* (New York, Dodd Mead, 1931) pp 209–229.

MIKES, GEORGE. "Stephen Leacock." In his *Eight Humorists* (London, Wingate, 1954) pp 41–65.

MILFORD, BARNEY. "There's Still a Lot of Leacock in Orillia," MACL MAG 68: 18–19, 80–82 (Feb. 15, 1955).

MILLER, MARGARET J. *Seven Men of Wit* (London, Hutchinson, 1960).

MURPHY, BRUCE. "Stephen Leacock—the Greatest Living Humorist," ONT LIB R 12: 67–69 (Feb. 1928).

NIMMO, BARBARA. Preface to *Last Leaves* by Stephen Leacock (New York, Dodd Mead, 1945) pp vii–xx.

O'HAGAN, HOWARD. "Stephie," QUEEN'S Q 68: 135–146 (Spring 1961).

PACEY, DESMOND. "Leacock as a Satirist," QUEEN'S Q 58: 208–219 (Summer 1951).

PHELPS, ARTHUR L. "Stephen Leacock." In his *Canadian Writers* (Toronto, McClelland & Stewart, 1951) pp 70–76.

PRIESTLEY, J. B. Introduction to *The Bodley Head Leacock* (London, Bodley Head, 1957) pp 9–13. [Canadian edition has title *The Best of Leacock* (Toronto, McClelland & Stewart, 1957.]

ROSS, DAVID W. "Stephen Leacock, Scholar and Humorist" (Thesis, Columbia University, 1947).

ROSS, MALCOLM. Preface to *Sunshine Sketches of a Little Town* by Stephen Leacock (Toronto, McClelland & Stewart, 1960) pp ix–xvi. [New Canadian Library no 15.]

SANDWELL, B. K. "He Made Humour Almost Respectable," CAN AUTH & BKMN 23: 13–16 (Fall 1947).

———— "Here Stephen Leacock Lives and Writes," SAT N 58: 4 (Oct. 10, 1942).

———— "Leacock Recalled: How the 'Sketches' Started," SAT N 67: 7 (Aug. 23, 1952).

———— "Leacock for Canadians," SAT N 64: 1–2 (Feb. 1, 1949).

———— "Stephen Butler Leacock, 1869–1944," ROY SOC CAN PROC & TRANS 3rd ser 38: 105–106 (1944).

———— "Stephen Leacock, Worst-Dressed Writer Made Fun Respectable," SAT N 59: 17 (April 8, 1944).

SEDGEWICK, G. G. "Stephen Leacock as a Man of Letters," UNIV TOR Q 15: 17–26 (Oct. 1945).

STEVENSON, O. J. "Laughter Holding Both His Sides." In his *A People's Best* (Toronto, Musson, 1927) pp 95–100.

VINING, C. "Mr. Leacock: a Profile," MACL MAG 68: 33 (Oct. 15, 1955).

WATT, FRANK W. "Critic or Entertainer?" CAN LIT no 5: 33–42 (Summer 1960).

WATTERS, R. E. "Leacock in Limbo," CAN LIT no 3: 68–70 (Winter 1960).

———— "A Special Tang: Stephen Leacock's Canadian Humour," CAN LIT no 5: 21–32 (Summer 1960). [Also in *Canadian Anthology*, ed. C. F. Klinck and R. E. Watters, rev. ed. (Toronto, Gage, 1966) pp 540–547.]

WHEELWRIGHT, J. "Poet as Funny Man," POETRY (Chicago) 50: 210–215 (July 1937).

LEMELIN, Roger, 1919–

COLLIN, W. E. "Roger Lemelin: The Pursuit of Grandeur," QUEEN'S Q 61: 195–212 (Summer 1954).

KEATE, STUART. "The Boy from the Town Below," MACL MAG 63: 17, 26, 28 (Feb. 1, 1950).

LEMELIN, ROGER. "My First Novel," QUEEN'S Q 61: 189–194 (Summer 1954).

———— "The 'Not-so-innocent' Abroad," SAT N 65/66: 12–13, 37 (Nov. 7, 1950).

LeMOINE, Sir James McPherson, 1825–1912

ANON. Obituary, ROY SOC CAN PROC & TRANS 3rd ser 6: v–vii (1912).

McLEAN, EDITH. "Sir J. M. LeMoine," WOMEN'S CAN HIST SOC OTTAWA TRANS 4: 27–34 (1911).

MUDDIMAN, B. "Grape Festivals of Spencer Grange," CAN MAG 40: 501–511 (April 1913).

RENAULT, RAOUL. *Bibliographie de Sir James M. LeMoine* (Quebec, Brousseau, 1897).

TARDIVEL, JULES PAUL. *Borrowed and Stolen Feathers; or, A Glance through Mr. J. M. LeMoine's Latest Work, "The Chronicles of the St. Lawrence"* (Quebec, "Le Canadien," 1878).

LePAN, Douglas, 1914–

ANON. "Poet at Work," TIME (Can. ed.) 56: 17 (Sept. 11, 1950).

BROWN, E. K. Review of *The Wounded Prince*, UNIV TOR Q 18: 257–258 (April 1949).

FRYE, NORTHROP. Review of *The Net and the Sword*, UNIV TOR Q 23: 256–258 (April 1954).

LEPROHON, Rosanna Eleanor (Mullins), 1832–1879

BROTHER ADRIAN (HENRI DENEAU). "The Life and Works of Mrs. Leprohon" (Thesis, University of Montreal, 1948).

LEVINE, Norman, 1923–

LEVINE, NORMAN. "Why I am an Expatriate," CAN LIT no 5: 49–54 (Summer 1960).

LIGHTHALL, William Douw, 1857–1954

ANON. "A Tribute," CAN AUTH & BKMN 30: 30 (Summer 1954).

ELSON, JOHN MEBOURNE. "Who's Who in Canadian Literature: William Douw Lighthall," CAN BKMN 12: 151–154 (Aug. 1930).

GIBBON, JOHN MURRAY. "William Douw Lighthall," EDUC RECORD (Quebec) 59: 172–177 (July–Sept. 1943). [Also in *Leading Canadian Poets*, ed. W. P. Percival (Toronto, Ryerson, 1948) pp 107–116.]

SOMERVILLE, R. S. "Canadian Celebrities: 69, Mr. W. D. Lighthall," CAN MAG 26: 552–555 (April 1906).

SURVEYER, E. F. "William D. Lighthall, 1857–1954," ROY SOC CAN PROC & TRANS 3rd ser 49: 113–115 (1955).

LIVESAY, Dorothy (Mrs. Duncan C. McNair), 1909–

COLLIN, W. E. "Dorothy Livesay," CAN FORUM 12: 137–138, 140 (Jan. 1932). [Also in his *The White Savannahs* (Toronto, Macmillan, 1936) pp 147–173.]

CRAWLEY, ALAN. "Dorothy Livesay—an Intimate Biography," EDUC RECORD (Quebec) 61: 169–173 (July–Sept. 1945). [Also in *Leading Canadian Poets*, ed. W. P. Percival (Toronto, Ryerson, 1948) pp 117–124.]

O'DONNELL, KATHLEEN. "Dorothy Livesay" (Thesis, University of Montreal, 1959).

PACEY, DESMOND. Introduction to *Selected Poems of Dorothy Livesay 1926–1956* (Toronto, Ryerson, 1957) pp. xi–xix.

PRATT, E. J. "Dorothy Livesay," GANTS DU CIEL 11: 61–65 (printemps 1946).

SCHULTZ, GREGORY PETER. "The Periodical Poetry of A. J. M. Smith, F. R. Scott, Leo Kennedy. A. M. Klein, and Dorothy Livesay, 1925–1950" (Thesis, University of Western Ontario, 1957).

STEINBERG, M. W. "Dorothy Livesay: Poet of Affirmation," BC LIB Q 24: 9–13 (Oct. 1960).

STEPHAN, RUTH. "A Canadian Poet," POETRY (Chicago) 65: 220–222 (Jan. 1945).

WEAVER, ROBERT. "The Poetry of Dorothy Livesay," CONTEMP VERSE 26: 18–22 (Fall 1948).

LIVESAY, Mrs. Florence Hamilton (Randall), 1874–1953

WEEKES, MARY. "An Afternoon with the Livesays at Their Home in Clarkson," SAT N 60: 33 (Sept. 23, 1944).

LLOYD, Cecil Richard Francis, 1884–1938

ANON. "Who's Who in Canadian Literature: Cecil Francis Lloyd," CAN BKMN 10: 291–292 (Oct. 1928).

CLAY, CHARLES. "Bookman Profiles: C. F. Lloyd," CAN BKMN 20: 15–18 (Sept. 1938).

——— "Cecil Francis Lloyd: 1884–1938," CAN POETRY 3: 11–13 (Oct. 1938).

LLOYD, C. F. "Poet's Early Days in Canada," SAT N 53: 5 (Aug. 13, 1938).

LOCKHART, Arthur John, 1850–1926 [pseud: "Pastor Felix"]

U.K. "The Rev. Arthur J. Lockhart ('Pastor Felix')," DOM ILLUS 5: 70 (Aug. 2, 1890).

LOGAN, John Daniel, 1869–1929
 ANON. Obituary, COMMONWEAL 9: 387 (Feb. 6, 1929).
 [ELSON, J. M.] "Passing of J. D. Logan," CAN BKMN 11: 43 (Feb. 1929).

LOWER, Arthur Reginald Marsden, 1889–
 UNDERHILL, FRANK H. "A Canadian Philosopher-Historian," CAN FORUM 27: 83–84 (July 1947).

LOWRY, Malcolm, 1909–1957
 AIKEN, CONRAD. *Ushant, An Essay* (N.Y., Duell, Sloan, 1952) *passim*. [Two of the characters of this semi-autobiographical work, Hambo and Blackstone, bear evident relation to Lowry. See pages 225–226, 229, 239–240, 249–250, 288, 291–297, 322–326, 338–340, 348–361.]
 ANON. "The Fate of the Consul," TIMES LIT SUPP (London) no 3061: 693 (Oct. 28, 1960).
 BIRNEY, EARLE. "First Supplement to Malcolm Lowry Bibliography," CAN LIT no 11: 90–95 (Winter 1962).
 ———— "Glimpses into the Life of Malcolm Lowry," TAM R no 19: 35–41 (Spring 1961).
 ———— "The Unknown Poetry of Malcolm Lowry," BC LIB Q 24: 33–40 (April 1961).
 BIRNEY, EARLE and MARGERIE LOWRY. "Bibliography of Malcolm Lowry: Part I, Works by Malcolm Lowry," CAN LIT no. 8: 81–88 (Spring 1961).
 ———— "Malcolm Lowry (1909–1957) A Bibliography: Part II, Works about Malcolm Lowry," CAN LIT no 9: 80–84 (Summer 1961).
 BONNEFOI, GENEVIÈVE. "Souvenir de Quauhnahuac," LES LETTRES NOUVELLES ns 5: 94–108 (juillet–août, 1960).
 CARROY, JEAN-ROGER. "Obscur Présent, le feu . . . ," LES LETTRES NOUVELLES ns 5: 83–88 (juillet–août, 1960).
 CLARK, ELEANOR. Review of *Under the Volcano*, NATION (New York) 164: 335–336 (March 22, 1947).
 D'ASTORG, BERTRAND. Revue de *Au-dessous du Volcan*, ESPRIT 18: 702–707 (Nov. 1950).
 DEACON, W. A. Review of *Under the Volcano*, GLOBE & MAIL (March 22, 1947).
 FLINT, R. W. Review of *Under the Volcano*, KENYON R 9: 474–477 (Summer 1947).
 FOUCHET, MAX-POL. "Non se puede . . . ," LES LETTRES NOUVELLES ns 5: 21–25 (juillet–août, 1960). [Reprinted CAN LIT no 8: 25–28 (Spring 1961).]
 FRANÇILLON, CLARISSE. "Malcolm, mon ami," LES LETTRES NOUVELLES ns 5: 8–19 (juillet–août, 1960).
 ———— "Souvenirs sur Malcolm Lowry," LES LETTRES NOUVELLES 5: 588–603 (Nov. 1957).
 HAYS, H. R. Review of *Under the Volcano*, NY TIMES BK R (Feb. 23, 1947) p 5.
 HEILMAN, ROBERT B. "The Possessed Artist and the Ailing Soul," CAN LIT no 8: 7–16 (Spring 1961).
 ———— Review of *Under the Volcano*, SEWANEE R 55: 483–492 (Summer 1947).

KIRK, DOWNIE. "More than Music: Glimpses of Malcolm Lowry," CAN LIT no 8: 31–38 (Spring 1961).

LOWRY, MALCOLM. "Letters from Malcolm Lowry," CAN LIT no 8: 39–46 (Spring 1961). [Two letters from Lowry, one to Albert Erskine, the other to David Markson.]

———— "Preface to a Novel," CAN LIT no 9: 23–29 (Summer 1961). [Translation of the preface to *Au-dessous du Volcan* (Paris, Club Français du Livre, 1949; reprinted Paris, Corrêa, 1960). The preface was prepared in French by Clarisse Françillon from Lowry's English notes (since lost) while she was working on the French translation of the novel. This preface is here translated into English by George Woodcock.]

McCONNELL, WILLIAM. "Recollections of Malcolm Lowry," CAN LIT no 6: 24–31 (Autumn 1960).

McCORMICK, JOHN. Discussion of *Under the Volcano* in his *Catastrophe and Imagination: An Interpretation of the Recent English and American Novel* (New York and Toronto, Longmans, 1957) pp 65–66, 85–89.

MAYBERRY, GEORGE. Review of *Under the Volcano*, NEW REPUBLIC 116: 35–36 (Feb. 24, 1947).

MYRER, ANTON. "Le monde au-dessous du volcan," LES LETTRES NOU-VELLES ns 5: 59–66 (juillet–août, 1960).

NADEAU, MAURICE. "Lowry," LES LETTRES NOUVELLES ns 5: 3–7 (juillet–août, 1960).

SANDWELL, B. K. Review of *Under the Volcano*, SAT N 63: 15 (Nov. 1, 1947).

SCHORER, MARK. Review of *Under the Volcano*, NY HERALD–TRIB BK R (Feb. 23, 1947) p 2.

SIMPSON, R. G. Review of *Under the Volcano*, NORTHERN R 1: 37–38 (Aug.–Sept. 1947).

SPRIEL, STEPHEN. "Le Cryptogramme Lowry," LES LETTRES NOU-VELLES ns 5: 67–81 (juillet–août, 1960).

WOODBURN, JOHN. Review of *Under the Volcano*, SAT R LIT 30: 9–10 (Feb. 22, 1947).

WOODCOCK, GEORGE. "French Thoughts on Lowry," CAN LIT no 6: 79–80 (Autumn 1960).

———— "Malcolm Lowry as Novelist," BC LIB Q 24: 25–32 (April 1961).

———— "Malcolm Lowry's 'Under the Volcano,'" MOD FICTION STUDIES 4: 151–156 (Summer 1948).

———— "On the Day of the Dead," NORTHERN R 6: 15–21 (Dec.–Jan. 1953–1954).

———— "Under Seymour Mountain," CAN LIT no 8: 3–6 (Spring 1961).

McARTHUR, Peter, 1866–1924

DEACON, WILLIAM ARTHUR. "The Affability of Peter McArthur," CAN BKMN 3: 43 (Sept. 1921).

———— *Peter McArthur* (Toronto, Ryerson, 1923).

HATHAWAY, R. H. "Vale! Peter McArthur," CAN BKMN 7: 8, 12 (Jan. 1925).

STEVENSON, O. J. "The Greatest Good." In his *A People's Best* (Toronto, Musson, 1927) pp 201–210.

WATT, FRANK W. "Peter McArthur and the Agrarian Myth," QUEEN'S Q 67: 245–257 (Summer 1960).

MACBETH, Mrs. Madge Hamilton (Lyons), 1878–1965 [pseuds: "Gilbert Knox," "W. S. Dill"]
   MACBETH, MADGE HAMILTON. *Boulevard Career* (Toronto, Kingswood House, 1957).
   ———— "My First Book," CAN AUTH & BKMN 29: 3–4 (Autumn 1953).
   ———— *Over My Shoulder* (Toronto, Ryerson, 1953).
   PRICE, ELIZABETH BAILEY. "Madge Macbeth Won Success as Writer by 'Cruel, Heart-Breaking Struggle,'" MACL MAG 38: 50–51 (Jan. 1, 1924).

MACBETH, Roderick George, 1858–1934
   CHALMERS, D. A. "A Western Canadian Author and His Latest Work," BC MO 13: 23–26 (July 1918).

McCAIG, Donald, 1832–1905
   BOYLE, DAVID. "Milestones, Moods and Memories," CAN MAG 2: 493–496 (March 1894).

McCLUNG, Mrs. Nellie Letitia (Mooney), 1873–1951
   ANON. "Nellie McClung," CAN AUTH & BKMN 27: 34 (1951).
   ———— "A Page about People," MACL MAG 40: 18 (May 15, 1927).
   ARMITAGE, MAY L. "Mrs. Nellie McClung," MACL MAG 28: 37–38 (July 1915).
   EGGLESTON, WILFRID. "Nellie McClung: Crusader," CAN AUTH & BKMN 19: 21 (Sept. 1943).
   HENRY, LORNE J. "Nellie L. McClung (1873–)." In his *Canadians: A Book of Biographies* (Toronto, Longman's, 1950) pp 91–97.
   JAQUES, E. "Years between," COUNTRY GUIDE 61: 42–43 (Dec. 1942).
   LAMBERT, NORMAN P. "A Joan of the West," CAN MAG 46: 265–268 (Jan. 1916).
   McCLUNG, NELLIE L. *Clearing in the West: My Own Story* (Toronto, Allen, 1935).
   ———— "Nellie McClung in Hollywood," CHATELAINE 4: 16 (Sept. 1932).
   ———— *The Stream Runs Fast* (Toronto, Allen, 1945).
   McCOURT, EDWARD A. "Nellie L. McClung." In his *The Canadian West in Fiction* (Toronto, Ryerson, 1949) pp 71–76.
   STRANGE, K. "Nellie McClung Celebrates Her Golden Wedding Jubilee in B.C.," SAT N 62: 37 (Sept. 14, 1946).
   ZIEMAN, MARGARET K. "Nellie was a Lady Terror," MACL MAG 66: 20–21, 62–66 (Oct. 1, 1953).

MacCOLL, Evan, 1808–1898
   MACKENZIE, ALEXANDER. "A Biographical Sketch." In *Poems and Songs* by Evan MacColl, 2nd ed. (Kingston, British Whig, 1888) pp 9–24.

McCRAE, John, 1872–1918
   BYERLY, ALPHEUS E. *The McCraes of Guelph* (Elora, Ont., "Express," 1932).
   GORDON, W. "On English Poetry of the War," QUEEN'S Q 27: 62–84 (July–Sept. 1919).

MacBeth, Rev. R. G. "The McCraes of Guelph," BC MO 15: 13 (Jan. 1920).

MacNaughton, John. "In Memoriam Lieut.-Col. John McCrae," UNIV MAG (Montreal) 17: 235–246 (April 1918).

Macphail, Sir Andrew. "John McCrae: An Essay in Character." In *In Flanders Fields* by John McCrae (Toronto, Ryerson, 1919) pp 49–141.

Rhodenizer, V. B. "In Flander's Fields: Poet Psychology," CAN BKMN 5: 263 (Oct. 1923).

Stevenson, O. J. "When We Save We Lose." In his *A People's Best* (Toronto, Musson, 1927) pp 13–20.

Wharton, Lewis and Lorne Pierce. "Who's Who in Canadian Literature: John McCrae," CAN BKMN 8: 237–240 (Aug. 1926).

McCULLOCH, Thomas, 1776–1843

Frye, H. Northrop. Introduction to *The Stepsure Letters* by Thomas McCulloch (Toronto, McClelland & Stewart, 1960) pp iii–ix. [New Canadian Library no 16.]

Harvey, D. C. "Thomas McCulloch." In *Canadian Portraits*, ed. R. G. Riddell (Toronto, Oxford, 1940) pp 22–28.

Irving, John A. "The Achievement of Thomas McCulloch." In *The Stepsure Letters* by Thomas McCulloch (Toronto, McClelland & Stewart, 1960) pp 150–156. [New Canadian Library no 16.]

Lochhead, Douglas G. "A Bibliographical Note." In *The Stepsure Letters* by Thomas McCulloch (Toronto, McClelland & Stewart, 1960) pp 156–159. [New Canadian Library no 16.]

McCulloch, William. *The Life of Thomas McCulloch* (Truro, N.S., the Albion, 1920).

MacIntosh, F. C. "Some Nova Scotian Scientists," DAL R 10: 199–213 (July 1930).

McCULLY, Laura Elizabeth, 1886–1924

Hassard, Albert. "Laura McCully: Poet," CAN BKMN 6: 191–192 (Sept. 1924).

MACDONALD, James Edward Hervey, 1874–1932

Buchanan, D. W. "J. E. H. Macdonald—Painter of the Forest," CAN GEOG J 33: 148–149 (Sept. 1946).

Duval, P. "Montreal Show Honors a Great Canadian Painter," SAT N 63: 2 (Dec. 13, 1947).

Hunter, Edmund R. *J. E. H. Macdonald: A Biography and Catalogue of His Work* (Toronto, Ryerson, 1940).

Jackson, A. Y. "J. E. H. Macdonald," CAN FORUM 13: 136–139 (Jan. 1933).

Mulligan, M. A. "J. E. H. Macdonald (1873–1932)," CAN COMMENT 6: 27 (Nov. 1937).

Pierce, Lorne. *A Postscript of J. E. H. Macdonald* (Toronto, Ryerson, 1940).

Robson, Albert Henry. *J. E. H. Macdonald* (Toronto, Ryerson, 1937).

MACDONALD, Mrs. Jane Elizabeth Gostwycke (Roberts), 1864–1922

de Mille, A. B. "Canadian Celebrities: XVI, The Roberts Family," CAN MAG 15: 426–430 (Sept. 1900).

Roberts, Lloyd. *The Book of Roberts* (Toronto, Ryerson, 1923).

MacDONALD, John James, 1849–   [pseud: James MacRae]
  DEACON, W. A. "James MacRae: The Man from Glengarry." In his *The Four Jameses* (Ottawa, Graphic, 1927) pp 157–177.

MACDONALD, Mrs. Lucy Maud (Montgomery) 1874–1942
  ANON. Obituary, CURRENT BIOG (1942).
  ———— Obituary, PUB WKLY 141: 1675 (May 2, 1942).
  ———— Obituary, WILSON LIB BUL 16: 788 (June 1942).
  MONTGOMERY, LUCY MAUD. *The Green Gables Letters from L. M. Montgomery to Ephraim Weber, 1905–1909*, ed. Wilfrid Eggleston (Toronto, Ryerson, 1960).
  PHELPS, ARTHUR L. "L. M. Montgomery." In his *Canadian Writers* (Toronto, McClelland & Stewart, 1951) pp 85–93.
  RHODENIZER, V. B. "Who's Who in Canadian Literature: L. M. Montgomery," CAN BKMN 9: 227–228 (Aug. 1927).
  RIDLEY, HILDA M. *The Story of L. M. Montgomery* (Toronto, Ryerson, 1956).
  SCLANDERS, IAN. "Lucy of Green Gables," MACL MAG 64: 12–13, 33–36 Dec. 15, 1951).
  WEBER, E. "L. M. Montgomery as a Letter Writer," DAL R 22: 300–310 (Oct. 1942).
  ———— "L. M. Montgomery's 'Anne,'" Bibliog. DAL R 24: 64–73 (April 1944).

MACDONALD, Wilson Pugsley, 1880–1967
  ANON. Biographical Note, CAN AUTH & BKMN 34: 13 (Spring 1958).
  ———— "Poems of Wilson Macdonald," CAN AV 11: 10 (Dec. 1938).
  FRASER, A. ERMATINGER. "Who's Who in Canadian Literature: Wilson Macdonald," CAN BKMN 9: 3–6 (Jan. 1927).
  HUGHES, J. M. "Wilson Macdonald: A Sketch of Personality," ACTA VIC 55: 9–14 (Feb.–March 1931).
  KNISTER, RAYMOND. "A Poet in Arms for Poetry," CAN MAG 68: 28, 38–39 (Oct. 1927).
  ———— "Wilson Macdonald," WILLISON'S MO 2: 188–189 (Oct. 1926).
  MACDONALD, WILSON. "My First Book," CAN AUTH & BKMN 29: 5 (Summer 1953).
  MACKAY, L. A. "Wilson Macdonald," CAN FORUM 13: 262–263 (April 1933). [Discussion: 13: 357–358 (June 1933).]
  MONTGOMERY, M. JOAN [Joan Roberts]. "Wilson Macdonald," EDUC RECORD (Quebec) 59: 35–40 (Jan.–March 1943). [Also in *Leading Canadian Poets*, ed. W. P. Percival (Toronto, Ryerson, 1948) pp 125–134.]
  ORR, M. "Poet of Brotherhood," CAN BKMN 18: 10 (July 1936).
  QUINLAN, ANNA. "A Survey of Wilson MacDonald" (Thesis, Ottawa University, 1936).
  RIMMER, T. D. "A Canadian Genius," CAN BKMN 8: 365–367 (Dec. 1926).

McDOUGALL, Alexander, 1804–1855
  CHISHOLM, SIR JOSEPH. "Hon. Alexander McDougall," DAL R 15: 293–314 (Oct. 1935).

McEVOY, Bernard, 1842–1932
STEVENSON, LIONEL. "Verses for My Friends," BC MO 23: 9–10 (Aug. 1924).

McFARLANE, Charles Leslie, 1902–
MAHAFFY, R. U. "Verve and Versatility," SAT N 66: 25 (Aug. 14, 1951).
MOORE, H. N. "Leslie McFarlane," MACL MAG 53: 2 (March 15, 1940).

McGEE, Thomas D'Arcy, 1825–1868
ANON. "The Last Days of McGee," WESTERN HOME MO 31: 19, 56 (July 1930).
BRADY, ALEXANDER. *Thomas D'Arcy McGee* (Toronto, Macmillan, 1925).
CLARKE, HENRY J. *A Short Sketch of the Life of the Hon. D'Arcy McGee* (Montreal, Lovell, 1868).
CONNOLLY, REV. T. L. *Funeral Oration on the Late Hon. Thomas D'Arcy McGee* ... (Halifax, Compton, 1868).
CROSS, ETHELBERT F. H. "An Exile from Erin." In his *Fire and Frost* (Toronto, Bryant, 1898) pp 78–88.
FRENCH, H. J. O. *The Life of the Hon. D'Arcy McGee* (Montreal, 1868). [Pamphlet.]
HARVEY, DANIEL COBB. *Thomas D'Arcy McGee, the Prophet of Canadian Nationality: A Popular Lecture* ... (Winnipeg, University of Manitoba, 1923).
———— "The Centenary of D'Arcy McGee," DAL R 5: 1–10 (April 1925).
HASSARD, A. R. "Great Canadian Orators: I, D'Arcy McGee," CAN MAG 53: 263–269 (Aug. 1919).
HENDERSON, JOHN. "Thomas D'Arcy McGee," In his *Great Men of Canada* (Toronto, Southam, 1928) pp 205–218.
KEEP, G. R. C. "D'Arcy McGee and Montreal," CULTURE 12: 16–28 (mars 1951).
McGIBBON, ROBERT D. *Thomas D'Arcy McGee: An Address* ... *before the St. Patrick's Society of Sherbrooke* ... *March 17th, 1884* (Montreal, Dawson Bros., 1884).
MARKEY, JOHN. "Thomas D'Arcy McGee: Poet and Patriot," CAN MAG 46: 67–72 (Nov. 1915).
O'DONNELL, KATHLEEN. "Thomas D'Arcy McGee's Irish and Canadian Ballads" (Thesis, University of Western Ontario, 1956).
O'LEARY, M. GRATTAN. "Observing the First Centenary of D'Arcy McGee," MACL MAG 38: 21, 50, 56 (April 1, 1925)
O'NEILL, K. "Thomas D'Arcy McGee, Statesman, Journalist, Poet," CATHOLIC WORLD 130: 681–686 (March 1930).
PHELAN, JOSEPHINE. *The Ardent Exile: The Life and Times of Thos. D'Arcy McGee* (Toronto, Macmillan, 1951).
SADLIER, MARY ANNE. Biographical Sketch and Introduction to *The Poems of Thomas D'Arcy McGee* (New York, D. & J. Sadlier, 1869) pp 15–58.
SISTER MARY LOUISE. "Thomas D'Arcy McGee as a Man of Letters" (Thesis, University of New Brunswick, 1960).
SKELTON, ISABEL. *The Life of Thomas D'Arcy McGee* (Gardenvale, Que., Garden City Press, 1925).
SPAIGHT, GEORGE. *Trial of Patrick J. Whelan for the Murder of the Hon. D'Arcy McGee* ... (Ottawa, Desbarats, 1868).

TAYLOR, FENNINGS. "Hon. D'Arcy McGee." In *Portraits of British North Americans*, ed. W. Notman (Montreal, Notman, 1865) vol 2, pp 1–28.
—— *The Hon. D'Arcy McGee: A Sketch of His Life and Death*, new ed., rev. and enl. (Montreal, Lovell, 1868).

MacGEORGE, Robert Jackson, 1811?–1884
TALMAN, J. J. "Three Scottish-Canadian Poets [MacGeorge, Menzies, McQueen]," CAN HIST R 28: 166–177 (June 1947).

MacGILLIVRAY, Carrie Holmes, –1949
DUMBRILLE, DOROTHY. "Breath of Yesterday," CAN AUTH & BKMN 25: 19–20 (Summer 1949).

MACHAR, Agnes Maule, 1837–1927 [pseud: "Fidelis"]
CUMBERLAND, R. W. "Agnes Maule Machar," QUEEN'S Q 34: 331–339 (Jan. 1927).
—— "Agnes Maule Machar," WILLISON'S MO 3: 34–37 (June 1927).
GUILD, LEMAN A. "Canadian Celebrities: 73, Agnes Maule Machar (Fidelis)," CAN MAG 27: 499–501 (Oct. 1906).
MacCALLUM, F. L. "Agnes Maule Machar," CAN MAG 62: 354–356 (March 1924).

MACHRAY, Robert, 1831–1904
COOMBES, G. FREDERICK. "Illustrated Interviews: XI, Most Rev. Archbishop Machray," WESTMINSTER (Vancouver) n.s. 4: 1–8 (Jan. 1904).
MACHRAY, ROBERT. *Life of Robert Machray . . . Archbishop of Rupert's Land . . . by his Nephew . . .* (London, Macmillan, 1909).
MUNRO, B. "A Great Pioneer," QUEEN'S Q 46: 176–184 (Summer 1939).

McILWRAITH, Jean Newton, 1859–1938
MacMURCHY, MARJORY. "Canadian Celebrities: XXIV, Miss Jean N. McIlwraith," CAN MAG 17: 131–134 (June 1901).
WILSON, ELIZABETH. "Beloved Friend," SAT N 54: 28 (Dec. 17, 1938).

MacINNES, Thomas Robert Edward, 1867–1951
DEACON, WILLIAM ARTHUR. "Tom MacInnes," EDUC RECORD (Quebec) 63: 161–166 (July–Sept. 1947). [Also in *Leading Canadian Poets*, ed. W. P. Percival (Toronto, Ryerson, 1948) pp 135–144.]
PACEY, DESMOND. "Service and MacInnes," NORTHERN R 4: 12–17 (Feb.–March 1951).
POUND, A. M. "Who's Who in Canadian Literature: Tom MacInnes," CAN BKMN 8: 363–364 (Dec. 1926).
PROUTY, W. H. "A Biographical and Critical Study of Tom MacInnes" (Thesis, University of New Brunswick, 1956).

McINTYRE, James, 1827–1906
DEACON, W. A. "James McIntyre (1827–1906)." In *Canadian Portraits*, ed. R. G. Riddell (Toronto, Oxford, 1940) pp 124–130.
—— "James McIntyre: The Cheese Poet." In his *The Four Jameses* (Ottawa, Graphic, 1927) pp 45–87.

MacKAY, Isabel Ecclestone (MacPherson), 1875–1928
DUDEK, LOUIS. "A Note on Isabel Ecclestone MacKay," FIRST STATEMENT vol 1 no 15: 3–4 [undated].

MacKay, Isabel Ecclestone. [Autobiographical Note], CAN MAG 50: 531–532 (April 1918).

Patterson, Myrtle. "Who's Who in Canadian Literature: Isabel Ecclestone MacKay," CAN BKMN 9: 371–372 (Dec. 1927).

MACKENZIE, Sir Alexander, 1764–1820

Burpee, Lawrence J. "Alexander Mackenzie Reaches the Arctic Coast." In his *Search for the Western Sea* (Toronto, Musson, 1908) [rev. ed. 1935] pp 415–471.

Cameron, M. M. "Essai sur Mackenzie de Chateaubriand," CANADIEN FRANÇAIS 28: 497–511 (Jan. 1941).

Dillon, R. H. "Alexander Mackenzie's Letter," BC HIST Q 16: 209–210 (July–Oct. 1952).

Fleming, R. H. 'The Origin of 'Sir Alexander Mackenzie and Company,' " CAN HIST R 9: 137–147 (June 1928).

Godsell, P. H. "Cradle of Exploration," CAN MAG 80: 12ff (Oct. 1933).

Gordon, Charlotte. "Sir Alexander Mackenzie," CAN FORUM 7: 361–362 (Sept. 1927).

Macdonald, Adrian. "Sir Alexander Mackenzie." In his *Canadian Portraits* (Toronto, Ryerson, 1925) pp 18–36.

Montgomery, F. "Alexander Mackenzie's Literary Assistant," CAN HIST R 18: 301–304 (Sept. 1937).

Parker, Elizabeth. "Early Explorers of the West," CAN ALPINE J 29: 20–30 (1944–1945).

Plaskett, J. S. "Astronomy of the Explorers," BC HIST Q 4: 63–78 (April 1940).

Sage, W. N. *Sir Alexander Mackenzie and His Influence on the History of the North West* (Kingston, Queen's University, 1922). [Department of History and Political and Economic Science, Bul. no 43.]

Swannell, F. C. "On Mackenzie's Trail," BEAVER 289: 9–14 (Summer 1958).

Wade, Mark S. *Mackenzie of Canada* (London, Blackwood, 1927).

Wallace, William S. *The Pedlars from Quebec* ... (Toronto, Ryerson, 1954).

Woollacott, Arthur Philip. *Mackenzie and His Voyageurs* (Toronto, Dent, 1927).

Wrong, Humphrey Hume. *Sir Alexander Mackenzie, Explorer and Fur-Trader* (Toronto, Macmillan, 1927).

Zillmer, R. T. "In the Footsteps of Mackenzie," CAN ALP J 26: 111–126 (Jan. 1938).

MACKENZIE, William Lyon, 1795–1861

Dent, John C. *The Story of the Upper Canadian Rebellion* . . . (Toronto, Robinson, 1885) 2 vols.

Fraser, Blair. "The Furious Rebel of Muddy York," MACL MAG 61: 16–17, 24–31 (July 1, 1948).

Hathaway, E. J. "William Lyon Mackenzie in Toronto," CAN MAG 43: 131–141 (June 1914).

Kilbourn, William. *The Firebrand: William Lyon Mackenzie and the Rebellion in Upper Canada* (Toronto, Clarke Irwin, 1956).

King, John. *The Other Side of the "Story": Being Some Reviews of Mr.*

J. C. Dent's . . . "Story of the Upper Canadian Rebellion" . . . (Toronto, Murray, 1886).

LINDSEY, CHARLES. *The Life and Times of Wm. Lyon Mackenzie* (Toronto, Randall, 1862). [Later ed. G. G. S. Lindsey, with additions, in "Makers of Canada" series (Toronto, Morang, 1908).]

SMITH, WILLIAM. *Political Leaders of Upper Canada* (Toronto, Nelson, 1931).

WALLACE, WILLIAM S. *The Family Compact* . . . (Toronto, Glasgow Brook, 1915).

YEIGH, FRANK. "Some Reminders of William Lyon Mackenzie," CAN MAG 19: 195–203 (July 1902).

McKISHNIE, Archibald P., 1875–1946

FORTH, GERTRUDE E. "Who's Who in Canadian Literature: Archie P. McKishnie," CAN BKMN 10: 41–42 (Feb. 1928).

McLACHLAN, Alexander, 1818–1896

BEGG, REV. W. P. "Alexander McLachlan's Poems and Ballads," ROSE-BEL CAN MO 12: 355–362 (Oct. 1877).

BURTON, JEAN. "Alexander McLachlan—the Burns of Canada," WILLISON'S MO 3: 268–269 (Dec. 1927).

DEWART, EDWARD H. "Introductory Essay." In *The Poetical Works of Alexander McLachlan* (Toronto, Briggs, 1900) pp 9–15.

DUFF, JAMES. "Alexander McLachlan," QUEEN'S Q 8: 132–144 (Oct. 1900).

[HAMILTON, ALEX.?] "Biographical Sketch." In *The Poetical Works of Alexander McLachlan* (Toronto, Briggs, 1900) pp 17–28.

McCAIG, D. "Alexander McLachlan," CAN MAG 8: 520–523 (Nov. 1897).

MACLEAN, John, 1851–1928

K., W. "Who's Who in Canadian Literature: John Maclean," CAN BKMN 8: 269–270 (Sept. 1926).

WATSON, ROBERT. "Dr. John Maclean as an Author," CAN BKMN 10: 101–102 (April 1928).

McLELLAN, Mrs. Joyce Anne (Marriott) 1913–

COLLIN, E. "Drought on the Prairies," POETRY (Chicago) 58: 53–57 (April 1941).

DE BRUYN, JAN. "Anne Marriott, Poet of Joy," BC LIB Q 22: 23–29 (Jan. 1959).

MacLENNAN, (John) Hugh, 1907–

ANON. "New Writers," PUB WKLY 140: 1843 (Nov. 8, 1941).

BALLANTYNE, M. G. "Theology and the Man on the Street: a Catholic Commentary on 'Cross Country,' " CULTURE 10: 392–396 (déc. 1949).

DAVIES, ROBERTSON. "MacLennan's Rising Sun," SAT N 74: 29–31 (March 28, 1959).

DUNCAN, DOROTHY. "My Author Husband," MACL MAG 58: 7, 36, 38, 40 (Aug. 15, 1945).

GOETSCH, PAUL. *Das Romanwerk Hugh MacLennans; eine Studie zum literarischen Nationalismus in Kanada* (Hamburg, Gruyter, 1961).

MACLENNAN, HUGH. "My First Book," CAN AUTH & BKMN 28: 3–4 (1952).

———— "The Story of a Novel," CAN LIT no 3: 35–39 (Winter 1960).

McPHERSON, HUGO. Introduction to *Barometer Rising* by Hugh MacLennan (Toronto, McClelland & Stewart, 1958) pp ix–xv. [New Canadian Library no 8.]

———— "The Novels of Hugh MacLennan," QUEEN'S Q 60: 186–198 (1953–1954).

PHELPS, ARTHUR L. "Hugh MacLennan." In his *Canadian Writers* (Toronto, McClelland & Stewart, 1951) pp 77–84.

VALLERAND, JEAN. "Hugh MacLennan ou la tendresse dans la littérature canadienne," LE DEVOIR (samedi, 28 novembre, 1959) p 11.

WALBRIDGE, E. F. "Hugh MacLennan," WILSON LIB BUL 20: 700 (June 1946).

WATTERS, R. E. "Hugh MacLennan and the Canadian Character." In *As a Man Thinks...*, ed. E. Morrison and W. Robbins (Toronto, Gage, 1953) pp 228–243.

WOODCOCK, GEORGE. "Hugh MacLennan," NORTHERN R 3: 2–10 (April–May 1950).

McLENNAN, William, 1856–1904

BRODIE, ALLAN DOUGLAS. "Canadian Short-Story Writers," CAN MAG 4: 334–344 (Feb. 1895).

V., E. Q. "Canadian Celebrities: V, William McLennan," CAN MAG 13: 251–253 (July 1899).

MacMECHAN, Archibald McKellar, 1862–1933

FRASER, A. L. "An Appreciation," CAN BKMN 15: 107 (Aug. 1933).

GORDON, W. "Archibald MacMechan," QUEEN'S Q 40: 635–640 (Nov. 1933).

SEDGEWICK, G. G. "A.M.," DAL R 13: 451–458 (Jan. 1934). [Also in *Our Sense of Identity*, ed. Malcolm Ross (Toronto, Ryerson, 1954) pp 147–155.]

STEWART, HERBERT L. "Archibald MacMechan," EDUC RECORD (Quebec) 60: 29–31 (Jan.–March 1944). [Also in *Leading Canadian Poets*, ed. W. P. Percival (Toronto, Ryerson, 1948) pp 145–151.]

MacMURCHY, Marjory. *See* WILLISON, Lady Marjory (MacMurchy)

McNAIR, Mrs. Dorothy (Livesay). *See* LIVESAY, Dorothy

MacNAUGHTON, John, 1858–1943

CALVIN, D. D. "John," QUEEN'S Q 40: 357–364 (Aug. 1933).

WILSON, R. A. "John MacNaughton: Humanist," QUEEN'S Q 54: 84–89 (Spring 1947).

WOODHEAD, W. D. "John MacNaughton," QUEEN'S Q 50: 165–173 (Summer 1943).

MACPHAIL, Sir Andrew, 1864–1938

ANON. Obituary, SAT N 53: 1 (Oct. 1, 1938).

EDGAR, PELHAM. "Sir Andrew Macphail," QUEEN'S Q 54: 8–22 (Feb. 1947).

———— "Sir Andrew Macphail: An Appraisal," CAN AUTH 16: 7, 21 (Autumn 1938).

———— "Sir Andrew Macphail," Obituary, ROY SOC CAN PROC & TRANS 3rd ser 33: 147–149 (1939).

LEACOCK, STEPHEN. "Andrew Macphail," QUEEN'S Q 45: 445–452 (Nov. 1938).

STEVENSON, J. A. "Sir Andrew Macphail," CAN DEFENCE Q 16: 206–210 (Jan. 1939).

MACPHERSON, Jay, 1931–

REANEY, JAMES. "The Third Eye: Jay Macpherson's 'The Boatman,' " CAN LIT no 3: 23–34 (Winter 1960). [Also in *Canadian Anthology*, ed. C. F. Klinck and R. E. Watters, rev. ed. (Toronto, Gage, 1966) pp 534–540.]

McPHERSON, John, 1817–1845

HARVEY, D. C. "Centenary of John McPherson," DAL R 25: 343–353 (Oct. 1945).

MacQUEEN, Thomas, 1803–1861

HAYDON, ANDREW. "Thomas MacQueen: Poet, Journalist, Politician." In his *Pioneer Sketches in the District of Bathurst* (Toronto, Ryerson, 1925) vol 1, pp 237–285.

TALMAN, J. J. "Three Scottish-Canadian Newspaper-Editor Poets [MacQueen, Menzies, MacGeorge]," CAN HIST R 28: 166–177 (June 1947).

MacRAE, James [pseud.]. *See* MacDONALD, John James

MAIR, Charles, 1838–1927

CHARLESWORTH, HECTOR W. "Patriots and the Poets of the West." In his *More Candid Chronicles* (Toronto, Macmillan, 1928) pp 18–36.

COPP, E. A. "Canada First Party (Charles Mair)" (Thesis, Queen's University, 1926).

DENISON, GEORGE TAYLOR. *The Struggle for Imperial Unity: Recollections and Experiences* (London, Macmillan, 1909).

DOOLEY, D. J., and F. N. SHRIVE. "Voice of the Burdash," CAN FORUM 37: 80–82 (July 1957).

FRASER, A. E. "A Poet Pioneer of Canada," QUEEN'S Q 35: 440–450 (May 1928).

GARVIN, J. W. "Who's Who in Canadian Literature: Charles Mair," CAN BKMN 8: 335–337 (Nov. 1926).

MACBETH, R. G. "A Tribute to Charles Mair," CAN BKMN 7: 45 (March 1925).

MACKAY, I. E. "Charles Mair, Poet and Patriot," CAN MAG 59: 162–165 (June 1922).

MORGAN, H. R. "Dr. Charles Mair," WILLISON'S MO 2: 110–111 (Aug. 1926).

NORWOOD, ROBERT. "Charles Mair." In *Leading Canadian Poets*, ed. W. P. Percival (Toronto, Ryerson, 1948) pp 152–157.

WHEELER, CHRISTINE GORDON. "The Bard of Bathurst," CAN BKMN 18: 10–11 (Jan. 25, 1936).

MANDEL, Eli W., 1922–

McMASTER, R. D. "The Unexplained Interior: A Study of E. W. Mandel's *Fuseli Poems*," DAL R 40: 392–396 (Fall 1960).

MANION, Robert James, 1881–1943
O'LEARY, M. GRATTAN. "Cabinet Portraits," MACL MAG 43: 10, 50 (Oct. 1, 1930).
——— "Doctor Manion," MACL MAG 51: 9, 36 (Aug. 15, 1938).

MARQUIS, Thomas Guthrie, 1864–1936
ANON. "Shepherd of Canadian Poets," CAN BKMN 17: 106 (Sept. 1935).
SWIFT, S. C. "Thomas Guthrie Marquis," CAN BKMN 18: 2, 6 (May 1936).

MARRIOTT, Anne. See McLELLAN, Mrs. Joyce Anne (Marriott)

MARSHALL, William Edward, 1859–1923
BOURINOT, ARTHUR S. "William E. Marshall: His Verse and Some Letters," DAL R 30: 196–204 (July 1950). [Also in his *Five Canadian Poets* (Montreal, Quality Press, 1956) pp 15–21.]
MACPHAIL, SIR ANDREW. "In Memoriam: William E. Marshall," DAL R 3: 152–154 (July 1923).

MARTIN, George, 1822–1900
ANON. "George Martin, Esq., Author of *Marguerite; or, The Isle Demons and Other Poems*," DOM ILLUS 5: 166 (Sept. 6, 1890).

MASSEY, Vincent, 1887–1967
ANON. [Biography]. In *Current Biography 1951* (New York, H. W. Wilson, 1952) pp 412–414.
BERTON, PIERRE. "There'll Always be a Massey," MACL MAG 64: 7–9, 71–77 (Oct. 15, 1951).
L., R. T. "Mr. Massey," MACL MAG 46: 18 (Aug. 15, 1933).
McGILLICUDDY, OWEN E. "A Massey Goes to Washington," MACL MAG 40: 13, 40, 42 (Feb. 1, 1927).

MATHER, Barry, 1909–
FRANCIS, ROBERT. "Barry Mather: The Poor Man's Pepys," SAT N 67: 12 (Sept. 6, 1952).

MAYSE, Arthur William Caswell, 1912–
ANON. "Arthur Mayse," MACL MAG 53: 2 (Feb. 15, 1940).

MENZIES, George, 1796?–1847
TALMAN, J. J. "Three Scottish-Canadian Newspaper-Editor Poets [MacQueen, Menzies, MacGeorge]," CAN HIST R 28: 166–177 (June 1947).

MIDDLETON, Jesse Edgar, 1872–1960
ANON. "Bookman Profiles," CAN BKMN 20: 23–26 (Dec. 1938).

MILLER, Peter, 1921–
MULLINS, S. G. "The Poetry of Peter Miller," CULTURE 21: 398–408 (déc. 1960).

MINER, Jack (John Thomas), 1865–1944
ANON. "How Jack Miner Started His Bird Sanctuary," FOR & OUTDOORS 51: 17 (April 1955).
BAKER, A. B. "Facts on the Balance of Nature," FOR & OUTDOORS 51: 23–24 (Oct. 1955).
BODSWORTH, FRED. "Billy Sunday of the Birds," MACL MAG 65: 12–13, 56–60 (May 1, 1952).

CORSAN, GEORGE H. "Goosie, Goosie, Gander!—At Home at Miner's," MACL MAG 39: 18–19 (March 1, 1926).

RANKIN, NORMAN S. "Jack Miner, Philosopher and Bird-Lover," CAN MAG 59: 479–486 (Oct. 1922).

TIGRETT, J. B. "Duck's Best Friend is Jack Miner," SAT EVE POST 216: 26–27 (March 18, 1944).

WADE, M. "Jack Miner's Philosophy," FOR & OUTDOORS 44: 18–21 (April 1948).

MITCHELL, William Ormond, 1914–

ANON. Biographical Note, MACL MAG 61: 2 (July 15, 1948).

McCOURT, EDWARD A. "William O. Mitchell." In his *The Canadian West in Fiction* (Toronto, Ryerson, 1949) pp 99–102.

PHELPS, ARTHUR L. "W. O. Mitchell." In his *Canadian Writers* (Toronto, McClelland & Stewart, 1951) pp 94–102.

MOFFATT, Mrs. Gertrude (MacGregor), 1884–1923

M., J. "Who's Who in Canadian Literature: Gertrude MacGregor Moffatt," CAN BKMN 10: 163–164 (June 1928).

MONTGOMERY, L. M. *See* Macdonald, Mrs. Lucy Maud (Montgomery)

MOODIE, Mrs. Susanna (Strickland), 1803–1885

DAVIES, ROBERTSON. *At My Heart's Core* (Toronto, Clarke Irwin, 1950). [A dramatized character study.]

HUME, BLANCHE. "Grandmothers of Canadian Literature," WILLISON'S MO 3: 474–477 (May 1928).

——— *The Strickland Sisters* (Toronto, Ryerson, 1928).

KLINCK, CARL, F. "A Gentlewoman of Upper Canada," CAN LIT no 1: 75–77 (Summer 1959).

McCOURT, E. A. "Roughing It with the Moodies," QUEEN'S Q 52: 77–89 (Feb. 1945).

McDOUGALL, ROBERT L. Introduction to *Life in the Clearings . . .* by Susanna Moodie (Toronto, Macmillan, 1959) pp vii–xxiii.

MARKHAM, MARY. "An Index to *The Literary Garland*, 1838–1851, with Three Essays on Colonial Fiction" (Thesis, University of Western Ontario, 1949).

NEEDLER, G. H. *Otonabee Pioneers: The Story of the Stewarts, the Stricklands, the Traills and the Moodies* (Toronto, Burns & Mac-Eachern, 1953).

——— "The Otonabee Trio of Women Naturalists—Mrs. Stewart, Mrs. Traill, Mrs. Moodie," CAN FIELD NATURALIST 60: 97–101 (Sept.–Oct. 1946).

PARTRIDGE, F. G. "The Stewarts and the Stricklands, the Moodies and the Traills," ONT LIB R 40: 179–181 (Aug. 1956).

STRICKLAND, JANE MARGARET. *Life of Agnes Strickland* (Edinburgh, Blackwood, 1887) *passim.*

WEAVER, EMILY. "Mrs. Traill and Mrs. Moodie, Pioneers in Literature," CAN MAG 48: 473–476 (March 1917).

MOORE, William Henry, 1872–1960

ANON. *"Polly Masson* and Our Polygot Politics," CAN BKMN 1: 43–44 (Oct. 1919).

MORGAN-POWELL, Samuel, 1898–
    LECOCQ, THELMA. "Montreal's Morgan-Powell," MACL MAG 56: 19–20, 30–32 (Sept. 15, 1943).

MORRIS, Eric Cecil, 1914–
    LANE, OSCAR. "Mr. Morris and Allegories," INDEX vol 1 no 1: 18–20 (March 1946).

MOUNTAIN, George Jehoshaphat, 1789–1863
    ANON. "His Lordship Goes Voyaging [to the Red River Colony, 1844]," BEAVER 275: 10–13 (June 1944).
    MOCKRIDGE, CHARLES HENRY. *The Bishops of the Church of England in Canada* . . . (Toronto, Brown, 1896).
    MOUNTAIN, ARMINE WALE. *A Memoir of Jehoshaphat Mountain* . . . (Montreal, Lovell, 1866).
    RIDDELL, W. R. "A Forgotten Canadian Poet," ONT HIST SOC PAPERS 21: 245–258 (1924).
    TAYLOR, FENNINGS. *The Last Three Bishops Appointed by the Crown for the Anglican Church of Canada* (Montreal, Lovell, 1869).

MOWAT, Angus McGill, 1892–
    ANON. "Youth in the Driver's Seat," SAT N 57: 6 (March 14, 1942).
    R., G. F. "Major Angus Mowat, Inspector Public Libraries," ONT LIB R 24: 259–260 (Aug. 1940).

MUIR, Alexander, 1830–1906
    COOPER, J. A. "Canada's National Song," CAN MAG 6: 176–179 (Dec. 1895).
    MORRISON, J. A. "The Author of 'The Maple Leaf,'" DAL R 26: 85–92 (April 1946).
    WHITE, A. C. "Canada's Most Loved Patriotic Songs," ETUDE 61: 226ff (April 1943).

MULLINS, Rosanna Eleanor. *See* LEPROHON, Rosanna Eleanor (Mullins)

MUNRO, Kathryn [pseud.]. *See* TUPPER, Kathryn

MURPHY, Mrs. Emily Cowan (Ferguson), 1868–1933 [pseud.: "Janey Canuck"]
    ANON. Obituary, CAN AUTH 11: 11 (Dec. 1933).
    —— "The Passing of Janey Canuck," CAN BKMN 15: 163 (Nov. 1933).
    SANDERS, BYRNE HOPE. "Emily Murphy." In her *Canadian Portraits— Famous Women* (Toronto, Clarke Irwin, 1958) pp 113–142.
    —— *Emily Murphy, Crusader ("Janey Canuck").* With introduction by Nellie L. McClung (Toronto, Macmillan, 1945).
    THOMSON, THERESA E. " 'Janey Canuck'—In Memoriam," CAN AUTH & BKMN 19: 15 (Dec. 1934).
    WILSON, A. E. "Emily Murphy, Crusader," ECHOES 170–189: 12 (June 1946).

MURRAY, George, 1830–1910
    ANON. Obituary, ROY SOC CAN PROC & TRANS 3rd ser 4: ix–xi (1910).
    DOUGHTY, A. G. "Verses and Versions," CAN MAG 5: 476–478 (Sept. 1895).

MURRAY, Sinclair [pseud.]. *See* SULLIVAN, Edward Alan

NELSON, Edwin Gregson, 1849–1904
 CODY, H. A. " 'My Own Canadian Home' [Sketch of Edwin Gregson Nelson]," MACL MAG 26: 52–56 (Aug. 1913).

NICOL, Eric, 1919–
 BAKER, RONALD JAMES. "Eric Nicol: The Low Calling of a New Hero," BC LIB Q 23: 31–34 (April 1960).

NIVEN, Frederick John, 1878–1944
 ADCOCK, ST. JOHN. *The Glory That was Grub Street: Impressions of Contemporary Authors* (London, Low, Marston, 1928), pp 247–257.
 BURPEE, L. J. "Frederick Niven," DAL R 24: 74–76 (April 1944).
 GIBSON, GRETCHEN. "Frederick Niven had Novelist's Memory and Loved His West," SAT N 59: 24 (April 1, 1944).
 McCOURT, EDWARD A. "The Transplanted." In his *The Canadian West in Fiction* (Toronto, Ryerson, 1949) pp 39–54.
 NEW, WILLIAM H. "Individual and Group Isolation in the Fiction of Frederick John Niven: Setting as a Basis for a Study of Conflict and Resolution" (Thesis, University of British Columbia, 1963).
 NIVEN, FREDERICK JOHN. *Coloured Spectacles* [An Autobiography] (London, Collins, 1938).
 REID, ALEXANDER. "A Scottish Chekhov?" SCOTLAND'S MAG 58: 45–46 (March 1962).
 STEVENSON, Y. H. "Frederick Niven, 'Kootenay Scribe'," CAN AUTH & BKMN 17: 7–8 (April 1940).

NORRIS, Mary Ann, 1801–1880
 FLEWWELLING, SUSAN. "The Diary of Mary Ann Norris, 1818–1838," DAL R 29: 439–450 (Jan. 1950); 30: 90–103 (April 1950).

NORWOOD, Robert Winkworth, 1874–1932
 ADENEY, MARCUS. "Who's Who in Canadian Literature: Robert Norwood," CAN BKMN 9: 163–166 (June 1927).
 ANON. Obituary, CAN AUTH 10: 55 (Sept. 1932).
 ———— Obituary, PUB WKLY 122: 1440 (Oct. 8, 1932).
 CHAFFEE, E. B. Obituary, CHRISTIAN CENT 49: 1245 (Oct. 12, 1932).
 FOLEY, JEAN STEELE. "A Poet's Gospel of Beauty," CAN MAG 60: 169–173 (Dec. 1922).
 GARVIN, JOHN. "Robert Norwood," CAN BKMN 14: 107–109 (Oct. 1932).
 MOORE, PHYLLIS. "The Man of Kerioth," CAN BKMN 3: 53–55 (June 1921).
 MUNRO, K. "Vale," CAN BKMN 14: 127 (Nov. 1932).
 POMEROY, ELSIE M. "The Poetry of Robert Norwood," EDUC RECORD (Quebec) 62: 12–19 (Jan.–Mar. 1946). [Also in *Leading Canadian Poets*, ed. W. P. Percival (Toronto, Ryerson, 1948) pp 158–167.]
 WATSON, ALBERT DURRANT. *Robert Norwood* (Toronto, Ryerson, 1923).

O'BRIEN, Cornelius, 1843–1906
 ANON. Obituary, ROY SOC CAN PROC & TRANS 2nd ser 12: vi–vii (1906).

HUGHES, KATHERINE. *Archbishop O'Brien: Man and Churchman* (Ottawa, Crain, 1906).

McLENNAN, C. P. "Church Memories of Halifax," DAL R 22: 170–184 July 1942).

ODELL, Jonathan, 1737–1818

ANDERSON, JOAN (JOHNSTON). "A Collection of the Poems of Jonathan Odell with a Biographical and Critical Introduction" (Thesis, University of British Columbia, 1961).

HILLS, G. M. *History of the Church in Burlington, New Jersey* (Trenton, N.Y., Sharp, 1876; 2nd ed. enl. and illus., 1885).

[HONEYMAN, A. VAN DOREN]. "Jonathan Odell," *Dictionary of American Biography* 13: 623–624.

LAWRENCE, J. W. *The Judges of New Brunswick and Their Times* (Saint John, Jack, 1907).

LEARY, LEWIS. "Francis Hopkinson, Jonathan Odell, and 'The Temple of Cloacina,'" AMER LIT 15: 183–191 (May 1943).

LEE, F. B. *New Jersey as a Colony and as a State* . . . (New York, Publishing Soc. New Jersey, 1902) pp 299–305.

PARRINGTON, VERNON LOUIS. "The Tory Satirists: I, Jonathan Odell." In his *Main Currents in American Thought* (New York, Harcourt Brace, 1927) 1: 255–259.

POOL, MINNIE A., (comp.) *Odell Genealogy, United States and Canada* (Monroe, Wis., E. A. Odell, 1935).

REDE, KENNETH. "A Note on the Author of *The Times*," AMER LIT 2: 79–82 (March 1930).

SABINE, LORENZO. *Biographical Sketches of Loyalists of the American Revolution* (Boston, Little Brown, 1864) pp 122–123.

TYLER, MOSES COIT. "Jonathan Odell . . . Satirist." In his *The Literary History of the American Revolution* (New York, Putnam, 1897) vol 2, pp 98–129. [Reprinted: New York, Ungar Publishing Co., 1957.]

OGILVY, Maud

BRODIE, ALLAN DOUGLAS. "Canadian Short-Story Writers," CAN MAG 4: 334–344 (Feb. 1895).

O'HAGAN, Thomas, 1855–1939

McMANUS, EMILY. "O'Hagan's Poems: A Study," CAN MAG 1: 665–668 (Oct. 1893).

STEVENSON, LIONEL. "Who's Who in Canadian Literature: Thomas O'Hagan," CAN BKMN 11: 107–109 (May 1929).

O'HIGGINS, Harvey Jerrold, 1876–1929

ANON. Biographical Sketch, SCHOLASTIC 25: 5 (Jan. 12, 1935).

———— "The Gossip Shop," AMER BKMN 53: 282 (1921).

———— Obituary, HARPER'S 158: 660 (April 1929).

LAURISTON, VICTOR. "Three Musketeers of the Pen in New York of the Nineties," SAT N 61: 32–33 (Jan. 12, 1946).

OSLER, Sir William, 1849–1919

ABBOTT, MAUDE ELIZABETH SEYMOUR, ed. *Classified and Annotated Bibliography of Sir William Osler's Publications* (Montreal, McGill University, 1938).

ALLISON, S. D. "Crowe Reminiscent of Osler," ROTARIAN 83: 58 (Nov. 1953).

ANON. "A Great Physician," REVIEW 1: 249 (Aug. 2, 1919).

———— "A Great Teacher," INDIA 58: 1082–1083 (May 11, 1905).

BEILEN, A. "William Osler, a Leader Among Clinicians," HYGEIA 14: 441–442 (May 1936).

BETT, WALTER R. *Osler: The Man and the Legend* (London, Heinemann, 1951).

BROWN, W. LANGDON. "Physician's Reminiscences," DAL R 18: 295–300 (Oct. 1938).

COLGATE, W. G. "Where Osler Went to School," CAN MAG 81: 36 (April 1934).

CUSHING, HARVEY. *The Life of Sir William Osler* (Oxford, Clarendon Press, 1925) 2 vols.

———— "William Osler, the Man." In his *Consecratio Medici and Other Papers* (Boston, Little Brown, 1928) pp 97–117.

DAVIES, B. "Sir William Osler Combined Humanist and Doctor," SAT N 64: 28–29 (May 24, 1949).

FRANCIS, W. W. "Sir William Osler and His Library," D. C. LIBRARIES (Washington, D.C.) pp 25–28 (Jan. 1937).

GWYN, NORMAN B. "Canada's Greatest Physician," CAN MAG 69: 12–13, 41–44 (Jan. 1926).

HENRY, LORNE J. "Sir William Osler (1849–1919)." In his *Canadians: A Book of Biographies* (Toronto, Longmans, 1950) pp 53–60.

MACDONALD, ADRIAN. "Sir William Osler." In his *Canadian Portraits* (Toronto, Ryerson, 1925) pp 192–208.

MACNEIL, IAN. "The Scamp Who Became the Great Physician," MACL MAG 64: 14–15, 36–37 (June 1, 1951).

NEWMAN, SIR GEORGE. "Physician of Two Continents." In his *Interpreters of Nature* (London, Faber & Gwyer, 1927) pp 227–247.

NORDLUND, F. L. "Osler the Man," HYGEIA 13: 778–780 (Sept. 1935).

PRATT, VIOLA WHITNEY. "Sir Frederick Osler." In her *Canadian Portraits: Famous Doctors* (Toronto, Clarke Irwin, 1956) pp 3–46.

REID, EDITH G. *The Great Physician* (New York, Oxford, 1931).

SHEPARD, FRANCIS JOHN. *Sir William Osler, Bart.* (Montreal, 1921).

SHERMAN, STUART PRATT. "William Osler: The High Calling of Medicine." In his *Critical Woodcuts* (New York, Scribner's, 1926) pp 222–234.

THAYER, WILLIAM SYDNEY. "Osler," NATION (NY) 110: 104–106 (Jan. 24, 1920).

———— *Osler and Other Papers* (Baltimore, Johns Hopkins Press, 1931).

VAN DYKE, HENRY. "Healing Gift." In his *Camp-fires and Guide-posts: A Book of Essays* . . . (New York, Scribner's, 1921) pp 300–309.

W., R. "Shelley, Emerson, and Sir William Osler," NOTES & QUERIES 190: 120–121 (March 23, 1946).

WHITE, W. "Biographical Essays of Sir William Osler and Their Relation to Medical History," BUL HIST MED 7: 28–48 (Jan. 1939).

———— "Osler on Shakespeare, Bacon, and Burton, with Reprint of His Creators, Transmuters, and Transmitters . . .," BUL HIST MED 7: 392–408 (April 1939).

———— "Osleriana since 1926: Bibliography of Writings about Osler," MED LIB ASSOC BUL 28: 189–197 (June 1940).

———— "Sir William Osler as a Critic of the Novel," MED RECORD 148: 340–342 (Nov. 2, 1938).

———— *Sir William Osler, Historian and Literary Essayist* (Detroit, Wayne University Press, 1951). [Reprinted from *Medical Journal of Australia*, vol 3 no 13 (Sept. 23, 1950).]

———— "Whitman and Sir William Osler," AMER LIT 11: 73–77 (March 1939).

WILKINSON, ANNE. *Lions in the Way. A Discursive History of the Oslers* (Toronto, Macmillan, 1956).

OSTENSO, Martha, 1900–1963
ANON. "Writer of Novel Wants to do Play," CHRISTIAN SCI MO 29: 12 (Aug. 17, 1937).

COLMAN, MORRIS. "Martha Ostenso, Prize Novelist," MACL MAG 38: 56–58 (Jan. 1, 1925).

MACLELLAN, W. E. "Real 'Canadian Literature'," DAL R 6: 18–23 (Oct. 1926).

OXLEY, James Macdonald, 1855–1907
BRODIE, ALLAN DOUGLAS. "Canadian Short-Story Writers," CAN MAG 4: 334–344 (Feb. 1895).

PACKARD, Frank Lucius, 1877–1942
ANON. Obituary, CURRENT BIOG (1942).

———— Obituary, PUB WKLY 141: 1187 (March 21, 1942).

———— Obituary, WILSON LIB BUL 16: 598 (April 1942).

OVERTON, GRANT. "Frank L. Packard Unlocks a Book." In his *Cargoes for Crusoes* (New York, Appleton, 1924) pp 330–347.

PAGE, Patricia Kathleen, 1916–
ANON. Biographical Note, CAN AUTH & BKMN 34: 9 (Spring 1958).

MEREDITH, WILLIAM. "A Good Modern Poet and a Modern Tradition," POETRY (Chicago) 70: 208–211 (July 1947).

SHAW, NEUFVILLE. "The Poetry of P. K. Page," EDUC RECORD (Quebec) 64: 152–156 (July–Sept. 1948).

SMITH, A. J. M. "New Canadian Poetry," CAN FORUM 26: 252 (Feb. 1947).

SUTHERLAND, JOHN. "The Poetry of P. K. Page," NORTHERN R 1: 13–23 (Dec. 1946–Jan. 1947).

PARKER, Sir Gilbert, 1862–1932
ANON. "The Birthplace of Gilbert Parker," CAN MAG 28: 308–309 (Jan. 1907).

———— "The Northwest and Gilbert Parker," NATION 96: 181–182 (Feb. 20, 1913).

———— Obituary, PUB WKLY 122: 880 (Sept. 10, 1932).

———— [Parker's Literary Works], OUTLOOK 103: 43–44 (Jan. 4, 1913).

———— "The Real Charley Steele ... [and David Claridge]," BKMN (New York) 37: 481–483 (July 1913).

———— [Sketch and Portrait], CURRENT LIT 37: 420–422 (Nov. 1904).

BLACK, F. D. "He Made the Most of His Great Natural Gifts," CAN MAG 66: 14–15 (Aug. 1926).

CARMAN, BLISS. "Gilbert Parker," CHAP-BOOK 1: 338–343 (Nov. 1, 1894).

COMER, CORNELIA A. P. "The Novels of Gilbert Parker," CRITIC 33: 271–274 (Oct. 1898).

COOPER, J. A. "Canadian Celebrities: Sir Gilbert Parker," CAN MAG 25: 494–496 (Oct. 1905).

FRIDEN, GEORG. *The Canadian Novels of Sir Gilbert Parker: Historical Elements and Literary Technique* (Copenhagen, E. Munksgaard; Upsala, A-B. Lundenquistska Bokhandeln, 1953). [Upsala Canadian Studies No. 2.]

GARVIN, JOHN. "Sir Gilbert Parker and Canadian Literature," CAN BKMN 14: 92 (Sept. 1932).

HORNING, L. E. "Gilbert Parker," ACTA VIC 11: 252–254 (March 1896).

HUME, BLANCHE. "Who's Who in Canadian Literature: Sir Gilbert Parker," CAN BKMN 10: 131–134 (May 1928).

INGRAHAM, MARY KINLEY. "Letters from Sir Gilbert Parker," CAN BKMN 15: 3–4 (Jan. 1933).

LOGAN, J. D. "Sir Gilbert Parker as a Poet," CAN MAG 62: 179–182 (Jan. 1924).

MCARTHUR, JAMES, *et al.* "Sir Gilbert Parker—The Man and the Novelist," BK NEWS 27: 325–334 (Jan. 1908).

MACPHAIL, SIR ANDREW. "Sir Gilbert Parker: An Appraisal," ROY SOC CAN PROC & TRANS 3rd ser 33: sect II, 123–135 (1939).

PARKER, GILBERT. "Fiction—Its Place in the National Life," NORTH AMER R 186: 495–509 (Dec. 1907).

RUTLEDGE, J. L. "Gilbert Parker the Novelist," ACTA VIC 27: 404–408 (April 1904).

STEVENSON, O. J. "The Storied Windows and the Painted Walls." In his *A People's Best* (Toronto, Musson, 1927) pp 37–46.

THOROLD, W. J. "Gilbert Parker," MASSEY'S 3: 117–123 (Feb. 1897).

VERTE, INNA. "The Birthplace of Sir Gilbert Parker," CAN BKMN 14: 113 (Oct. 1932).

PENFIELD, Wilder Graves, 1891–

BLOOM, M. T. "Explorer of the Human Brain," READER'S DIGEST 73: 138–140 (July 1958).

HUTTON, ERIC. "Penfield," MACL MAG 69: 11–15, 68–74 (Feb. 18, 1956).

PENFIELD, WILDER. "Historical Novelist Closer to Truth—Penfield Notes," CAN AUTH & BKMN 35: 11 (Spring 1959).

PRATT, VIOLA WHITNEY. "Wilder Graves Penfield, O.M." In her *Canadian Portraits: Famous Doctors* (Toronto, Clarke Irwin, 1956) pp 95–160.

SIMARD, L. C. Biographical Note, ROY SOC CAN PROC & TRANS 3rd ser 45: 39 (1951).

PHARIS, Gwen. *See* RINGWOOD, Gwen Pharis.

PHELPS, Arthur, 1887–1970

CYCLOPS. "Fresh Treatment of Canadian Writers," CAN AUTH & BKMN 27: 40–41 (1951).

PHILLIPPS-WOLLEY, Sir Clive Oldnall, 1854–1918
    SCOTT, DUNCAN CAMPBELL. "Sir Clive Phillipps-Wolley," ROY SOC CAN PROC & TRANS 3rd ser 13: xiii–xiv (1919).

PICKTHALL, Marjorie Lowry Christie, 1883–1922
    ADCOCK, A. ST. JOHN. "Marjorie Pickthall," BKMN (London) 62: 127–129 (June 1922).
    COLLIN, W. E. "Dream-Gardens." In his *The White Savannahs* (Toronto, Macmillan, 1936) pp 43–79.
    ——— "Marjorie Pickthall 1883–1922," UNIV TOR Q 1: 352–380 (April 1932).
    DUNLOP, W. R. "The Poems of Marjory Pickthall," BC MO 20: 6 (March 1923).
    GORDON, ALFRED. "Marjorie Pickthall as an Artist," CAN BKMN 4: 157–159 (May 1922).
    GORDON, B. K. "Marjorie Pickthall's Poetry," CAN BKMN 3: 52, 54 (Nov. 1922).
    HASSARD, ALBERT R. "The Dawn of Marjorie Pickthall's Genius," CAN BKMN 4: 159–161 (May 1922).
    LOGAN, J. D. "The Genius of Marjorie Pickthall: An Analysis of Aesthetic Paradox," CAN MAG 59: 154–161 (June 1922).
    ——— *Marjorie Pickthall, Her Poetic Genius and Art* (Halifax, Allen, 1922).
    LUGRIN, N. DE B. "Marjorie Pickthall as a Companion," CAN MAG 64: 72–73 (April 1925).
    MACDONALD, JOHN HARRY. "Marjorie Pickthall" (Thesis, Dalhousie University, 1927).
    PIERCE, LORNE. "Marjorie Pickthall," ACTA VIC 67: 21–30 (June 1943).
    ——— "Marjorie Pickthall," EDUC RECORD (Quebec) 63: 31–35 (Jan.–March 1947). [Also in *Leading Canadian Poets*, ed. W. P. Percival (Toronto, Ryerson, 1948) pp 168–176.]
    ——— *Marjorie Pickthall: A Book of Remembrance* (Toronto, Ryerson, 1925).
    ——— *Marjorie Pickthall: A Memorial Address* (Toronto, Ryerson, 1943).
    PRATT, E. J. "Marjorie Pickthall," CAN FORUM 13: 334–335 (June 1933).
    RITCHIE, ELIZA. "Marjorie Pickthall: In Memoriam," DAL R 2: 157–158 (July 1922).
    SCOTT, D. C. "Poetry and Progress," CAN MAG 60: 187–195 (Jan. 1923).
    SISTER ST. CECILIA. "Marjorie Pickthall, the Ethereal Minstrel of Canada" (Thesis, Ottawa University, 1941).
    STEVENSON, O. J. "A Golden Page." In his *A People's Best* (Toronto, Musson, 1927) pp 159–168.
    STRINGER, ARTHUR. "Wild Poets I've Known: Marjorie Pickthall," SAT N 56: 41 (June 14, 1941).
    TOYE, D. E. "The Poetry of Marjorie Pickthall," ACTA VIC 47: 15–18 (Jan. 1923).
    WHITNEY, V. L. "Marjorie Pickthall," ACTA VIC 39: 332–341 (March 1915).
    WILSON, ANNE ELIZABETH. "Magnificent Prose of Marjorie Pickthall," CAN BKMN 4: 185 (June 1922).

PIERCE, Lorne Albert, 1890–1961
ANON. "The Romantic Puritan," SAT N 70: 1, 24–26 (Nov. 26, 1955).
PIERCE, LORNE. *An Editor's Creed* (Toronto, Ryerson, 1960).
—— *The House of Ryerson* (Toronto, Ryerson, 1954).
—— *On Publishers and Publishing* (Toronto, Ryerson, 1951).
—— "The Ryerson Press," CAN LIB ASSOC BUL 9: 135–137 (March 1953).

PIERS, Mrs. Constance (Fairbanks), 1866–1939
ANON. Obituary, CAN AUTH 16: 13, 22 (April 1939).

PRATT, Edwin John, 1883–1964
ANON. Biographical Note, CAN AUTH & BKMN 34: 16 (Spring 1958).
—— "Garland for E. J. Pratt on His Seventy-Fifth Birthday," TAM R no 6: 65–80 (Winter 1958).
BÉNET, WILLIAM ROSE. Introduction to the American edition of Pratt's *Collected Poems* (New York, Knopf, 1945) pp ix–xiv.
BENSON, NATHANIEL A. "Who's Who in Canadian Literature: Edwin J. Pratt," CAN BKMN 9: 323–326 (Nov. 1927).
BIRNEY, EARLE. "Canadian Poem of the Year: *Brébeuf and His Brethren*," CAN FORUM 20: 180–181 (Sept. 1940).
—— "Distinguished Canadian Poem," CAN FORUM 21: 278–279 (Dec. 1941).
—— "E. J. Pratt and His Critics." In *Our Living Tradition*, Second and Third Series, ed. Robert L. McDougall (Toronto, published in association with Carleton University by University of Toronto Press, 1959) pp 123–147. [Reprinted, in part, in *Canadian Anthology*, ed. C. F. Klinck and R. E. Watters, rev. ed. (Toronto, Gage, 1966) pp 528–534.]
BROWN, E. K. "E. J. Pratt." In his *On Canadian Poetry*, rev. ed. (Toronto, Ryerson, 1944) pp 143–164.
—— "First of Canadian Poets," CAN FORUM 17: 321–322 (Dec. 1937).
—— "The Originality of E. J. Pratt." In *Canadian Accent*, ed. Ralph Gustafson (London, Penguin, 1944) pp 32–44.
—— "Pratt's Collected Work; Review Article," UNIV TOR Q 14: 211–213 (Jan. 1945).
COLLIN, W. E. "Pleiocene Heroics." In his *The White Savannahs* (Toronto, Macmillan, 1936) pp 119–144.
DUDEK, LOUIS. "A Garland for E. J. Pratt: Poet of the Machine Age," TAM R no 6: 74–80 (Winter 1958).
EDGAR, PELHAM. "E. J. Pratt," EDUC RECORD (Quebec) 59: 178–180 (July–Sept. 1943). [Also in *Leading Canadian Poets*, ed. W. P. Percival (Toronto, Ryerson, 1948) pp 177–183.]
—— "Edwin John Pratt," GANTS DU CIEL 11: 31–45 (printemps 1946). [English version in *Across My Path*, ed. Northrop Frye (Toronto, Ryerson, 1952) pp 109–117.]
FRYE, NORTHROP. Introduction to *The Collected Poems of E. J. Pratt*, 2nd ed. (Toronto, Macmillan, 1958) pp xiii–xxviii.
—— "La Tradition narratif dans la poesie canadienne-anglaise," GANTS DU CIEL 11: 19–30 (printemps 1946). [English version subsequently published in *Canadian Anthology*, ed. C. F. Klinck and R. E. Watters, rev. ed. (Toronto, Gage, 1966) pp 523–528.]

G., D. C. "Newfoundland Verse," ACTA VIC 48: 12–14 (Oct. 1923).

HILLYER, R. "Poetic Sensitivity to Time," SAT R LIT 28: 11 (April 28, 1946).

HORWOOD, HAROLD. "E. J. Pratt & William Blake: an Analysis," DAL R 39: 197–207 (Summer 1959).

KING, C. A. "The Mind of E. J. Pratt," CAN FORUM 36: 9–10 (April 1956).

KNOX, R. S. "A New Canadian Poet," CAN FORUM 3: 278–279 (June 1923).

LECOCQ, THELMA. "Ned Pratt—Poet," MACL MAG 57: 18, 24, 26, 28 (Nov. 15, 1944). [Also in *Our Sense of Identity*, ed. Malcolm Ross (Toronto, Ryerson, 1954) pp 192–200.]

McGRATH, M. HELEN. "Bard from Newfoundland: The Story of Dr. E. J. Pratt," ATLAN ADV 49: 13–15, 17+ (Nov. 1958).

MACKAY, L. A. "The Poetry of E. J. Pratt," CAN FORUM 24: 208–209 (Dec. 1944).

MACKINNON, MURDO. "A Garland for E. J. Pratt: The Man and the Teacher," TAM R no 6: 71–74 (Winter 1958).

PACEY, DESMOND. "E. J. Pratt." In his *Ten Canadian Poets* (Toronto, Ryerson, 1958) pp 165–193.

PHELPS, ARTHUR. L. "E. J. Pratt." In his *Canadian Writers* (Toronto, McClelland and Stewart, 1951) pp 1–9.

PRATT, E. J. "My First Book," CAN AUTH & BKMN 28: 5–6 (1952–1953).

ROSS, M. L. "Dr. E. J. Pratt: A Poet's Quarter-Century," SAT N 73: cover, 14–15+ (Feb. 1, 1958).

SCOTT, W. T. "Poetry and Event," POETRY (Chicago) 66: 329–334 (Sept. 1945).

SISTER MARY ROSALINDA. "*Brébeuf and His Brethren*: A great Canadian Poem" (Thesis, Ottawa University, 1959).

SISTER ST. DOROTHY MARIE. "The Epic Note in the Poetry of Edwin John Pratt" (Thesis, Ottawa University, 1956).

———— "The Poetic Imagery of Edwin Pratt" (Thesis, Ottawa University, 1958).

SMITH, A. J. M. "A Garland for E. J. Pratt: The Poet," TAM R no 6: 66–71 (Winter 1958).

SUTHERLAND, JOHN. "E. J. Pratt: a Major Contemporary Poet," NORTHERN R 5: 36–64 (April–May 1952).

———— "Foremost Poet of Canada," POETRY (Chicago) 82: 350–354 (Sept. 1953).

———— "The Poetry of E. J. Pratt," FIRST STATEMENT 2: 27–30 (Feb.–March 1945).

———— *The Poetry of E. J. Pratt: A New Interpretation* (Toronto, Ryerson, 1956).

SYLVESTRE, GUY. "Un grande poète canadien anglais," LE DEVOIR (Montreal) 36: 8 (12 mai 1945).

WATT, FRANK W. "Edwin John Pratt," UNIV TOR Q 29: 77–84 (Oct. 1959).

WELLS, H. W. "Canada's Best-Known Poet: E. J. Pratt," COLLEGE ENGLISH 7: 452–456 (May 1946).

WELLS, H. W. and C. F. KLINCK. *Edwin John Pratt: The Man and His Poetry* (Toronto, Ryerson, 1947).

RACEY, Arthur George, 1870–1942
RAINE, NORMAN REILLY. "A Cartoonist Looks at Life," MACL MAG 38: 18–19, 63–65 (Oct. 1, 1925).
SMITH, F. CLIFFORD. "Canadian Celebrities: XVIII, Mr. A. G. Racey, Cartoonist," CAN MAG 16: 38–41 (Nov. 1900).

RADDALL, Thomas Head, 1903–
BEVAN, ALLAN. Introduction to *At the Tide's Turn and Other Stories* by Thomas H. Raddall (Toronto, McClelland & Stewart, 1959) pp v–ix [New Canadian Library no 9.]
PHELPS, ARTHUR L. "Thomas Raddall." In his *Canadian Writers* (Toronto, McClelland & Stewart, 1951) pp 60–69.
RADDALL, THOMAS HEAD. "Literary Art," DAL R 34: 138–146 (Summer 1954).
———— "My First Book," CAN AUTH & BKMN 28: 5–8 (Autumn 1952).
———— "My Home Town," MACL MAG 57: 19–20, 36, 38 (Sept. 1, 1944).
———— "Sword and Pen in Kent," DAL R 32: 145–152 (Autumn 1952).
WALBRIDGE, E. F. "Biographical Sketch," WILSON LIB BUL 25: 576 (April 1951).
WRIGHT, ETHEL CLARK. "A Conflict of Loyalties," DAL R 23: 83–86 (April 1943).

RAMSAY, Andrew John, 1849?–1907
DAVIES, R. "A Harp That Once," QUEEN'S Q 50: 374–381 (Winter 1943–1944).

RAND, Theodore Harding, 1835–1900
CLARKE, HERBERT G. "Theodore Harding Rand's Poems," McMASTER U MO 6: 353–359 (May 1897).
SAUNDERS, E. M. "Theodore Harding Rand," McMASTER U MO 2: 1–9 (June 1892).
WHITESIDE, ERNESTINE R. "Canadian Poetry and Poets, III [Rand]," McMASTER U MO 8: 114–118 (Dec. 1898).

RAY, Anna Chapin, 1865–1945
ANON. Obituary, PUB WKLY 149: 178 (Jan. 12, 1946).
———— Obituary, WILSON LIB BUL 20: 392 (Feb. 1946).

READE, John, 1837–1919
ANON. Obituary, ROY SOC CAN PROC & TRANS 3rd ser 13: xiii–xiv (1919).
BOYD, JOHN. "John Reade: An Appreciation of the 'Dean of Canadian Letters,'" CAN MAG 53: 74–77 (May 1919).
GHENT, PERCY P. *John Reade and His Friends* (Toronto, Belcher, 1925).

REANEY, James, 1926–
ANON. Biographical Note, CAN AUTH & BKMN 34: 11 (Spring 1958).
SUTHERLAND, JOHN. "Canadian Comment," NORTHERN R 3: 36–42 (April–May 1950).

REEVE, Winnifred Eaton Babcock, 1879– [pseud: "Onoto Watanna"]
PRICE, ELIZABETH BAILEY. "Onoto Watanna, an Amazing Author," MACL MAG 35: 64–66 (Oct. 15, 1922).

———— "Onoto Watanna has Written a New Book," CAN BKMN 4: 123–125 (April 1922).

RICHARDSON, Evelyn, 1902–
RICHARDSON, EVELYN. "Lighthouse-Keeping: Eight Years Later," SAT N 68: 32 (May 2, 1953).
———— "No Ivory in Light Towers," DAL R 35: 234–244 (Autumn 1955).

RICHARDSON, John, 1796–1852
ANON. "Early Canadian Novels," CAN MAG 27: 375–376 (Aug. 1906).
———— "John Richardson, His Sweethearts," HARPER'S WKLY 55: 16, 17 (Oct. 7, 1911).
BAKER, RAY P. "John Richardson and the Historical Romance." In his *A History of English-Canadian Literature to the Confederation* (Cambridge, Harvard University Press, 1920) pp 125–139.
BURWASH, I. "John Richardson, 1796–1852, Young Volunteer of 1812," CAN MAG 39: 218–225 (July 1912).
CARSTAIRS, JOHN STEWART. "Richardson's War of 1812," CAN MAG 29: 72-74 (May 1901).
CASSELMAN, A. C. [Biography]. In *War of 1812* by John Richardson (Toronto, Historical Pub. Co., 1902) pp xi–lvii.
KLINCK, CARL F. Introduction to *Major Richardson's "Kensington Gardens in 1830"* (Toronto, Bibliographical Society of Canada, 1957) pp vii–xiii.
LANDE, LAWRENCE M. "Major John Richardson." In his *Old Lamps Aglow* (Montreal, the Author, 1957) pp 228–240.
PACEY, DESMOND. "A Colonial Romantic, Major John Richardson, Soldier and Novelist," Part I, CAN LIT no 2: 20–31 (Autumn 1959); Part II, CAN LIT no 3: 47–56 (Winter 1960).
RIDDELL, WILLIAM RENWICK. *John Richardson* (Toronto, Ryerson, [1926?]).

RICHLER, Mordecai, 1931–
COHEN, NATHAN. "A Conversation with Mordecai Richler," TAM R no 2: 6–23 (Winter 1957).
———— "Heroes of the Richler View," TAM R no 6: 47–49, 51–60 (Winter 1958).
RICHLER, MORDECAI. "How I Became an Unknown with My First Novel," MACL MAG 71: 18–19, 40–42 (Feb. 1, 1958).
———— "Like Children to the Fair," In *Alienation,* ed. Timothy O'Keefe, (London, MacGibbon & Kee, 1960) pp 158–167.
SCOTT, P. D. "Choice of Certainties," TAM R no 8: 73–82 (Summer 1958).
TALLMAN, WARREN. "Richler and the Faithless City," CAN LIT no 3: 62–64 (Winter 1960).

RIDDELL, William Renwick, 1852–1945
HAWKES, ARTHUR. "Telling the Canadian Story," CAN MAG 71: 22, 34–35 (Jan. 1929).
SURVEYER, E. FABRE. "The Honourable William Renwick Riddell," ROY SOC CAN PROC & TRANS 3rd ser 39: 111–114 (1945).

RINGWOOD, Gwen Pharis, 1910–
BRODERSEN, G. L. "Gwen Pharis—Canadian Dramatist," MAN ARTS R 4: 3–20 (Spring 1944).

ROBERTS, Charles George Douglas, 1860–1943

ANON. "The Animal Story," EDINBURGH R 214: 94–118 (July 1911).

———— "Charles G. D. Roberts," ACTA VIC 55: 15 (March–April 1931).

———— "Diamond Jubilee," CAN BKMN 15: 38 (March 1933).

———— "The New Roberts' Animal Book," CAN BKMN 4: 53 (Jan. 1922).

———— Obituary, CAN POETRY 7: 5–6 (Dec. 1943).

———— [Obituary]. In *Current Biography 1944* (New York, Wilson, 1945) p 599.

———— Obituary, TIME 42, 76 (Dec. 6, 1943).

———— Obituary, WILSON LIB BUL 18: 367 (Jan. 1944).

———— "Seventy-Fifth Birthday," CAN BKMN 17: 109 (Sept. 1935).

ARCHER, WILLIAM. "Charles G. D. Roberts." In his *Poets of the Younger Generation* (London, Lane, 1902) pp 362–372.

BENET, W. R. "The Phoenix Nest," SAT R LIT 27: 24 (March 4, 1944).

BENSON, NATHANIEL A. "Dean of Canadian Letters," SAT N 47: 5 (April 25, 1931).

———— "Sir Charles G. D. Roberts," EDUC RECORD (Quebec) 56: 80–84 (June 1937). [Also in *Leading Canadian Poets*, ed. W. P. Percival (Toronto, Ryerson, 1948) pp 184–192.]

BURROUGHS, JOHN. "Roberts' Red Fox," OUTING 48: 512a–512b (July 1906).

CAPPON, JAMES. *Charles G. D. Roberts* (Toronto, Ryerson, 1925).

———— "Roberts and the Influence of His Times," CAN MAG 24: 224–231 (Jan. 1905); 24: 321–328 (Feb. 1905); 24: 419–424 (March 1905); 24: 514–520 (April 1905).

———— *Roberts and the Influences of His Time* (Toronto, Briggs, 1905).

CARMAN, BLISS. "Contemporaries: V, Charles G. D. Roberts," CHAP-BOOK 2: 163–171 (Jan. 1, 1895).

DEACON, WILLIAM ARTHUR. "Sir Charles G. D. Roberts: An Appreciation," CAN AUTH & BKMN 19: 4 (Dec. 1934).

DE MILLE, A. B. "Canadian Celebrities: The Roberts Family," CAN MAG 15: 426–430 (Sept. 1900).

EDGAR, PELHAM. "Charles G. D. Roberts," ACTA VIC 52: 33–34 (Jan. 1928).

———— "Sir Charles G. D. Roberts and His Times," UNIV TOR Q 13: 117–126 (Oct. 1943). [Also in his *Across My Path*, ed. Northrop Frye (Toronto, Ryerson, 1952) pp 99–108.]

———— "Sir Charles G. D. Roberts, 1860–1943," ROY SOC CAN PROC & TRANS 3rd ser 38: 111–114 (1944).

FORBES, E. A. "The Development of Style and Thought in the Poetry of Charles G. D. Roberts, 1877–1897" (Thesis, University of New Brunswick, 1953).

GAMMON, DONALD B. "The Concept of Nature in Nineteenth Century Canadian Poetry, with Special Reference to Goldsmith, Sangster and Roberts" (Thesis, University of New Brunswick, 1948).

HARKINS, EDWARD F. "The Literary Career of Roberts." In his *Little Pilgrimages among the Men Who Have Written Famous Books* (Boston, Page, 1902) pp 299–315.

HENRY, LORNE J. "Sir Charles G. D. Roberts (1860–1943)." In his *Canadians: a Book of Biographies* (Toronto, Longmans, 1950) pp 69–75.

HERRIMAN, DOROTHY C. "Sir Charles G. D. Roberts: 80 Years Young 1860–1940," CAN AUTH 16: 5 (Jan. 1940).

HORNING, L. E. "Animal Stories," ACTA VIC 25: 277–279 (Feb. 1902).

KIRKCONNELL, WATSON. "Sir Charles Roberts: A Tribute," CAN AUTH & BKMN 19: 3 (Dec. 1943).

LAMPMAN, ARCHIBALD. "Two Canadian Poets [C. G. D. Roberts and G. F. Cameron]," with a prefatory note by E. K. Brown, UNIV TOR Q 13: 406–423 (July 1944).

LESPERANCE, JOHN. "The Poets of Canada," ROY SOC CAN PROC & TRANS 1st ser 2: 42ff (1884).

LIVESAY, DOROTHY. "Open Letter to Sir Charles G. D. Roberts," CAN BKMN 21: 34–35 (April 1939).

LOCK, D. R. "Charles G. D. Roberts," WORLD WIDE 31: 1187 (July 25, 1931).

LUCAS, ALEC. Introduction to *The Last Barrier and Other Stories* by Charles G. D. Roberts (Toronto, McClelland & Stewart, 1958) pp v–x. [New Canadian Library no 7.]

MARQUIS, T. G. "Professor Charles G. D. Roberts, M.A.," THE WEEK 5: 558–559 (July 26, 1888).

———— "Roberts," CAN MAG 1: 572–575 (Sept. 1893).

———— "Songs of the Common Day," THE WEEK 10: 1023 (Sept. 22, 1893).

MASSEY, VINCENT. "Roberts, Carman, Sherman: Canadian Poets," CAN AUTH & BKMN 23: 29–32 (Fall 1947).

MIDDLETON, J. E. "Dean of Canadian Letters," SAT N 58: 20–21 (June 19, 1943).

MUDDIMAN, B. "Vignette in Canadian Literature," CAN MAG 40: 451–458 (March 1913). [Also in REV OF REV 47: 490–491 (April 1913).]

O'HAGAN, THOMAS. "Two Canadian Poets," DOM ILLUS 1: 263 (Oct. 27, 1888).

PACEY, DESMOND. "Sir Charles G. D. Roberts." In his *Ten Canadian Poets* (Toronto, Ryerson, 1958) pp 34–58.

PIERCE, LORNE ALBERT. "Charles G. D. Roberts." In his *Three Fredericton Poets: Writers of the University of New Brunswick and the New Dominion* (Toronto, Ryerson, 1933) pp 11–17.

POIRIER, M. "The Animal Stories of E. Thompson Seton and Charles G. D. Roberts," QUEEN'S Q 34: 298–312 (Jan.–Mar. 1927); 34; 398–419 (April–June 1927).

POLLOCK, F. L. "Canadian Writers in New York," ACTA VIC 22: 434–439 (April 1899).

POMEROY, ELSIE. *Sir Charles G. D. Roberts: A Biography* (Toronto, Ryerson, 1943).

———— *Tributes through the Years: The Centenary of the Birth of Sir Charles G. D. Roberts, January 10, 1960* (Toronto, privately printed, 1959).

REID, R. L. "Charles G. D. Roberts, Poet and Novelist," BC MO 24: 7 (March 1925).

RHODENIZER, V. B. "Who's Who in Canadian Literature: Charles G. D. Roberts," CAN BKMN 8: 267–269 (Sept. 1926).

RITTENHOUSE, JESSIE B. "Charles G. D. Roberts." In her *The Younger American Poets* (Boston, Little Brown, 1904) pp 132–150.

ROBERTS, LLOYD. *The Book of Roberts* (Toronto, Ryerson, 1923).

Ross, P. D. "A Very Great Canadian," CAN AUTH & BKMN 19: 12 (Sept. 1943).

SMYTHE, A. A. E. "Charles G. D. Roberts," CAN BKMN 7: 25 (Feb. 1925).

STEPHEN, A. M. "The Poetry of C. G. D. Roberts," QUEEN'S Q 36: 48–64 (Jan. 1929).

STEVENSON, O. J. "New Visions and New Ventures." In his *A People's Best* (Toronto, Musson, 1927) pp 85–94.

STRINGER, ARTHUR. "Eminent Canadians in New York: II, The Father of Canadian Poetry," NATL MO 4: 61–64 (Feb. 1904).

———— "Wild Poets I've Known: Charles G. D. Roberts," SAT N 57: 25 (April 11, 1942).

SYKES, W. J. "Charles G. D. Roberts," ACTA VIC 17: 112–115 (Jan. 1894).

WHITESIDE, ERNESTINE R. "Canadian Poetry and Poets [Roberts]," McMASTER U MO 8: 21–28 (Oct. 1898).

ROBERTS, Goodridge Bliss, 1904–
ANDERSON, P. "A Note on Goodridge Roberts," NORTHERN R 1: 23 (Dec.–Jan. 1945–1946).

DE MILLE, A. B. "Canadian Celebrities: XVI, The Roberts Family," CAN MAG 15: 426–430 (Sept. 1900).

ROBERTS, Theodore Goodridge, 1877–1953
BAILEY, ALFRED G. "Theodore Goodridge Roberts," FIDDLEHEAD 18: 3 (1953).

———— "Theodore Goodridge Roberts: His Prose and Poetry," EDUC RECORD (Quebec) 61: 17–22 (Jan.–Mar. 1945). [Also in *Leading Canadian Poets*, ed. W. P. Percival (Toronto, Ryerson, 1948) pp 193–201.]

DE MILLE, A. B. "Canadian Celebrities: XVI, The Roberts Family," CAN MAG 15: 426–430 (Sept. 1900).

MACDONALD, GOODRIDGE. "Theodore Goodridge Roberts, Poet and Novelist," CAN AUTH & BKMN 29: 9–12 (Spring 1953).

POLLOCK, F. L. "Canadian Writers in New York," ACTA VIC 22: 434–439 (April 1899).

WADE, H. G. "Who's Who in Canadian Literature: Theodore Goodridge Roberts," CAN BKMN 13: 215–217 (Nov. 1931).

ROBINS, John D., 1884–1952
ANON. "John D. Robins," CAN FORUM 32: 218 (Jan. 1953).

ROSS, Alexander, 1783–1856
BRYCE, GEORGE. "Alexander Ross," CAN MAG 49: 163–168 (June 1917).

———— "Alexander Ross, Fur Trader, Author and Philanthropist," QUEEN'S Q 11: 46–56 (July 1903).

OLIVER, EDMUND HENRY. *The Canadian North West . . .* (Ottawa, Govt. Print. Bureau, 1914–1915) 2 vols.

ROSS, Sir George William, 1841–1914
> HASSARD, ALBERT R. "Great Canadian Orators: XII, Sir George Ross," CAN MAG 56: 170–172 (Dec. 1920).
>
> LOCKE, GEORGE N. "Goldwin Smith and Sir George W. Ross." In *The Yearbook of Canadian Art, 1913–*, comp. by the Arts & Letters Club of Toronto (Toronto, Dent, n.d.) pp 37–43.
>
> ROSS, MARGARET. *Sir George W. Ross* (Toronto, Ryerson, 1923).

ROSS, (James) Sinclair, 1908–
> ANON. "Canadian Writer," COUNTRY GUIDE 61: 38 (April 1942).
>
> DANIELLS, ROY. Introduction to *As For Me and My House* by Sinclair Ross (Toronto, McClelland & Stewart, 1957) pp v–x. [New Canadian Library no 4.]
>
> McCOURT, EDWARD A. "Sinclair Ross." In his *The Canadian West in Fiction* (Toronto, Ryerson, 1949) pp 94–99.
>
> STUBBS, R. S. "Presenting Sinclair Ross," SAT N 56: 17 (Aug. 9, 1941).

ROSS, Philip Dansken, 1858–1949
> O'LEARY, GRATTAN. "Ross Runs a Paper Worth Quoting," MACL MAG 37: 18, 55–57 (Nov. 1, 1924).

ROSS, W. W. Eustace, 1894–1966
> MOORE, M. "Experienced Simplicity," POETRY (Chicago) 38: 280–281 (Aug. 1931).

ROY, Gabrielle (Carbotte), 1909–
> ANON. "Happy Accident," TIME 49: 36 (March 17, 1947).
>
> BROWN, A. "Gabrielle Roy and the Temporary Provincial," TAM R no 1: 61–70 (Autumn 1956).
>
> DUNCAN, DOROTHY. "Le Triomphe de Gabrielle," MACL MAG 60: 23, 51, 54 (April 14, 1947).
>
> McPHERSON, HUGO. Introduction to *The Tin Flute* by Gabrielle Roy (Toronto, McClelland & Stewart, 1958) pp v–xi [New Canadian Library no 5.]
>
> ——— "The Garden and the Cage," CAN LIT no 1: 46–57 (Summer 1959).

SALVERSON, Mrs. Laura (Goodman), 1890–1970
> ANON. "Laura Goodman Salverson," CAN BKMN 9: 100 (April 1927).
>
> ——— "Merit Rewarded," ICELANDIC CANADIAN 2: 17 (March 1944).
>
> ——— "Novel of the Kensington Stone," CAN AUTH & BKMN 25: 24 (Summer 1949).
>
> FULLER, MURIEL. "Laura Goodman Salverson," CAN AUTH & BKMN 35: 12 (Winter 1958–1959).
>
> McCOURT, EDWARD A. "Laura Goodman Salverson." In his *The Canadian West in Fiction* (Toronto, Ryerson, 1949) pp 88–94.
>
> McDONALD, W. S. "A Great Canadian Novel," CAN AUTH 16: 13 (Autumn 1938).
>
> SALVERSON, LAURA G. An Autobiographical Sketch, ONT LIB R 14: 69–73 (Feb. 1930).

SANDWELL, Bernard Keble, 1876–1954
ANON. "The Front Page," CAN FORUM 31: 99 (Aug. 1951).
———— Obituary, CAN FORUM 34: 219 (Jan. 1955).
———— Obituary, FIN POST 48: 3 (Dec. 11, 1954).
———— Obituary, SAT N 70: 3 (Dec. 25, 1954).
DAVIES, ROBERTSON. Introduction to *The Diversions of Duchesstown and Other Essays* by B. K. Sandwell (Toronto, Dent, 1955) pp ix-xii.
FORD, ARTHUR B. "B. K. Sandwell," CAN AUTH & BKMN 30: 1–3 (Autumn 1954).
LECOCQ, T. "Good-Humored Oracle," MACL MAG 59: 18, 24–25 (April 1, 1946).
UNDERHILL, F. H. "Bernard Keble Sandwell, 1876–1954," ROY SOC CAN PROC & TRANS 3rd ser 49: 133–135 (1955).
WOODSIDE, C. W. "Last of the Nineteenth Century Liberals," SAT N 70: 19 (Dec. 25, 1954).

SANGSTER, Charles, 1822–1893
BAKER, R. P. "Charles Sangster." In his *A History of English-Canadian Literature to the Confederation* (Cambridge, Harvard University Press, 1920) pp 159–165.
BOURINOT, ARTHUR S. "Charles Sangster (1822–1893)," EDUC RECORD (Quebec) 62: 179–185 (July–Sept. 1946). [Also in *Leading Canadian Poets*, ed. W. P. Percival, (Toronto, Ryerson, 1948) pp 202–212. Also in his *Five Canadian Poets* (Montreal, Quality Press, 1956) pp 8–14.]
DEWART, EDWARD HARTLEY. "Charles Sangster," CAN MAG 7: 28–34 (May 1896).
———— "Charles Sangster, a Canadian Poet of the Last Generation." In his *Essays for the Times* (Toronto, Briggs, 1898) pp 38–51.
GAMMON, DONALD B. "The Concept of Nature in Nineteenth Century Canadian Poetry, with Special Reference to Goldsmith, Sangster and Roberts" (Thesis, University of New Brunswick, 1948).
HAMILTON, W. D. "An Edition of the Hitherto Uncollected Poems of Charles Sangster, together with a Biographical and Critical Introduction and Notes" (Thesis, University of New Brunswick, 1958).
HORNING, L. E. "Canadian Literature," THE WEEK 11: 1038–1040 (Sept. 28, 1894).
MACKLEM, JOHN. "Who's Who in Canadian Literature: Charles Sangster," CAN BKMN 10: 195–196 (July 1928).
MORGAN, HENRY J. *Sketches of Celebrated Canadians* (Quebec, Hunter Rose, 1862) pp. 684–693.
PACEY, DESMOND. "Charles Sangster." In his *Ten Canadian Poets* (Toronto, Ryerson, 1958) pp 1–33.

SAUNDERS, Margaret Marshall, 1861–1947
ANON. "Marshall Saunders' Birthday," CAN BKMN 13: 89 (April 1931).
———— "Marshall Saunders and Her Friends," CHATELAINE 3: 13ff (June 1931).
———— Obituary, WILSON LIB BUL 2: 572 (April 1947).
BOWKER, KATHLEEN K. "An Artist in Life," CAN BKMN 5: 275, 279 (Oct. 1923).

ELSON, JOHN MEBOURNE. "Who's Who in Canadian Literature: Miss Marshall Saunders," CAN BKMN 12: 223–228 (Nov. 1930).

HOWARD, DOROTHY. "Marshall Saunders: A Tribute to Canada's Most Revered Author," SAT N 62: 21 (March 1, 1947).

KIRKCONNELL, WATSON. "Tribute to Marshall Saunders," CAN AUTH & BKMN 30: 24–25 (Spring 1954).

STEVENSON, O. J. "Lift up Thy Voice for the Dumb." In his *A People's Best* (Toronto, Musson, 1927) pp 229–234.

SCHOFIELD, William Henry, 1870–1920

KEYS, D. R. "Canadian Celebrities: 71, William Henry Schofield, Ph.D.," CAN MAG 27: 299–302 (Aug. 1906).

SCOTT, Duncan Campbell, 1862–1947

ANON. Biographical Note, CAN AUTH & BKMN 34: 11 (Spring 1958).

———— "Duncan Campbell Scott's 85th Birthday," CAN AUTH & BKMN 23: 35 (Dec. 1947).

———— "Great Poet, Great Man [Editorial]," SAT N 63: 5 (Jan. 24, 1948).

———— Obituary, CAN FORUM 27: 244 (Feb. 1948).

———— Obituary, PUB WKLY 153: 170 (Jan. 10, 1948).

ARCHER, WILLIAM. "Duncan Campbell Scott." In his *Poets of the Younger Generation* (London, Lane, 1902) pp 385–395.

BOURINOT, ARTHUR S. "The Ever-Eager Heart," CAN AUTH & BKMN 25: 8–9 (Autumn 1949). [Also in his *Five Canadian Poets* (Montreal, Quality Press, 1956) pp 1–3.]

————, ed. *More Letters of Duncan Campbell Scott*, Second Series (Ottawa, Bourinot, 1960).

———— *Some Letters of Duncan Campbell Scott, Archibald Lampman and Others* (Ottawa, Bourinot, 1959).

BROCKINGTON, LEONARD W. "Duncan Campbell Scott's Eightieth Birthday," SAT N 57: 25 (Aug. 1, 1942).

BRODIE, A. D. "Canadian Short Story Writers," CAN MAG 4: 334–344 (Feb. 1895).

BROWN, E. K. "Duncan Campbell Scott." In his *On Canadian Poetry*, rev. ed. (Toronto, Ryerson, 1944) pp 118–143.

———— "Duncan Campbell Scott, an Individual Poet," MAN ARTS R 2: 51–54 (Spring 1941).

———— Memoir. In *Selected Poems of Duncan Campbell Scott* (Toronto, Ryerson, 1951) pp xi–xlii.

BURRELL, MARTIN. "Canadian Poet." In his *Betwixt Heaven and Charing Cross* (New York, Macmillan, 1928) pp 253–261.

CLARKE, GEORGE HERBERT. "Duncan Campbell Scott, 1862–1948," ROY SOC CAN PROC & TRANS 3rd ser 42: 115–119 (1948).

EDGAR, PELHAM. "Duncan Campbell Scott," DAL R 7: 38–46 (April 1927).

———— "Duncan C. Scott," THE WEEK 12: 370–371 (March 15, 1895).

———— "The Poetry of Duncan Campbell Scott," EDUC RECORD (Quebec) 58: 8–11 (Jan.–Mar. 1942). [Also in *Leading Canadian Poets*, ed. W. P. Percival (Toronto, Ryerson, 1948) pp 213–219.]

———— "Travelling with a Poet." In his *Across My Path*, ed. Northrop Frye (Toronto, Ryerson, 1952) pp 58–74.

GARVIN, J. W. "The Poems of Duncan Campbell Scott," CAN BKMN 8: 364–365 (Dec. 1926).

KNISTER, RAYMOND. "Duncan Campbell Scott," WILLISON's MO 2: 295–296 (Jan. 1927).

MACBETH, MADGE. "A Word of Remembrance about Duncan Campbell Scott," CAN AUTH & BKMN 24: 13 (Fall supplement, 1948).

MUDDIMAN, BERNARD. "Duncan Campbell Scott," CAN MAG 43: 63–72 (May 1914).

PACEY, DESMOND. "Duncan Campbell Scott." In his *Ten Canadian Poets* (Toronto, Ryerson, 1958) pp 141–164.

——— "The Poetry of Duncan Campbell Scott," CAN FORUM 28: 107–109 (Aug. 1948).

SMITH, ARTHUR JAMES MARSHALL. "Duncan Campbell Scott." In *Our Living Tradition*, Second and Third Series, ed. Robert L. McDougall (Toronto, published in association with Carleton University by University of Toronto Press, 1959) pp 73–94.

——— "Duncan Campbell Scott, a Reconsideration," CAN LIT no 1: 13–25 (Summer 1959).

——— "The Poetry of Duncan Campbell Scott," DAL R 28: 12–21 (April 1948).

STEVENSON, LIONEL. "Who's Who in Canadian Literature: Duncan Campbell Scott," CAN BKMN 11: 59–62 (March 1929).

STEVENSON, O. J. "Music's Magic Spell." In his *A People's Best* (Toronto, Musson, 1927) pp 109–118.

STRAFFORD, EZRA H. "The Poet of Summer," THE WEEK 11: 801–802 (July 20, 1884).

SYKES, W. J. "The Poetry of Duncan Campbell Scott," QUEEN'S Q 46: 51–64 (Feb. 1939).

WRIGHT, PERCY H. "Who is Our Poet Laureate?" SAT N 53: 20 (Dec. 4, 1937).

SCOTT, Francis Reginald, 1899–

ANON. Biographical Note, CAN AUTH & BKMN 34: 9 (Spring 1958).

BELL, W. "Profs and Propaganda," SAT N 54: 10 (Aug. 19, 1939).

COLLIN, W. E. "Pilgrim of the Absolute." In his *The White Savannahs* (Toronto, Macmillan, 1936) pp 177–204.

DUDEK, LOUIS. "F. R. Scott and the Modern Poets," NORTHERN R 4: 14–15 (Dec.-Jan. 1950–51).

LEFOLII, K. "Poet Who Outfought Duplessis," MACL MAG 72: 16–17, 70+ (April 11, 1959).

PACEY, DESMOND. "F. R. Scott." In his *Ten Canadian Poets* (Toronto, Ryerson, 1958) pp 223–253.

SCHULTZ, GREGORY PETER. "The Periodical Poetry of A. J. M. Smith, F. R. Scott, Leo Kennedy, A. M. Klein and Dorothy Livesay, 1925–1950" (Thesis, University of Western Ontario, 1957).

SCOTT, Frederick George, 1861–1944

ADAMS, THOMAS. "Frederick G. Scott," CAN MAG 11: 160–164 (June 1898).

ANON. Obituary, CHRISTIAN CENT 61: 284 (March 1, 1944).

BRODIE, ALLAN DOUGLAS. "Canadian Short-Story Writers," CAN MAG 4: 334–344 (Feb. 1895).

CATES, JOHN. "Canon Scott, Beloved Padré of World War I," SAT N 59: 16 (Jan. 29, 1944).

EVANS, H. "Canon Scott," MACL MAG 51: 15, 46–47 (Nov. 1, 1938).

HAMMOND, MELVIN O. "The Poet of Laurentians," CAN MAG 32: 456–460 (March 1909).

LOWE, A. "Beloved Companion," CAN MAG 74: 3–4 (Sept. 1930).

PERCIVAL, W. P. "Frederick George Scott," EDUC RECORD (Quebec) 56: 4–7 (Jan.–March 1937) [Also in *Leading Canadian Poets*, ed. W. P. Percival (Toronto, Ryerson, 1948) pp 220–226.]

RAYMOND, W. O. "Frederick George Scott (1861–1944)," ROY SOC CAN PROC & TRANS 3rd ser 38: 119–123 (1944).

STEVENSON, O. J. "Poet and Padré." In his *A People's Best* (Toronto, Musson, 1927) pp 177–184.

WETHERELL, J. E. "A New Book of Poems," CAN MAG 4: 287–288 (Jan. 1895).

SEDGEWICK, Garnett Gladwin, 1882–1949

SAGE, W. N. "Garnett Gladwin Sedgewick (1882–1949)," ROY SOC CAN PROC & TRANS 3rd ser 44: 101–103 (1950).

SEDGEWICK, G. G. "Musquodoboit," DAL R 19: 467–471 (Jan. 1940).

SELLAR, Robert, 1841–1919

LANCTOT, G. "Un Régionaliste Anglais de Québec, Robert Sellar," BULLETIN DES RECHERCHES HISTORIQUES 41: 172–174 (mars 1935).

SERVICE, Robert William, 1874–1958

ANON. Biographical Note, CAN AUTH & BKMN 34: 11 (Spring 1958).

———— Biographical Note, MACL MAG 66: 71 (Dec. 15, 1953).

———— "Rhyming was His Ruin," TIME 46: 103–104 (Oct. 1, 1945).

FINNIE, R. "When the Ice-Worms Nest Again," MACL MAG 58: 10, 62 (Nov. 1, 1945).

HAMER-JACKSON, CELESTA. "Robert W. Service," EDUC RECORD (Quebec) 59: 226–228 (Oct.–Dec. 1943). [Also in *Leading Canadian Poets,* ed. W. P. Percival (Toronto, Ryerson, 1948) pp 227–233.]

HELLMAN, G. T. "Whooping It Up," NEW YORKER 22: 34–38 (March 30, 1946); 22: 32–36 (April 6, 1946).

HORNING, L. E. "Robert W. Service," ACTA VIC 41: 295–301 (June 1917).

MIGONE, PIETRO. "Robert Service, Poet of the Canadian North" (Thesis, University of Ottawa, 1949).

PACEY, DESMOND. "Service and MacInnes," NORTHERN R 4: 12–17 (Feb.–March 1951).

PHELPS, ARTHUR L. "R. W. Service." In his *Canadian Writers* (Toronto, McClelland & Stewart, 1951) pp 28–35.

SERVICE, ROBERT W. *Harper of Heaven* (New York, Dodd Mead, 1948).

———— *The Ploughman of the Moon: An Adventure into Memory* (New York, Dodd Mead, 1945).

———— "So I Have a Mild Face," MACL MAG 54: 9, 28, 30 (Jan. 15, 1941).

STOUFFER, R. P. "Robert W. Service," ACTA VIC 39: 55–63 (Nov. 1914).

SETON, Ernest Thompson, 1860–1946
 ANON. "The Animal Story," EDINBURGH R 214: 94–118 (July 1911).
 ———— "Happy Hunting Ground," TIME 48: 30 (Nov. 4, 1946).
 ———— Obituary, NEW MEXICO HIST R 22: 107 (Jan. 1947).
 ———— Obituary, NEWSWEEK 28: 58 (Nov. 4, 1946).
 ———— Obituary, WILSON LIB BUL 21: 266 (Dec. 1946).
 ———— "Returned to Winnipeg to Deliver a Series of Lectures," SAT N
 54: 6 (Oct. 21, 1939).
 ———— "Salute to an Old Friend," SAT EVE POST 211: 22 (Dec. 31,
 1938).
 ———— "Wilderness Mosaic," NEWSWEEK 42: 78–79 (Aug. 24, 1953).
 BODSWORTH, C. F. "Backwoods Genius with the Magic Pen," MACL
 MAG 72: 22+ (June 6, 1959).
 CHAPMAN, F. M. "Champion of E. T. Seton," SAT R LIT 16: 9 (Oct. 2,
 1937).
 ———— "Naturalist, Artist, Author, Educator," BIRD LORE 37: 245–247
 (July 1935).
 GARST, SHANNON and WARREN GARST. *Ernest Thompson Seton, Naturalist*
 (New York, Messner, 1959).
 POIRIER, M. "The Animal Stories of E. Thompson Seton and Charles G.
 D. Roberts," QUEEN'S Q 34: 298–312 (Jan.–March 1927); 34:
 398–419 (April–June 1927).
 SETON, ERNEST THOMPSON. *Trail of an Artist-Naturalist: The Autobiog-*
 raphy of— (New York, Scribner's, 1940).
 VOGT, W. "Popularizing Nature," SAT R LIT 16: 9 (Sept. 18, 1937).
 WILEY, FARIDA A., ed. *Ernest Thompson Seton's America.* Selections ...
 ed. with an intro. by F. A. Wiley and with biographical contributions
 by Julia Seton (New York, Devin-Adair, 1954).
 ZAHNISER, H. "Nature in Print," NATURE MAG 46: 450–451 (Nov.
 1953).

SHAPIRO, Lionel, 1908–1958
 SHAPIRO, L. S. B. "Myth That's Muffling Canada's Voice," MACL MAG
 68: 12–13, 43–45 (Oct. 29, 1955).

SHARP, Luke [pseud.]. *See* BARR, Robert

SHEARD, Mrs. Virna (Virginia Stanton), 1865?–1943
 FRENCH, DONALD G. "Virna Sheard," CAN BKMN 12: 4–5 (Jan. 1930).

SHEPPARD, Edmund Ernest, 1855–1924
 BUTCHART, R. "Sheppard, Man and Journalist," SAT N 53: 8–9 (Jan. 1,
 1938).
 CHARLESWORTH, HECTOR. "When Journalists were Picturesque." In his
 Candid Chronicles (Toronto, Macmillan, 1925) pp 72–86.
 CLARK, G. "Mack's Son Remembers," SAT N 53: 4a (Jan. 1, 1938).

SHERMAN, Francis Joseph, 1871–1926
 ANON. "Francis J. Sherman, Poet and Banker," ROY BANK MAG pp
 3–10 (June–July, 1935).
 HATHAWAY, R. H. "Francis Sherman: Canadian Poet," WILLISON'S MO
 2: 383–384 (March 1927).
 MASSEY, VINCENT. "Roberts, Carman, Sherman: Canadian Poets," CAN
 AUTH & BKMN 23: 29–32 (Fall 1947).

PIERCE, LORNE ALBERT. "Francis Sherman." In his *Three Fredericton Poets: Writers of the University of New Brunswick and the New Dominion* (Toronto, Ryerson, 1933) pp 25–30.

ROBERTS, CHARLES G. D. "Presidential Address—Francis Sherman," ROY SOC CAN PROC & TRANS 3rd ser 28: 1–9 (May 1934) [1935]. [Reprinted as "Francis Sherman," DAL R 14: 419–427 (Jan. 1935).]

WILSON, L. R. "The Life and Poetry of Francis Sherman, 1871–1920" (Thesis, University of New Brunswick, 1959).

SHORTT, Adam, 1859–1931

HAYDON, THE HON. ANDREW. "Adam Shortt," QUEEN'S Q 38: 609–623 (Autumn 1931).

MACKINTOSH, W. A. "Adam Shortt, 1859–1931," CAN J ECON 4: 164–176 (May 1938).

SIBBALD, Susan (Mein), 1783–1866

HETT, FRANCIS P. *Georgina: A Type Study of Early Settlement and Church Building in Upper Canada* (Toronto, Macmillan, 1939).

———— ed. *The Memoirs of Susan Sibbald . . .* (London, Lane, 1926).

SIMCOE, Elizabeth Posthuma (Gwillim), 1766–1850

ROBERTSON, JOHN ROSS, ed. *The Diary of Mrs. John Graves Simcoe . . .* (Toronto, Briggs, 1911).

WEAVER, EMILY P. "Mrs. Simcoe and Her Diary," CAN MAG 37: 346–356 (Aug. 1911).

SIME, Jessie Georgina, 1880–

ANON. "A Montreal Woman on Women," CAN BKMN 2: 57–58, 59–62 (April 1920).

SINCLAIR, Gordon Allan, 1900–

M., G. "Brash Boy," SAT N 65: 20 (March 7, 1950).

SINCLAIR, GORDON. "The Inside Story of Gordon Sinclair," MACL MAG 62: 12–13, 39–42 (Dec. 1, 1949).

SINCLAIR, Lister S., 1921–

ANON. Biographical Note, TIME (Can. ed.) 55: 19–20 (Feb. 20, 1950).

FRANKLIN, BERT. "Patriarch at 27," MACL MAG 61: 8, 50–52 (Nov. 1, 1948).

WATSON, J. L. "At the Top in Radio Drama ["Encounter by Moonlight"]," SAT N 63: 31 (March 20, 1948).

SKINNER, Constance Lindsay, 1879?–1939

ANON. Biographical Note, SCHOLASTIC 32: 5 (Feb. 26, 1938).

———— Obituary, LIBRARY J 64: 313 (April 15, 1939).

———— Obituary, PUB WKLY 135: 1289 (April 1, 1939).

———— Obituary, TIME 33: 72 (April 10, 1939).

———— Obituary, WILSON LIB BUL 13: 580 (May 1939).

LE BOURDAIS, D. M. "The Saskatchewan," CAN FORUM 30: 88–89 (July 1950).

SMITH, Arthur James Marshall, 1902–

BROWN, E. K. "A. J. M. Smith and the Poetry of Pride," MAN ARTS R 4: 30–32 (Spring 1944).

COLLIN, W. E. "Arthur Smith," GANTS DU CIEL 11: 47–60 (printemps 1946).

——— "Difficult Lonely Music." In his *The White Savannahs* (Toronto, Macmillan, 1936) pp 235–263.

KLEIN, A. M. "The Poetry of A. J. M. Smith," CAN FORUM 23: 257–258 (Feb. 1944).

PACEY, DESMOND. "A. J. M. Smith." In his *Ten Canadian Poets* (Toronto, Ryerson, 1958) pp 194–222.

SCOTT, F. R. "A. J. M. Smith," EDUC RECORD (Quebec) 64: 24–29 (Jan.–March 1948). [Also in *Leading Canadian Poets* ed. W. P. Percival (Toronto, Ryerson, 1948) pp 234–244.]

S., J. "Literary Colonialism," FIRST STATEMENT 2: 3 (Feb. 1944).

SCHULTZ, GREGORY PETER. "The Periodical Poetry of A. J. M. Smith, F. R. Scott, Leo Kennedy, A. M. Klein and Dorothy Livesay, 1925–1950" (Thesis, University of Western Ontario, 1957).

SUTHERLAND, JOHN. "Mr. Smith and 'The Tradition.'" In his *Other Canadians* (Montreal, First Statement Press, 1947) pp 5–12.

SMITH, Goldwin, 1823–1910

ADAM, GRAEME M. "Professor Goldwin Smith," CAN MAG 24: 113–119 (Dec. 1904).

ANON. "'Sir Francis Bond Head,' a Footnote: Notes and Documents," CAN HIST R 19: 297–299ff (Sept. 1938).

ARMYTAGE, W. H. G. "Goldwin Smith, Some Unpublished Letters," QUEEN'S Q 54: 452–460 (Nov. 1947).

COLQUHOUN, A. H. U. "Goldwin Smith in Canada," CAN MAG 35: 315–323 (Aug. 1910).

COOPER, J. J. *Goldwin Smith, D.C.L.* (Reading, 1912). [Pamphlet.]

FERGUSON, A. S. "Goldwin Smith," QUEEN'S Q 21: 352–357 (Jan. 1914).

GRANT, W. L. "Goldwin Smith at Oxford," CAN MAG 35: 304–314 (Aug. 1910).

HATHAWAY, E. J. "Professor Goldwin Smith," INDEPENDENT 68: 1338–1341 (June 16, 1910).

HAULTAIN, THEODORE ARNOLD. *Goldwin Smith, His Life and Opinions* (London, Werner Laurie, 1913).

——— "Goldwin Smith's 'Reminiscences,'" CAN MAG 36: 302–306 (Jan. 1911).

———, ed. *A Selection from Goldwin Smith's Correspondence . . .* (Toronto, McClelland & Stewart, [1913?]).

LOCKE, GEORGE N. "Goldwin Smith and Sir George W. Ross." In *The Yearbook of Canadian Art, 1913–*, comp. by the Arts and Letters Club of Toronto (Toronto, Dent, n.d.) pp 37–43.

MAVOR, JAMES. "Goldwin Smith," MACL MAG 34: 12–13, 47–49 (March 1, 1921).

ROBERTS, C. G. D. "Goldwin Smith at Home." In *Authors at Home,* eds. J. L. and J. B. Gilder (New York, Wessels, 1888) pp 263ff.

ROSS, MALCOLM. "Goldwin Smith." In *Our Living Tradition,* First Series, ed. Claude T. Bissell (Toronto, University of Toronto Press, 1957) pp 29–47.

SMITH, GOLDWIN. "Memories of My Home," CAN MAG 36: 128–135 (Dec. 1910).

———— "My Early Connection with London Journalism," CAN MAG 36: 9–12 (Nov. 1910).

———— *Reminiscences*, ed. by Arnold Haultain (New York, Macmillan, 1910).

UNDERHILL, FRANK. "Goldwin Smith." In *Canadian Portraits*, ed. R. G. Riddell (Toronto, Oxford, 1940) pp 117–123.

———— "Goldwin Smith," UNIV TOR Q 2: 285–309 (Jan. 1933).

WALLACE, ELIZABETH. "Goldwin Smith: Journalist and Critic," CAN FORUM 35: 275 (March 1956).

———— "Goldwin Smith, Liberal," UNIV TOR Q 23: 155–172 (Jan. 1954).

———— "Goldwin Smith on History," J MOD HIST 26: 220–232 (Sept. 1954).

———— "Goldwin Smith and Social Reform," CAN HIST R 29: 363–369 (Dec. 1948).

———— *Goldwin Smith, Victorian Liberal* (Toronto, University of Toronto Press, 1957).

WALLACE, W. S. *"The Bystander* and Canadian Journalism," CAN MAG 35: 553–558 (Oct. 1910).

———— "The Bystander Papers," CAN BKMN 1: 35–39 (July 1919).

YEIGH, FRANK. "Goldwin Smith and the Round Table Club," WILLISON'S MO 3: 307–309ff (Jan. 1928).

SMITH, Kay, 1911–
ANON. "Three New Poets," FIRST STATEMENT vol 1, no 12: 1–4 [undated].

SMYTHE, Albert Ernest Stafford, 1861–1947
STEVENSON, LIONEL. "Who's Who in Canadian Literature: Albert E. S. Smythe," CAN BKMN 9: 291–293 (Oct. 1927).

SNIDER, Charles Henry Jeremiah, 1879–1971
MACKLEM, JOHN. "Who's Who in Canadian Literature: C. H. J. Snider," CAN BKMN 10: 327–329 (Nov. 1928).

STANSBURY, Joseph, 1740–1809
[GHENT, W. J.] "Joseph Stansbury," *Dictionary of American Biography* vol 17, pp 516–517.

TYLER, MOSES COIT. "Joseph Stansbury, Tory Song-Writer and Satirist." In his *The Literary History of the American Revolution* (New York, Putnam, 1897) 2: 79–96. [Reprinted: New York, Ungar Publishing Co., 1957.]

STEAD, Robert James Campbell, 1880–1959
BOWKER, KATHLEEN K. "Robert Stead: An Interview," CAN BKMN 5: 99 (April 1923).

McCOURT, EDWARD A. "Robert J. C. Stead." In his *The Canadian West in Fiction* (Toronto, Ryerson, 1949) pp 82–88.

STEELE, Sir Samuel Benfield, 1849–1919
MACBETH, R. G. "Sir Samuel Benfield Steele," CAN MAG 52: 972–975 (March 1919).

STEELE, SAMUEL B. *Forty Years in Canada: Reminiscences of the Great North-West* (London, Jenkins, 1915).

STEPHANSSON, Stephan Gudmondsson, 1853–1927
   KIRKCONNELL, WATSON. "Canada's Leading Poet, Stephan G. Stephansson, (1853–1927)," UNIV TOR Q 5: 263–277 (Jan. 1936).

STEPHEN, Alexander Maitland, 1882–1942
   STEPHEN, W. GORDON. "A. M. Stephen," EDUC RECORD (Quebec) 60: 148–153 (July–Sept. 1944). [Also in *Leading Canadian Poets,* ed. W. P. Percival (Toronto, Ryerson, 1948) pp 245–254.]
   STEVENSON, LIONEL. "Two Vancouver Poets," CAN BKMN 18: 407 (Jan. 25, 1936).
   ——— "Who's Who in Canadian Literature: A M. Stephen," CAN BKMN 11: 203–205 (Sept. 1929).
   WOOLLACOTT, A. P., "A Poet of the West," MACL MAG 44: 84, 87 (April 15, 1931).

STEWART, George, 1848–1906
   ANON. Obituary, ROY SOC CAN PROC & TRANS 2nd ser 12: vii–viii (1906).
   ANON. "George Stewart, Jr.," CAN ILLUS NEWS 21: 82 (Feb. 7, 1880).

STORY, George Morley, 1927–
   WHITE, J. A. "Newfoundland Word Man," ATLAN ADV 48: 40–41, 43–44 (Dec. 1957).

STRANGE, William, 1902–
   CHAMBERLAIN, FRANK. "Mart Kenney and William Strange, Radio's Two Top Men of War," SAT N 60: 20 (April 7, 1945).

STRINGER, Arthur John Arbuthnot, 1874–1950
   BROWN, HARRY W. "Arthur J. Stringer's Poems," CAN MAG 6: 88–91 (Nov. 1895).
   BRUCE, H. A. "Canadian Celebrities: XIV, Arthur J. Stringer," CAN MAG 15: 143–145 (June 1900).
   DAVIES-WOODROW, CONSTANCE. "Who's Who in Canadian Literature: Arthur Stringer," CAN BKMN 10: 259–261 (Sept. 1928).
   DEACON, WILLIAM ARTHUR. "What a Canadian Has Done for Canada." In his *Poteen* . . . (Ottawa, Graphic, 1926) pp 51–62. [Also in *Our Sense of Identity*, ed. Malcolm Ross (Toronto, Ryerson, 1954) pp 209–216.]
   LAURISTON, VICTOR. "Arthur Stringer," EDUC RECORD (Quebec) 58: 209–214 (Oct.–Dec. 1942). [Also in *Leading Canadian Poets*, ed. W. P. Percival (Toronto, Ryerson, 1948) pp 255–264.]
   ——— *Arthur Stringer, Son of the North: Biography and Anthology* (Toronto, Ryerson, 1941).
   ——— *Postscript to a Poet: Off the Record Tales about Arthur Stringer* (Chatham, Tiny Tree Club, 1941).
   ——— "Three Musketeers of the Pen in New York of the Nineties," SAT N 61: 32–33 (Jan. 12, 1946).
   ——— "Two Poets and a Parallel," CAN AUTH & BKMN 23: 37–38 (Fall 1947).
   ——— "Wife or Marie Dressler Stringer's Heroine?" SAT N 59: 15 (Feb. 5, 1944).

MANSFIELD, M. "Canadian Poet," POETRY (Chicago) 34: 108–110 (May 1929).

McCOURT, EDWARD A. "Arthur Stringer." In his *The Canadian West in Fiction* (Toronto, Ryerson, 1949) pp 76–81.

PHELPS, ARTHUR L. "Poetry with a Preface," CAN MAG 44: 467–470 (March 1915).

POMEROY, ELSIE. "The Poetry of Arthur Stringer," CAN POETRY 14: 22–23 (Spring 1951).

STRINGER, ARTHUR. "The Difficulty of Dressing Heroines," CAN BKMN 20: 9–14 (Oct. 1938).

SULLIVAN, (Edward) Alan, 1868–1947 [pseud.: Sinclair Murray]

ANON. "Alan Sullivan, Master Craftsman," CAN AUTH & BKMN 23: 39 (Fall 1947).

STEVENSON, J. A. "Alan Sullivan, Poet, Engineer," SAT N 62: 25 (Aug. 23, 1947).

SULLIVAN, ALAN. "In the Matter of Alan Sullivan," ONT LIB R 14: 35–36 (Nov. 1929).

SUMMERS, Mrs. Eve H. (Brodlique), 1867?–

BAYARD, MARY TEMPLE. "Eve Brodlique," CAN MAG 7: 515–518 (Oct. 1896).

SUTHERLAND, Alexander Hugh, 1870–1952

MORTON, JAMES. "Alexander H. Sutherland," CAN AUTH & BKMN 28: 40 (1952).

SWABEY, Maurice (1832?–1902)

[JACK, DAVID R.] Editorial: Biographical Sketch, ACADIENSIS 2: 246–248 (Oct. 1902).

SWANSON, Robert E.

OLSEN, W. H. "Interesting People," BC DIGEST 1: 68–69 (Dec. 1945).

THOMPSON, David, 1770–1857

BEGG, ALEXANDER. *History of British Columbia* (Toronto, Briggs, 1894) pp 95–98.

BURPEE, LAWRENCE J. "David Thompson, a Great Land Geographer," CAN GEOG J 30: 238–239 (May 1945).

———— "Notes on David Thompson," CAN HIST ASSOC ANNUAL REPORT (1923) pp 75–84.

———— *On the Old Athabaska Trail* (Toronto, Ryerson, 1926) pp 32–74.

———— "The Outwitting of Sakatow," CAN MAG 64: 3–5 (Jan. 1926).

———— "Over the Rockies with Thompson," NATL LIFE CANADA 3: 8–11 (Feb. 1924).

———— *The Search for the Western Sea* (Toronto, Musson, 1908; rev. ed. 1935) pp 529–559.

CANADIAN HISTORICAL ASSOCIATION. "David Thompson Monument," CAN HIST ASSOC ANNUAL REPORT (1927) pp 9–16.

COCHRANE, CHARLES NORRIS. *David Thompson, the Explorer* (Toronto, Macmillan, 1924).

CROFT, FRANK. "David Thompson's Lonely Crusade to Open the West," MACL MAG 70: 33, 38–43 (Nov. 9, 1957).

ELLIOTT, T. C. "David Thompson, Pathfinder," OREGON HIST Q 26: 191–202 (June 1925).

——— "David Thompson, Pathfinder, and the Columbia River," OREGON HIST Q 12: 195–205 (Sept. 1911).

——— "David Thompson and Beginnings in Idaho," OREGON HIST Q 21: 49–61 (June 1920).

——— "The Strange Case of David Thompson and Jeremy Pinch," OREGON HIST Q 40: 188–199 (June 1939).

FLEMING, SANDFORD. "Travels and Discoveries of Mr. David Thompson 1790–1811," ROY SOC CAN PROC & TRANS 1st ser 7: 108–109 (1889).

FULLER, G. W. *History of the Pacific Northwest* (New York, Knopf, 1931) pp 78–83.

——— *Inland Empire of the Pacific Northwest* (Spokane, Linderman, 1928) vol 1, pp 147–157.

GLOVER, RICHARD. "The Witness of David Thompson," CAN HIST R 31: 25–38 (March 1950).

HAMER-JACKSON, CELESTA. *Discoverers and Explorers of North America* (Toronto, Nelson, 1931) pp 271–280.

HOPWOOD, V. G. "Centenary of an Explorer—David Thompson's *Narrative* Re-considered," QUEEN'S Q 64: 41–49 (Spring 1957).

——— "More Light on David Thompson," BEAVER 288: 58 (Autumn 1957).

——— "New Light on David Thompson," BEAVER 288: 26–31 (Summer 1957).

HOWAY, FREDERIC WILLIAM. *British Columbia: The Making of a Province* (Toronto, Ryerson, 1928) pp 60–65.

JORDAN, MABEL E. "Canada Remembers David Thompson," CAN GEOG J 54: 114–117 (March 1957).

KARR, W. J. *Explorers, Soldiers and Statesmen* (Toronto, Dent, 1929) pp 152–159.

MACKAY, I. E. "The David Thompson Memorial," CAN MAG 60: 223–229 (Jan. 1923).

MACRAE, A. O. *History of the Province of Alberta* ([Calgary?], Western Canada History Co., 1912) vol 1, pp 51–59.

MORTON, ARTHUR S. *David Thompson* (Toronto, Ryerson, 1930). [Ryerson Canadian History Readers.]

——— "Did Duncan M'Gillivray and David Thompson Cross the Rockies in 1801?" CAN HIST R 18: 156–162 (June 1937).

——— "The North West Company's Columbia Enterprise and David Thompson," CAN HIST R 17: 266–288 (Sept. 1936).

PARKER, ELIZABETH. "Early Explorers of the West: David Thompson," CAN ALPINE J 29: 216–228 (1946).

SCHOLEFIELD, E. O. S. *British Columbia* (Vancouver, Clarke, 1914) vol 1, pp 308–317.

STEVENS, WILLIAM. "Opening of the Land Fur Trader." In *Builders of the West*, ed. F. W. Howay (Toronto, Ryerson, 1929) pp 198–203.

THOMPSON, DAVID. "Account of an Attempt to Cross the Rocky Moun- tains by M. J. Hughes, Nine Men and Myself, on the Part of the N.W. Company . . . 1800" [Original Manuscript].

——— "David Thompson's Account of His First Attempt to Cross the Rockies," ed. F. W. Howay, QUEEN'S Q 40: 333–356 (Aug. 1933).

——— "David Thompson's Journeys in Idaho," ed. T. C. Elliott, WASHINGTON HIST Q 11: 97–103, 163–173 (April–July 1920).

——— "David Thompson's Journeys in the Pend Oreille Country," ed. T. C. Elliott, WASHINGTON HIST Q 23: 18–24, 88–93, 173–176 (Jan.–July 1932).

——— "David Thompson's Journeys in the Spokane Country," ed. T. C. Elliott, WASHINGTON HIST Q 8: 183–187, 261–264 (July–Oct. 1917); 9: 11–16, 103–106, 169–173, 284–287 (Jan.–Oct. 1918); 10: 17–20 (Jan. 1919).

——— *David Thompson's Narrative of His Explorations in Western America 1784–1812*, ed. J. B. Tyrrell (Toronto, Champlain Society, 1916).

——— "The Discovery of the Source of the Columbia River," ed. T. C. Elliott, OREGON HIST Q 26: 23–49 (March 1925).

——— "Discoveries from the East Side of the Rocky Mountains to the Pacific Ocean," ed. by J. B. Tyrrell, CAN HIST R 15: 39–45 (March 1934).

——— *Journals Relating to Montana and Adjacent Regions 1808–1812*, ed. M. Catherine White (Missoula, Montana State University Press, 1950).

——— *New Light on the Early History of the Greater Northwest: The Manuscript Journals of Alexander Henry . . . and of David Thompson . . . 1799–1814*, ed. Elliott Coues (New York, Harper, 1897) 3 vols.

——— "Some Letters of David Thompson," ed. by L. J. Burpee, CAN HIST R 4: 105–126 (June 1923).

TYRRELL, J. B. *A Brief Narrative of the Journeys of David Thompson in North-Western America . . .* (Toronto, Copp Clark, 1888). [A paper read before the Canadian Institute, March 3rd, 1888.]

——— "David Thompson: A Great Geographer," GEOG J 37: 49–58 (Jan. 1911).

——— "David Thompson and the Columbia River," CAN HIST R 18: 12–27 (March 1937).

——— "David Thompson and the Rocky Mountains," CAN HIST R 15: 39–45 (March 1934).

——— *David Thompson, Canada's Greatest Geographer: An Appreciation in Connection with the Opening of the David Thompson Memorial Fort at Lake Windermere, B.C., August 30, 1922.* [8-page pamphlet.]

——— "The Re-discovery of David Thompson," ROY SOC CAN PROC & TRANS 3rd ser 22: sect II, 233–248 (1928).

WALLACE, W. S. "The Man Who Read the Stars." In his *By Star and Compass* (London, Oxford University Press, 1923) pp 168–179.

THOMPSON, Dora Olive, 1895?–1934

GARATT, MABELLA R. "Vale Brave Spirit," CAN BKMN 16: 152 (Nov. 1934).

THOMSON, Edward William, 1849–1924

BOURINOT, ARTHUR STANLEY. *Edward William Thomson (1849–1924): A Bibliography with Notes and Some Letters* (Ottawa, the Author, 1955).

————, ed. *The Letters of Edward William Thomson to Archibald Lampman (1891–1897)*, with notes, a bibliography, and other material on Thomson and Lampman (Ottawa, Bourinot, 1957).

HAMMOND, M. O. "Edward William Thomson," QUEEN'S Q 38: 123–139 (Jan. 1931).

MACLELLAN, W. E. "E. W. Thomson," DAL R 2: 374–375 (Oct. 1922).

PEACOCK, H. R. "A Biographical and Critical Study of Edward William Thomson" (Thesis, University of New Brunswick, 1949).

THOMSON, John Stuart, 1869–1950

MCLAREN, D. T. "Canadian Celebrities: X, J. Stuart Thomson," CAN MAG 14: 360–361 (Feb. 1900).

TRAILL, Mrs. Catharine Parr (Strickland), 1802–1899

BURNHAM, HAMPDEN. "Mrs. Traill," CAN MAG 4: 388–389 (Feb. 1895).

BURPEE, LAWRENCE J. "Catharine Parr Traill (1802–1899)." In his *A Little Book of Canadian Essays* (Toronto, Musson, 1909) pp 56–64.

———— "Last of the Stricklands: Mrs. Catharine Parr Traill," SEWANEE R 8: 207–217 (April 1909).

FITZGIBBON, AGNES. "Biographical Sketch [of Mrs. Traill]." In *Pearls and Pebbles; or, Notes of an Old Naturalist* by Catharine Parr Traill (London, Sampson Low, [1894]) pp iii–xxxvi.

HUME, BLANCHE. "Grandmothers of Canadian Literature," WILLISON'S MO 3: 474–477 (May 1928).

———— *The Strickland Sisters* (Toronto, Ryerson, 1928).

MCNEIL, J. L. "Mrs. Traill in Canada" (Thesis, Queen's University, 1948).

NEEDLER, G. H. *Otonabee Pioneers: The Story of the Stewarts, the Stricklands, the Traills and the Moodies* (Toronto, Burns & Mac-Eachern, 1953).

———— "The Otonabee Trio of Women Naturalists—Mrs. Stewart, Mrs. Traill, Mrs. Moodie," CAN FIELD NATURALIST 60: 97–101 (Sept.–Oct. 1946).

PARTRIDGE, F. G. "The Stewarts and the Stricklands, the Moodies and the Traills," ONT LIB R 40: 179–181 (Aug. 1956).

STRICKLAND, JANE MARGARET. *Life of Agnes Strickland* (Edinburgh, Blackwood, 1887) *passim.*

WEAVER, EMILY. "Mrs. Traill and Mrs. Moodie, Pioneers in Literature," CAN MAG 48: 473–476 (March 1917).

TRANTER, Gladdis Joy, 1902–

SHACKLETON, KATHLEEN. "Portrait of a Poet," SAT N 63: 28 (Feb. 21, 1948).

TROTTER, Bernard Freeman, 1890–1917

GIBBON, J. M. "Where is Canadian Literature?" CAN MAG 50: 333–340 (Feb. 1918).

LIGHTHALL, W. D. "Canadian Poets of the Great War," CAN BKMN 1: 14–22 (April 1919).

MUIR, THOMAS D. "Bernard Freeman Trotter," QUARTERLY (McMaster
  University) 45: 10–13 (Nov. 1935).
RICHARDSON, ARTHUR H. "Bernard Freeman Trotter," MCMASTER U
  MO 27: 3–7 (Oct. 1917).

TUPPER, Mrs. Kathryn (Munro), [pseud: Kathryn Munro]
  ANON. "Kathryn Munro," CAN BKMN 13: 43 (Feb. 1931).

VAN DER MARK, Christine, 1917–
  McCOURT, EDWARD A. "Christine Van Der Mark." In his *The Canadian
    West in Fiction* (Toronto, Ryerson, 1949) pp 102–107.

VINING, Charles Arthur McLaren, 1897–
  BENSON, N. A. "Charles Vining Has a Big Job, but He's Big Too," SAT
    N 58: 24–25 (Oct. 31, 1942).
  KING, T. R. "R. T. L. Himself," MACL MAG 48: 8 (Feb. 1, 1935).

WADDINGTON, Miriam, 1917–
  ANON. "Portrait," CAN AUTH & BKMN 34: 4 (Spring 1958).
  SOWTON, IAN. "The Lyric Craft of Miriam Waddington," DAL R 39: 237–
    242 (Summer 1959).

WALLACE, Frederick William, 1886–1958
  ANON.   "A Sea-Writer Shanghaied; The Work of Frederick William
    Wallace," CAN BKMN 1: 16–17 (July 1919).
  ROSS, I. M. "Author, Adventurer, Philosopher," CAN MAG 51: 78–79
    (May 1918).
  WALLACE, FREDERICK WILLIAM. *Roving Fisherman: An Autobiography*
    . . . (Gardenvale, Que., "Canadian Fisherman," 1955).

WARMAN, Cy, 1855–1914
  C., F. "Canadian Celebrities: XXXII, Cy Warman and His Work," CAN
    MAG 18: 410–412 (March 1902).

WARNOCK, Amelia Beers. *See* GARVIN, Mrs. Amelia Beers (Warnock)

WATANNA, Onoto [pseud.]. *See* REEVE, Mrs. Winnifred Eaton Babcock

WATSON, Albert Durrant, 1859–1926
  PIERCE, LORNE. *Albert Durrant Watson: An Appraisal* (Toronto, Ryerson,
    1923).

WATSON, James Wreford, 1915–   [pseud.: James Wreford]
  ANON. Biographical Note, CAN AUTH & BKMN 34: 9 (Spring 1958).

WATSON, Robert, 1882–1948
  C. "Robert Watson, Western Canadian Novelist," BC MO 15: 9 (Dec.
    1919).
  PERRY, ANNE ANDERSON. "Who's Who in Canadian Literature: Robert
    Watson," CAN BKMN 10: 99–101 (April 1928).

WATSON, Sheila, 1909–
CHILD, P. A. "Canadian Prose-Poem," DAL R 39 233–236 (Summer 1959).
THEALL, D. F. "A Canadian Novella," CAN FORUM 39: 78–80 (July 1959).

WATSON, Wilfred, 1911–
BILSLAND, JOHN WINSTANLEY. "Vision of Clarity: The Poetry of Wilfred Watson," CAN LIT no 4: 40–51 (Spring 1960).

WATT, Ernest Frederick Balmer, 1901–
MIDDLETON, J. E. · "Lieutenant Commander and Poet," SAT N 58: 33 (March 13, 1943).
ROBERTSON, C. B. "A Pen Portrait of Frederick B. Watt, Poet of the Sea," CAN MAG 70: 14 (Sept. 1928).

WEBB, Phyllis Jean, 1927–
ANON. Biographical Note, CAN AUTH & BKMN 34: 13 (Spring 1958).

WEBSTER, John Clarence, 1863–1950
ANON. Obituary, CAN HIST R 31: 216–217 (June 1950).
———— "Websters of Shediac," FOOD FOR THOUGHT 16: 249–253 (March 1956).
EARL, LAWRENCE. "The Man From Shediac," MACL MAG 55: 51–52, 57 (Sept. 15, 1942).
HARVEY, D. C. "John Clarence Webster (1863–1950)," ROY SOC CAN PROC & TRANS 3rd ser 44: 113–120 (1950).
SCLANDERS, I. "Little Dynamo," SAT N 65: 14 (Oct. 11, 1949).
STEAD, R. J. C. "John Clarence Webster," CAN GEOG J 40: 232–235 (May 1950).
WEBSTER, JOHN CLARENCE. *Those Crowded Years, 1863–1944* (Shediac, N.B., privately printed, 1944). [Reminiscences.]

WETHERALD, Agnes Ethelwyn, 1857–1940
BERNHARDT, CLARA. "Ethelwyn Wetherald," SAT N 55: 11 (April 13, 1940).
———— "Ethelwyn Wetherald: Appreciation," CAN AUTH & BKMN 17: 8 (April 1940).
GARVIN, J. W. "Ethelwyn Wetherald's Poetry, an Appreciation," CAN BKMN 13: 199–201 (Oct. 1931).
HALE, KATHERINE. "Ethelwyn Wetherald," EDUC RECORD (Quebec) 63: 82–86 (April–June 1947). [Also in *Leading Canadian Poets,* ed. W. P. Percival (Toronto, Ryerson, 1948) pp 265–271.]
MACDONALD, ELIZABETH ROBERTS. "Trees and a Poet," CAN MAG 53: 51–54 (May 1919).
MACKLEM, JOHN. "Who's Who in Canadian Literature: Ethelwyn Wetherald," CAN BKMN 11: 251–253 (Nov. 1929).
STEVENSON, O. J. "A Balm for Pain." In his *A People's Best* (Toronto, Musson, 1927) pp 193–200.

WICKSTEED, Gustavus William, 1799–1898
LANDE, LAWRENCE M. "Gustavus William Wicksteed." In his *Old Lamps Aglow* (Montreal, the Author, 1957) pp 200–207.

WILLISON, John Stephen, 1856–1927

CHARLESWORTH, HECTOR. "Two Canadian Memoirists." In his *The Canadian Scene* (Toronto, Macmillan, 1927), pp 106–124. [Also discusses George Henry Ham.]

COLQUHOUN, ARTHUR H. U. *Press, Politics and People: The Life and Letters of Sir John Willison, Journalist and Correspondent of* The Times (Toronto, Macmillan, 1935).

———— "Sir John Willison," DAL R 7: 159–162 (July 1927).

MACMURCHY, MARJORIE. "Sir John Willison's Reminiscences," CAN MAG 54: 271–272 (Jan. 1920).

V., E. Q. "Canadian Celebrities: XXXIX, Mr. J. S. Willison," CAN MAG 20: 222–224 (Jan. 1903).

WILLISON, JOHN STEPHEN. *Reminiscences, Political and Personal* (Toronto, McClelland & Stewart, 1919).

WILLISON, Lady Marjory (MacMurchy), –1938

BRODIE, ALLAN DOUGLAS. "Canadian Short-Story Writers," CAN MAG 4: 334–344 (Feb. 1895).

WILLSON, David, 1778–1866

CUNNINGHAM, RALPH. "A Note on David Willson's Temple," ALPHABET no 9: 39–42 (Nov. 1964).

HUGHES, JAMES L. *Sketches of Sharon Temple and of Its Founder, David Willson* (Toronto, Federal Print., [1918?]).

MCARTHUR, EMILY. *A History of the Children of Peace* (Newmarket, Express-Herald Print., n.d.).

MCFADDIN, CHARLES E. "A Study of the Buildings of the Children of Peace, Sharon, Ontario" (Thesis, University of Toronto, 1953).

SPOONER, HILARY. "Sharon Temple and the Children of Peace," ONT HIST 50: 219–227 (Autumn 1958).

SQUAIR, JOHN. "The Temple of Peace, David Willson of Sharon, 1778–1866," WOMEN'S CAN HIST SOC TORONTO TRANS no 20: 46–52 (1919–1920).

TREWHELLA, E. W. "The Story of Sharon," *Newmarket Era and Express,* Jan. 31, 1952.

WILLSON, DAVID. *A Collection of Items of the Life of David Willson. From the Year 1801 to 1852 . . .* (Newmarket, Porter, 1852).

———— *The Practical life of the Author, from the Year 1801 to 1860* (Newmarket, Jackson, 1860).

WILSON, Sir Daniel, 1816–1892

ANON. "Sir Daniel Wilson," R HIST PUB RELATING TO CANADA 5: 199–217 (1901). [Includes a bibliography.]

KINGSFORD, WILLIAM. "In Memoriam," ROY SOC CAN PROC & TRANS 1st ser 11: 55–65 (1893).

LANGTON, HUGH H. *Sir Daniel Wilson. A Memoir* (Toronto, Nelson, 1929).

WILSON, Ethel, 1890–

LIVESAY, DOROTHY. "Ethel Wilson: West Coast Novelist," SAT N 67: 20, 36 (July 26, 1952).

PACEY, DESMOND. "The Innocent Eye: The Art of Ethel Wilson," QUEEN'S Q 61: 42–52 (Spring 1954).

WATTERS, REGINALD EYRE. "Ethel Wilson, the Experienced Traveller," BC LIB Q 21: 21–27 (April 1958).

WILSON, ETHEL. "The Bridge or the Stokehold? Views of the Novelist's Art," CAN LIT no 5: 43–47 (Summer 1960).

———— "A Cat among the Falcons," CAN LIT no 2: 10–19 (Autumn 1959).

WISEMAN, Adele, 1928–

MULLINS, STANLEY G. "Traditional Symbolism in Adele Wiseman's *The Sacrifice*," CULTURE 19: 287–297 (sept. 1958).

WITHROW, William Henry, 1839–1908

ANON. "The Late Rev. Dr. Withrow," ROY SOC CAN PROC & TRANS 3rd ser 3: xlviii–l (1909).

WOODCOCK, George, 1912–

BILSLAND, J. W. "George Woodcock, Man of Letters," BC LIB Q 23: 23–28 (July 1959).

WREFORD, James [pseud.]. *See* WATSON, James Wreford

WRONG, George Mackinnon, 1860–1948

CALAIS, STUART. "Canadian Celebrities: 70, Professor George M. Wrong," CAN MAG 27: 208–210 (July 1906).

MARTIN, C. B. "George MacKinnon Wrong (1860–1948)," ROY SOC CAN PROC & TRANS 3rd ser 43: 147–149 (1949).

SAGE, W. N. "George M. Wrong: 1860–1948," BC HIST Q 12: 311–312 (Oct. 1948).

WALLACE, W. S. "The Life and Work of George M. Wrong," CAN HIST R 29: 229–237 (Sept. 1948). [Bibliography on pp 238–239.]